METHODOLOGY AND EPISTEMOLOGY OF MULTILEVEL ANALYSIS

METHODOS SERIES

VOLUME 2

This Book Series is devoted to examining and solving the major methodological problems social sciences are facing. Take for example the gap between empirical and theoretical research, the explanatory power of models, the relevance of multilevel analysis, the weakness of cumulative knowledge, the role of ordinary knowledge in the research process, or the place which should be reserved to "time, change and history" when explaining social facts. These problems are well known and yet they are seldom treated in depth in scientific literature because of their general nature.
So that these problems may be examined and solutions found, the series prompts and fosters the setting-up of international multidisciplinary research teams, and it is work by these teams that appears in the Book Series. The series can also host books produced by a single author which follow the same objectives. Proposals for manuscripts and plans for collective books will be carefully examined.
The epistemological scope of these methodological problems is obvious and resorting to Philosophy of Science becomes a necessity. The main objective of the Series remains however the methodological solutions that can be applied to the problems in hand. Therefore the books of the Series are closely connected to the research practices.

Methodology and Epistemology of Multilevel Analysis

Approaches from Different Social Sciences

edited by

Daniel Courgeau

Directeur of Research (Emeritus),
INED (Institute National d'Études Démographiques), Paris, France

KLUWER ACADEMIC PUBLISHERS
DORDRECHT / BOSTON / LONDON

A C.I.P. Catalogue record for this book is available from the Library of Congress.

ISBN 1-4020-1475-9

Published by Kluwer Academic Publishers,
P.O. Box 17, 3300 AA Dordrecht, The Netherlands.

Sold and distributed in North, Central and South America
by Kluwer Academic Publishers,
101 Philip Drive, Norwell, MA 02061, U.S.A.

In all other countries, sold and distributed
by Kluwer Academic Publishers,
P.O. Box 322, 3300 AH Dordrecht, The Netherlands.

Printed on acid-free paper

Printed in the Netherlands.

TABLE OF CONTENTS

LIST OF AUTHORS

EDITOR

Courgeau, Daniel, Institut National d'Études Démographiques, Paris (France)

AUTHORS

Courgeau, Daniel, Institut National d'Études Démographiques, Paris (France)

Diez Roux, Ana V., University of Michigan School of Public Health, Ann Arbor (United States of America)

Goldstein, Harvey, Mathematical Sciences, Institute of Education, University of London, London (Great Britain)

Fieldhouse, Ed, Centre for Census and Survey Research, Faculty of Economic & Social Studies, University of Manchester, Manchester (Great Britain)

Franck, Robert, Centre for the Philosophy of Science, Université Catholique de Louvain, Louvain-la-Neuve (Belgium)

Steel, David, School of Mathematics and Applied Statistics, University of Wollongong, Wollongong (Australia)

Tranmer, Mark, Centre for Census and Survey Research, Faculty of Economic & Social Studies, University of Manchester, Manchester (Great Britain)

Walliser, Bernard, Centre d'Enseignement et de Recherche en Analyse Socio-économique, École Nationale des Ponts et Chaussées, Paris (France)

ACKNOWLEDGEMENTS

We would like to thank the French *Institut National d'Études Démographiques* (Ined) and his Director François HÉRAN, whose help permitted us to organise a three day meeting in Paris, in order to compare the different approaches to multilevel analysis followed in demography, economy, educational sciences, epidemiology, human geography, philosophy and epistemology, and to agree on the final content of this volume.

Several other persons contributed to this book. Thanks are due to Nico KEILMAN for reading and commenting on a first draft of Chapter 2. Many thanks to Godfrey ROGERS who translated from French the Chapter 2, and to Jonathan MANDELBAUM who translated the *General introduction* and the *General conclusion* of this volume. An anonymous referee must also be thanked for his valuable remarks on a first version of the manuscript. Finally we wish to thank Cyril COURGEAU, who redraw the graphs, and Hella COURGEAU who produced and laid out the present edition.

Daniel COURGEAU

GENERAL INTRODUCTION

To give the subject of this volume—*multilevel analysis*—its proper place within the general context of the social sciences, it is useful to start with an overview of the issues and questions raised by these disciplines. Compared with the natural sciences, the social sciences are far from fully constituted, and it is important to realise how their relevance can be improved by taking multiple aggregation levels into account.

First, the social sciences begin with the observation of a human behaviour or phenomenon, and then seek to structure it into different fields, which will constitute the specific object of each science. As a rule, the objects are defined independently of the vantage-point and scale that we can adopt to observe them. For example, the object of economics is the production, distribution, and consumption of wealth, but there is no indication of whether the level chosen is the individual, a market, a firm, or a nation. Likewise, the object of demography is the quantitative study of human populations, their variations, and their condition, but demographers do not specify whether the study is at the level of a family, a local population, or a national population. In other words, the distinction between levels precedes the object of each of these sciences, and we shall see that they are all subjected to it.

Second, the social sciences need to discover the categories that will provide suitable starting points for their development. It may be tempting for any individual, who routinely experiences these various social facts, to remain content with their apparent meaning and with a naive explanation of the lived experience in its immediacy—either because the individual already realises its meaning, or because he or she feels its absence and is preparing to search for it among similar lived experiences (Granger, 1994). This is true of the many phenomena studied in the social sciences, such as the birth of a child in demography, a price rise in economics, the fact that a person develops AIDS in epidemiology, or the fact that a person solves a problem in psychology. Far from being convinced of the complexity and opaqueness of these phenomena, naive observers see them as being fraught with explanation, because of their possible experience of similar circumstances and because of their personal knowledge of the conditions and consequences of their everyday actions. But this explanation, specific to each individual, will differ from that of other individuals with other experiences. As a result, it will not provide any schematisation that can be adopted by all and be publicly intelligible. The social sciences must therefore set aside such explanations and identify conceptual categories that will allow them to objectivate human experience, even provisionally. Although these nascent sciences, by comparison with the "non-social" sciences, have not yet identified the categories with sufficient clarity,

D. Courgeau (ed.) Methodology and Epistemology of Multilevel Analysis, 1-23.

we can assume that the objectivation process is under way. We shall return to this point in the volume's conclusion.

Third, we need to realise that all scientific knowledge assumes a splitting of reality into a concrete aspect and a virtual aspect—the latter being a fairly abstract image of the events explored by the scientist. For the social sciences, the observation of individuals, groups or societies provides the "reality" that they will study. But unlike in the physical sciences, where there is only one type of virtuality—an abstract construct based on the formal properties of physical phenomena—virtuality in the social sciences undergoes a split as well. The first virtuality obtained is "an abstract construct, external by nature to the conscience of human actors albeit very *real*; it provides a scaffolding for the knowledge of facts" (Granger, 2001, p. 191): by placing this virtuality in the foreground, the social sciences attempt to *explain* human behaviours, developing the structure that will enable social scientists to describe the phenomena observed. The second virtuality resulting from the split is experienced by the actors: it is a complex of thoughts, affects, and intentions that make it possible to *understand* the behaviour of a given individual, without being entirely accessible to the social scientist. We are dealing here with a "clinical knowledge" that aims to grasp human facts in their singularity, in their individuality and not in their generality. However, it is this experienced virtuality that will confer meaning upon the abstract construct that the social scientist is trying to achieve. As we shall see, it is from life stories told by individuals themselves that biographical analysis will be able to take shape: the stories will provide the raw material from which we can construct a process underlying all these biographies.

We will not elaborate here on this "clinical knowledge" of singular human facts, which psychoanalysis and some currents of psychology and sociology are seeking to attain. The process of capturing the individual, in this case,

> consists in constructing and superimposing ever more detailed networks of conceptual representation, each of which represents only a generic virtuality. It is the assumed convergence of the superposition of these grids that would bring us closer to an understanding of the individual. But it would, at best, impart only a limit meaning to this scientific reality of the individual. When measured against its concrete aspect, the limit meaning remains indefinitely incomplete (Granger, 2001, p. 206).

We shall therefore give priority to a virtual theoretical representation—divorced from the procedures of an individualised and unique capture of phenomena—and a scientific description of human reality, using concepts chained together in causal relationships, which will lead to models. Among the sciences examined in closer detail in this volume are demography, economics, epidemiology, education, human geography and social statistics. These are in fact the main social sciences for which multilevel modelling proves to be the most relevant.

It is only when social scientists attempt to observe behaviours and objectivate the environment where they occur and the manner in which they operate that they will face the problem of aggregation—in a space that is both physical and social—and the problem of choosing a suitable time scale. There will be many questions as to the choice of the right aggregation level: Should the observation focus on aggregate or individual behaviours? Will the methods used to identify the relationships between the values measured be the same or totally different depending on the level of observation? Can several aggregation levels be used simultaneously? and so on. The social scientist will also need to address the issue of time: Will it be historical time, in which the events studied unfold, or, on the contrary, the time lived by the individual who experiences the events? Will the observation point be a precise moment of that "lived" time, in order to explain the behaviours occurring then by conditions prevailing immediately beforehand? Or, on the contrary, will the observation span an individual's entire life, involving constantly changing conditions? These issues have been present from the very beginning of social-science research. We shall address them throughout this volume, and try to find satisfactory solutions.

The multilevel approach—which has recently gained ground—tackles the issues from a fresh angle. Within the framework of a single model, it seeks to achieve a synthesis connecting individuals to the society in which they live. For this purpose, it uses intermediate levels, which can vary from one science to another: for example, class and school, in education; the village, the town, and the region, in human geography; the family, the household, and the contact circle, in demography. This approach recognises that the grouping of individuals according to these various levels introduces an influence of the group on its members and, conversely, an influence of members on the group's future. Ignoring this relationship may lead to an incorrect analysis of individual behaviours and an equally incorrect analysis of the behaviours of the entire group. Only by recognising these reciprocal influences can we arrive at a more correct analysis of behaviours. The aim of this volume is therefore to explore the contributions of the new approach to various social sciences, to dissect the methodological assumptions on which it is based, and to see if it helps to improve the state of knowledge in those sciences.

This multi-author volume is not simply a collection of independently-written papers. It is the product of close communication between the specialists involved in clarifying the advantages of multilevel analysis: their exchanges shed new light on the approach. We also asked a philosopher of science for a more epistemological contribution—which proved highly relevant—to our methodological work. Our joint efforts lasted more than two years and culminated in a three-day meeting at INED in March 2001. The forum gave us the opportunity to compare our different approaches—often in an impassioned spirit—and to agree on a fuller and more written-up version of our proceedings. We were also able to present the social sciences in a more varied manner so as to avoid excessive repetitions. Of course each author retains sole responsibility for his or her presentation; their opinions, which diverged on certain points, have been included here so as to highlight the constructive side of our disagreements.

Before opening the discussion to our contributors, we will try to outline a very broad opposition between *holism* and *individualism* in the social sciences, and to indicate the richness and relevance of the explanations they allow, as well as the apparent incompatibility of their premises. Next, we show

how more numerous and more complex levels of aggregation can emerge. We conclude with a prelude to the synthesis provided by multilevel analysis, on which the subsequent chapters will elaborate, and give a short presentation of the scope of this volume.

1. OPPOSITION BETWEEN HOLISM AND INDIVIDUALISM

The distinction between holism and individualism stems from the fact that a social system can be viewed from two opposite perspectives: either as a totality endowed with specific properties, irreducible to those of its members, or as a set of individuals, such that all social phenomena resolve into individual decisions and actions, without involving any supra-individual factors.

In the social sciences, the initial opposition is between society and the individual—although, as we demonstrate later on, the levels are far more diverse. The important point here is to examine in greater detail, on the basis of this initial distinction, how behaviours are taken into account and what consequences result from it.

1.1. Society

It seems preferable to begin with the social structure or form, which is already viewed as essential in some of Aristotle's writings. For the philosopher, the State as community (πόλιζ), under whatever government,

> is by nature clearly prior to the family and to the individual, since the whole is of necessity prior to the part; for example, if the whole body be destroyed, there will be no foot or hand, except in an equivocal sense, as we might speak of a stone hand; for when destroyed the hand will be no better than that (*Politics*, book I, part 2, trans. B. Jowett).

Considered as a whole, the community is not an artificial or conventional form, but originates in the demands of human nature: a man who cannot belong to a community "must be either a beast or a god".

In fact, for Aristotle, the individual cannot be the object of any science. He clearly states:

> But none of the arts theorise about individual cases. Medicine, for instance, does not theorise about what will help to cure Socrates or Callias, but only about what will help to cure any or all of a given class of patients: this alone is business: individual cases are so infinitely various that no systematic knowledge of them is possible (*Rhetoric*, book I, part 2, trans. W. Rhys Roberts).

It should be noted here that Aristotle often uses the term "art" (τέχνη) as a substitute for the term "science" (επιστημη), although he occasionally distinguishes between the two: art is more oriented toward "necessity or pleasure"; science is disinterested and aims not to indulge in the pleasures or necessities of life, but rather to discover the structure of things. Incidentally, the modern concept of social science is not present in Aristotle's thought (Granger, 1976).

Closer to us, the macrolevel *par excellence* is society or the State, rather than the community. To take a society as the macrolevel is to regard it as a perfectly defined and organised whole, clearly distinct from the sum of individuals who compose it, and displaying a powerful internal integration. We can thus deal with this society independently of other contemporaneous societies, and we can treat the social phenomena to be studied as external to individuals. Moreover, these phenomena are of a different nature than individual states of conscience. By contrast, we can compare different societies and highlight their distinguishing features.

We have seen earlier that the purpose of all social sciences is to explain a certain number of behaviours and to analyse the structures in which these phenomena appear. The behaviours and structures are specific to each science, for example: mortality, fertility, nuptiality, and migration, for demography; production, and consumption of wealth, for economics; the dissemination in space and time of diseases, for epidemiology. When we view phenomena at the level of a society, the concrete aspect is represented by the statistical reality of the facts observed in that society. We can classify the facts into two categories, which provide an explanatory framework: (1) the facts that will represent the origin of social facts and the initial conditions observed; (2) the facts that will represent the results obtained under these conditions. The aim here is to use a *model*—which will constitute an abstract virtuality—to describe not only the summary results, but also the processes that lead to these results from the initial conditions.

The origin of social facts must be sought in the formation of the social environment in which they occur. The initial conditions will therefore be supplied by the main characteristics of this environment, which can lead to the phenomena studied and are observed prior to them. The conditions can be measured by statistics describing the state of the society under examination at a given moment. The events studied, meanwhile, can be measured by the proportions of individuals who have experienced them in the following period, which is often very short. For example, the percentages of individuals having displayed a given behaviour (proportion of suicides; proportions of migrants, of persons who have contracted a particular disease, of farmers who have given up farming, etc.), will be linked to certain characteristics that may or may not lead to these behaviours (shares of Catholics and Protestants to explain suicide; percentage of managers or, on the contrary, of farmers to characterise migration; percentages of individuals living in insalubrious conditions or on the contrary in uncontaminated locations to characterise the propensity to contract a given disease; percentages of farm labourers or, on the contrary, of farmers on large holdings to characterise exits from farming).

Thus, when we start from society as an organised whole in order to produce a set of effects under social constraints, our aim will be to show the way in which the society produces a given economic, demographic, social, or other type of fact. More specifically, it is by linking the observed facts to the society of which they are a diverse expression that we will be able to explain and find a basis for their reciprocal effects (Franck, 1994).

Durkheim (1897/1930) sought to relate social facts to the society in which they occur, in order to explain and find a basis for the effect of the religious system, household system, and political system on suicide. To his end, he established a network of links between different factors representing these systems—factors for which we can perform suitable aggregate measurements (such as the percentages of Protestants or divorcees in each age group). His method for comparing suicides in different categories of individuals is that of concomitant variations already advocated by Mill (1843), which closely foreshadows what we now call a linear regression. Durkheim shows how, for different sub-populations, suicide varies as a function of religion, and of the domestic and political characteristics of the society in which the individual lives. However, it is not these characteristics themselves that explain the greater or lesser frequency of suicide, but the social structure itself in which the individuals live. He concludes that "suicide varies in inverse proportion to the degree of integration of the social groups to which the individual belongs" (Durkheim, 1897/1930, p. 223), i.e., the more structured the society, the fewer suicides will occur in it.

Likewise, demographers have long given priority to the analysis of aggregate data. This is possible, for example, by using civil-registration records to study a phenomenon in the year following a census. The phenomenon can then be related to the set of characteristics measured thanks to the census. First, the census provides data on various populations exposed to the risk of the events; one can thus calculate the corresponding rates for different regions, districts, or population categories covered by the civil records (by occupational category, for example). Again, we can also use linear-regression methods for more detailed analyses: Puig (1981) examines the immigration and emigration rates of French regions, measured by a question on the place of residence in the previous census; he relates the rates to several aggregate characteristics of these regions (percentage of farmers, unemployed, etc.). Puig effectively identifies a link between ratios, while assuming that it proxies the influence of these characteristics on an individual's decision to migrate "based on a trade-off between his or her resources and location preferences" (p. 49). We will examine the validity of such a hypothesis later.

Likewise, in epidemiology, the theory of miasmas developed in the first half of the nineteenth century can be regarded as a holistic approach to public-health issues associated with urban conditions, poverty, and hazardous occupations (McMichael, 1999). For this purpose, epidemiologists relied on statistical averages characteristic of a natural and physical environment. The result was a series of measures to improve sewage systems, water supply, regulations on housing standards, and—more generally—sanitation developments affecting public health.

In all these instances, society is regarded as a system composed of different categories such as religious, occupational, or political. The system explains why an observed social fact is the cause of a given social effect, or why it produces another given social fact. The problem is to define and bound this system properly by identifying the appropriate aggregate characteristics, which correspond to the collective states existing in the society (suicide rates, percentages of Protestants and Catholics, proportion of bachelors and widows, etc.). We will then be able to consolidate the relationship between these characteristics, such as the respective influence of Catholicism and Protestantism on suicide rates.

Another factor underlying this approach is historical time: as noted earlier, we will observe the situation at a given instant to explain the phenomena that occur at that time on the basis of conditions prevailing immediately before. The approach gives precedence to the analysis of concomitant phenomena and relationships observed at that moment: period analysis in demography, static analysis in sociology, structuralism in anthropology, etc. Of course a change from one period to the next is possible, as the structures have changed and the macro effects can also evolve. Again, however, these changes take place only at the aggregate level, without involving individual behaviours that occur in a "lived time".

The paradigms or rather the research programs that sustain such an approach in each social science must all, therefore, regard the individual as a non-relevant unit, and consider that only the individual's membership in different groups or categories will influence the occurrence rates of the phenomena studied. Of course, these paradigms will contain other elements specific to each social science. This defines a *methodological holism* in which some of the facts studied are a function of the social science examined, while others may be common to several of the sciences.

Indeed, it is a holism of this kind that enables us to envisage an interdependence of social facts in a given social structure. Accordingly, a particular social fact that we want to study may appear in different proportions in different regions studied, as can the preceding social facts to which we are trying to connect it. By contrast, to the extent that this structure characterises the society as a whole, a linear relationship between these proportions should emerge. In demography, for example, if we establish a relationship between regional emigration rates and percentages of farmers, the relationship should always involve the same parameters for all regions (Courgeau, 2002). We will thus be able to estimate the migration probabilities of the farmers and of other categories, that are independent of the region in which they live, by regressing the regional emigration rates on the regional percentages of farmers.

If, however, these hypotheses are not confirmed, we cannot take the conclusion for granted. All we can say from such an analysis is that a high percentage of farmers leads to a high emigration rate, which may involve farmers, persons of other professional categories or outside the labour force. This type of fallacious inference leads to what is customarily referred to as *ecological fallacy*, which consists in trying to detect individual behaviours by looking at aggregate measures (Robinson, 1950). Robinson showed, for example, that the correlations between two characteristics measured on a binary basis among individuals (being black and illiterate in the United States), or by proportions in regions (proportion of black and illiterate population), were generally not identical and could even carry opposite signs.

1.2. The individual

The other approach centres, instead, on the individual. However, given the diversity of meanings that the social sciences have assigned to individualism (Birnbaum and Leca, 1986), it is important to state at the outset that we shall set aside sociological, economic, legal, ethical, and philosophical individualism—described and discussed in greater detail in Valade (2001)—and focus exclusively on *methodological individualism*. This consists in explaining an observed phenomenon not as if it were determined by the society examined, but on the contrary as the outcome of individual actions or attitudes. It is essential, for example, to "reconstruct the motives of individuals concerned by the phenomenon in question, and to understand the phenomenon as the result of the aggregation of individual behaviours dictated by these motives" (Boudon, 1988, p. 31), all the more so as the individualism is rational here. Such an approach can be used for all phenomena, whether they belong to the realm of sociology, demography, economics, or any other social science.

It is important to realise that methodological individualism appeared in our western societies far later than holism, as it was largely derived from the ideas developed in the early Classical age, when "the autonomous individual constituted the ultimate unit of the social sciences, and all social phenomena were resolved into individual decisions and actions whose analysis in terms of supra-individual factors would be useless or impossible" (Valade, 2001, p. 370). However, its introduction raised a host of problems, which we now need to examine in detail.

Earlier, we noted the force of Aristotle's argument that "individual cases are so infinitely various that no systematic knowledge of them is possible". The individual is indeed intimately linked to the actors' virtual experience, comprising thoughts, affects, intentions, etc. not directly accessible to social scientists. Incidentally, this is why we do not elaborate here on the "clinical knowledge" of human facts. How can we, in such conditions, envisage the formalisation of a *virtual individual* as a theoretical object open to comprehensive modelling?

Our starting point is the observation of individual lives, by means of a biographical compendium that supplies all the events of use to the social science concerned, and provides an accurately dated record of the individual's existence. This observation in no way enables us to estimate individual random processes, whose probabilistic structure would be specific to each individual tracked. It does seem hard to assume that two individuals, even if similar in many ways, automatically follow the same path. Moreover, as we can only observe one realisation of this process for each individual—his or her own actual life course—we have no way of identifying its probabilistic structure. This is entirely consistent with Aristotle's earlier-quoted observation that an individual process is not identifiable.

We must therefore modify the interpretation of this process. For this, we shall distinguish between two stages in the development of a truly individual approach. As the full, complex process cannot be the object of scientific inquiry, the social scientist first needs to specify a *theoretical model*, characterised by only a small number of events. This theoretical model can be regarded as "a filter that retains from complex phenomena only that which must figure in the object of research" (Franck, 2002, p. 288).

Conventional economics, for example, relies on the postulate that agents display a strong rationality, which can be defined by explicit axioms. This makes it possible to elaborate a pure theory, derived from the consequences of the set axioms (Walliser, 2001). However, the strong-rationality postulate can be rejected in favour of a limited-rationality postulate, which leads to different theoretical models.

Similarly, the demographer can set up a theoretical model that constitutes a complex causal mechanism. To study the mortality of a population, for example, we can assume that "the age at death of an individual would be dependent on the states he or she has undergone in his or her life, on the time spent in each, and on their sequence" (Duchêne and Wunsch, 1991, p. 112). These states—characterised by the individual's education, family status, occupation, etc.—are assumed to act in synergy on the effect. Here, therefore, we examine not the effects of isolated characteristics but the incidence of the transitions between states in an individual life.

In a second step, we will seek to test such a theoretical model with the aid of a special *empirical model*, situated at an intermediate level between the complex process and theory. Let us again begin with observed reality, which comprises a number of individual paths. From this observation, can we estimate a probabilistic process that takes into account all the information contained in these paths? To the extent that any random process can be seen as a distribution of probabilities across a set of paths, we can say—in this case—that we observe the same random process repeatedly. Now, the probabilistic structure of the underlying process becomes identifiable from the observation of these different paths. We thus identify a collective process, which can be as complex as we like.

In the search for individual random processes, two *individuals observed* by the survey, possessing identical characteristics, have no reason to follow the same process. By contrast, in the search for a process underlying the population, two *statistical individuals*—seen as units of a repeated random draw, subject to the same selection conditions and exhibiting the same characteristics—automatically obey the same process. We can thus see more clearly how the use of observed biographies, which constitute the statistical reality of the human facts studied, can now be transformed into an abstract description of human reality by means of concepts deliberately stripped of at least some of the concrete circumstances of a virtual life-experience. These concepts fall into a sequence governed by the logical relationships of the process identified, forming a biographical model.

From the observation of a set of individual cases, we can use such an analysis to describe a mechanism that will link the phenomena studied to the individual characteristics, whether or not they are time-dependent. We now need to show what abstract relationships exist between the elements of a process that organises the life of the population studied. But for this enterprise we must replace the aggregate approach by an individual approach to human societies. This calls for new data-collection procedures and analytical methods. Let us now examine briefly how this is taking place in selected social sciences.

The economist Léon Walras (1874/1926) held that individuals respond independently to market prices, which form the only link between them. A collective entity—the auctioneer—matches consumers' orders (which define their effective demands) against the producers' supply, and can thus determine pure-competition prices: to reach equilibrium prices, the price of the goods whose effective demand exceeds effective supply must rise, and the price of the goods whose effective supply exceeds effective demand must fall. This approach is, however, based on very heroic assumptions that define a market operating under perfect competition, and hence an underlying economic structure: perfect market fluidity; immediate, full information for consumers and producers; free entry into the market, etc. Moreover, there is no statistical or temporal dimension involved here. Walras himself realised, however, the arbitrary nature of some his assumptions, when he stated that the calculation must stop at a certain point. This point, in his view, was marked by the appearance of free will, i.e., the emergence of a virtual life-experience no longer directly accessible to the investigator, as we noted earlier. Naturally the conditions of this model have been enlarged to the case where all individuals consciously interact with each other (Kirman, 1997). This enlargement, however, is still thwarted by the virtual life-experience or free will, even if its boundaries have receded.

Similarly, it is only in the early 1980s that demographers were able to adopt an approach effectively based on individual data supplied by the World Fertility Survey (WFS), INED's "Family, occupational, and migration biography" survey (also known as "Triple biography" or "3B"), and similar programs. The aim was no longer to take a snapshot of a population at a given moment, as in a census, but on the contrary to try to document over time either the history of the fertility of each woman in a sample, as in the WFS, or the more complex history of several types of phenomena tracked simultaneously in several areas of an individual's life, as in the 3B survey. But at the same time the methods for analysing aggregate data—essentially the linear regression methods—no longer allowed such biographies to be analysed. This obstacle was overcome by the introduction of new methods, initiated a few years earlier by probabilistic analysts (Cox, 1972); their development went hand in hand with their adoption in many fields, particularly the social sciences. Thanks to these methods of event history analysis, we can now examine the unfolding over time of several demographic phenomena while taking into account their possible reciprocal influences and, simultaneously, the role of various individual characteristics—time-dependent or not—on these behaviours (Courgeau and Lelièvre, 1986).

Meanwhile, by the late 1940s, medicine had succeeded in controlling the most important infectious diseases such as tuberculosis, smallpox, plague, and typhoid. Epidemiology was then confronted by new chronic diseases whose rapid spread and totally unknown origins were sufficiently frightening to replace earlier epidemics (M. and E. Susser, 1996). The chief weapon to combat these diseases was found in the vast cohort studies on smoker's cancer, coronary heart diseases, and so on. The studies accumulated a large set of characteristics of the persons untouched by the disease, of those already affected, and of those who contracted it in the course of the longitudinal study. The methods for observing and analysing such biographical data flourished, made it possible to identify the main risk factors, and helped reduce them. All these studies, performed in the last fifty years, seek to link the occurrence of a disease to various risks, using multivariate methods and survival analysis. This has made it possible to highlight the multicausal nature of public-health problems more effectively.

In all the examples we have given, the initial observation no longer involves society as a whole, but focuses on a number of individual cases from which we can estimate the structure of a given process. It is this process that now characterises the occurrence of one or more given phenomena. We will thus be able to describe the causal structure of the processes studied, such as the effect of a particular characteristic on the risks of disease in epidemiology, of migration in demography or human geography, of passing an exam in education, and so on. More generally, we should be able to describe with precision the interactions between many phenomena and the characteristics of the society studied.

This time, however, we will not find a historical time underlying the approach, as in the case of holism, but a time experienced by the individuals studied, which may even be frozen, as in the Walrasian model mentioned earlier or in a stationary Markov process. The individual time scale may run from the date of birth or a founding event such as marriage (for the analysis of legitimate fertility) or contamination (for the study of the outbreak of a disease). The event history approach allows the events that will shape the phenomena studied to be introduced as time-dependent characteristics. We will therefore be able to track evolutionary processes: for example, "the evolutionary processes of the determinants of agents under the influence of time, their past actions, and the actions of others" (Walliser and Prou, 1988, p. 201), in economics, or a process describing the sequence of fertility-period events in demography.

The paradigms or rather the research programs that underpin such an approach in the social sciences will now consider individual biographies as the empirical material on which they will work; however, their research objects will be the processes that give meaning to the biographies. It is important to remember here that, under the terms of this methodological individualism, we cannot grasp the virtual life experience of these actors themselves, but only an abstract process. Each of these paradigms, of course, will contain elements specific to each of the sciences in question.

In fact, it is a methodological individualism of this kind that enables us to contemplate an interdependence between different characteristics for a given statistical individual, situated in a given social structure and a given population. Consequently, if we break down the total population into different parts, the statistical individuals in each of these sub-populations will no longer have any reason to follow the previous overall process. They will now follow as many different processes as there are sub-populations. For example, if we establish a relationship between the probability of migration of farmers compared with other occupations in the total population, the relationships estimated for each region will no longer yield the same parameters as under the conditions of methodological holism (Courgeau, 2002). Under the latter, statistical individuals taken from the overall population will consistently follow the same process, whatever their region of residence. By contrast, we can say that statistical individuals picked from different regional sub-populations will no longer have any reason to follow the same process. Yet there will not be the slightest contradiction between these two samplings, as we will not be dealing with the same statistical individuals. In this case, the concomitant-variations method is not valid; we need methods using individual responses to estimate the parameters of each regional model.

It is fair to say that this approach enables us to factor in the influence of some individual characteristics on behaviours: the characteristics form a combination of variables whose identified effects on a given cohort and in a specific environment provide an explanation of these behaviours. Here, however, as we no longer consider the context in which these behaviours occur, a risk of *atomistic fallacy* appears. Indeed, there is no reason why this context—comprising both family and environment—should have no influence on observed behaviours, and it seems fallacious to examine individuals divorced from the constraints of the society and environment in which they live.

2. HOW ARE THE TWO APPROACHES LINKED?

We are now in the presence of two approaches: the aggregate or "macro" approach versus the individual or "micro" approach. On the face of it, they appear to be antagonistic in every way, both epistemologically and technically—i.e., in the measurement, analysis, and interpretation of results. Let us begin by examining each of these points in greater detail.

Insofar as the aggregate approach starts with the assumption that the essential factor is the social structure, the latter cannot be defined except through the fullest possible observation of society. Moreover, the structure basically evolves in historical time; it can remain static for long periods yet change quickly in times of crisis. We will therefore give precedence to a synchronous measurement method, with repetitions in the course of the historical time of the observation. This makes it clearer why the principal method for measuring aggregate data is the population census, which gathers a comprehensive set of information on a country's population. The information can, for example, be linked to civil-registration data for demographic studies. Other sources—comprehensive or not—are available for this population, allowing a measurement of phenomena not documented by the censuses. Often, the sources consist of period surveys of large numbers of individuals, which capture a number of phenomena and furnish evidence of the links between them. For example, the Labour-Force Surveys conducted in European Union countries provide an annual overview of a population's activity measured through such variables as employment and unemployment, wages, occupation, educational attainment, and job search.

As the individual approach emphasises individual actions and decisions, these cannot be identified except by the most detailed possible observation of behaviours provided by a biographical database. Moreover, the time scale to be considered will be the individual's personal time frame, not historical time. We can thus see more clearly why the measurement of individual data, because of the scope of the information that it involves, leads to retrospective or prospective biographical surveys that can cover only a small number of respondents, given the level of detail of the questions required. The surveys supply all the events in an individual's life that are relevant to the planned study; the events are situated in diachronic time. As a rule, they are highly detailed biographical surveys that will capture the dates of occurrence of events in such different areas as family life and working life. Sometimes the events will be located in a physical and social space, along with a certain number of the individuals' characteristics, which can also change over time.

As we can see, the two types of measurement are very different, but they will nevertheless capture two aspects of an identical reality, specific to each social science. They are most often used separately, as the measures rest on different concepts such as holism or methodological individualism. However, if we could transcend these concepts, we could envisage a simultaneous treatment of both measures. We shall discuss this later. For now, let us turn to the analytical methods.

For aggregate data, the analysis of social structures leads to the identification of concomitant variations between relevant indicators: "the mere parallelism of the values taken by the two phenomena, provided that it has been established in an adequate number of sufficiently varied cases, is the proof of a relationship between them" (Durkheim, 1895/1937, p. 129). In this case, to show the possible links between an aggregate characteristic that we want to analyse and other aggregate characteristics that may help explain the phenomenon studied, the best method is to use regressions—in particular, linear regressions. The units of analysis generally consist of groups of individuals living in the same district, the same region, etc., especially when we are working on comprehensive census data. Within the group, we do not know the joint distribution of the individual variables. All we know is the marginal distribution of each of these characteristics. We will be able to identify the links between them by means of regression analysis on the groups—which, as explained earlier, we regard as arbitrary for our purposes. Such an analysis will also be conducted in a historical time frame, typically at a particular point, in order to interlink the social facts.

For individual data, on the contrary, the aim is to connect a life-long behaviour to personal events or characteristics that can also vary over time. Other methods must therefore be used. Here are some of the most common: logistic regression methods for binary data or polytomous data observed at a specific moment (binary: the individual has experienced a given event or not; polytomous: the variable examined may exist in several forms); event history analysis methods for binary characteristics observed throughout individuals' life courses (the date of an event they have experienced); or longitudinal analysis methods for continuous data such as an individual's size throughout his or her life. However, linear-regression methods can still be used for continuous individual data (such as an individual's score on a test). In all these cases we can find links between the individual characteristics by working on a "lived time".

Again, we can see how different these analytical methods are, and how hard it is to use them simultaneously. The first relate aggregate characteristics to each other; the second interlink individual characteristics. The first will place them in a historical-time context, the second in a time lived by the individual. We must therefore try to transcend these incompatibilities in order to establish models that will reconcile the analytical methods.

Let us set aside, for the moment, the time dimension of the phenomena studied, which we will examine in greater detail later. Figure 1 illustrates the two types of model and gives a clearer picture of the difficulties we face in trying to move from one to the other.

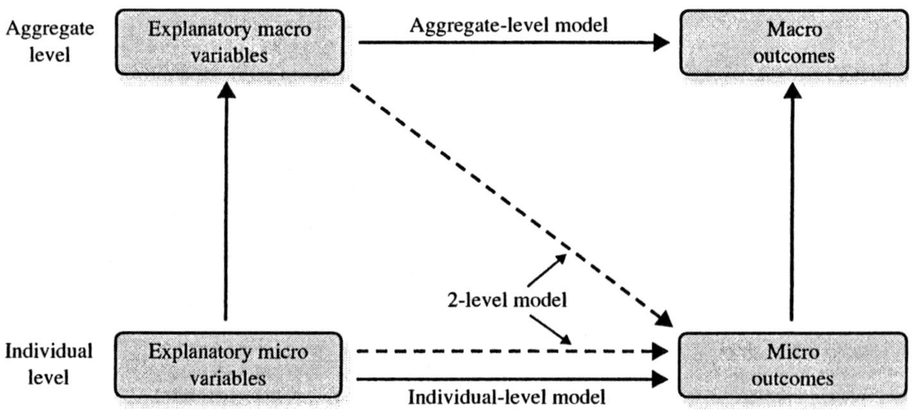

Figure 1. Connection between different models

The aggregate-level model, represented by the top horizontal solid-line arrow, shows the result obtained at the macro level, for example the proportions of individuals having experienced the event studied: the proportions are explained by the rule and institutions governing these behaviours in the society considered, which are measured, for example, by aggregate characteristics. In contrast, the individual model, represented by the lower horizontal solid-line arrow, links the obtained result to the micro level—for example, the probability that a statistical individual will experience the event, a probability explained by the individual characteristics governing the behaviour.

Using simple, concrete examples, we shall now attempt to describe the difficulties encountered when trying to move between these two levels in different social sciences. Here, we deal with the shift from the individual level to the aggregate level, as indicated by the two vertical solid-line arrows of figure 1. We shall not examine all the possibilities in detail, but we will show, in a few selected cases, the reasons for divergence between individual and aggregate models.

First, let us assume that all the individual characteristics are continuous data, for example, in education, the score in a test taken by an eleven-year-old pupil as a function of the pupil's score at age eight (Goldstein, 1995). We may regard the children's school as the aggregate level at which we can compute the average scores of pupils aged eight and eleven. The aggregate variables are, again, continuous variables. We should also recall that these schools are used, at the aggregate level, solely to estimate overall parameters, which are assumed to be independent of their choice.

Can we assume that the relationship observed between individual scores is reproduced identically between aggregate scores? Supposing, for example, that a linear regression is correctly demonstrated between individual scores, can we estimate the parameters of a similar regression on the aggregate data? We can show mathematically that the parameters of a regression on aggregate data cannot, in most cases, be deduced from those of a regression on individual data, as they depend on other quantities linked to the grouping used (Duncan *et al.*, 1961). For these quantities not to affect the shift from individual to aggregate regressions, very special conditions must prevail—which is rarely the case. For example, if the scores at age eight are identical in each class and if each class has the same number of pupils, then the parameters of a regression on individual data and on aggregate data are identical. These parameters, therefore, may broadly be described as independent: in some cases, the parameter may be positive at the individual level and negative at the aggregate level. Moreover, if the relationship between the scores is more complex than a linear relationship, then the relationship between the aggregate data will not even be of the same kind as the relationship between individual data. For example, when the score at age eleven is linked to the score at age eight by an exponential relationship, it is easy to see that the aggregate scores will not be linked by an exponential relationship. We must therefore recognise in all these situations, where a linear or non-linear regression applies at the individual level, that the relationship at the aggregate level will measure something totally different from the aggregation of individual behaviours.

Let us now assume that we are working on binary individual data, i.e., the individual possesses or does not possess a particular characteristic, as regards both the variable to be explained and the explanatory variables. For example, in demography, let us suppose that we are seeking to relate an inter-regional migration to the fact that the individual is a farmer or not (Courgeau, 2002). We can treat the individual's region of residence as the aggregate level. This enables us to compute percentages of migrants and farmers in each region. We will then see a change in the nature of the variables and hence in the models applicable at the individual and aggregate levels. There is a shift from a dichotomous model (logit or probit) to a regression model involving aggregate characteristics. How can we tie the parameters of these models together? For example, we have been able to show that if we estimate a logit model at the individual level, then the model at the aggregate level is a linear regression between the percentages, whose parameters are expressed in a fairly simple but non-linear manner as a function of the individual parameters (Courgeau, 2002). In the case of the Norwegian data used in that article, the parameters estimated at the individual and aggregate levels will be very different and even contradictory, for at the aggregate level the migration probability of farmers exceeds that of other occupations, whereas at the individual level it is lower. Again, these differences can be explained only by simultaneously including in the same individual model the fact of being a farmer and the percentage of farmers living in the region. We are no longer dealing with an aggregate model.

Lastly, let us assume we are working on an individual biographical model, which will be seeking to estimate the effect of various individual characteristics, most of them binary and potentially time-dependent, on the instantaneous rate of a given event. Such an instantaneous rate measures the limit, when the time interval considered tends toward zero, of the ratio between the probability of the event's occurrence and the length of that time interval t. In that case the instantaneous rate of a given event will no longer even have an equivalent at the aggregate level, unless we define an instantaneous rate of this event estimated on each of the sub-populations of the areas. If we follow this approach, the characteristics to be examined must be individual characteristics, not the areas' aggregate characteristics. This is equivalent to working at the individual level, using the division into areas as well. As we can see, the result is that we take into account the aggregate and individual characteristics to explain an individual behaviour. Again, the model is not of the aggregate type.

As the three examples above have shown, we cannot treat an aggregate-level model as directly deducible from a model estimated at the individual level. The criteria for grouping individuals are too far from being strictly random, and the resulting models generally do not resemble individual models. In addition, the aggregate-level model may incorporate more general characteristics that cannot be linked to individual characteristics. For instance, the population density of a locality or region, or the number of hospital beds there, have no equivalent at the individual level. They can, however, be aggregated at higher levels: the number of hospital beds in a region is the sum of the number of beds in each locality of the region. Other collective characteristics are well defined at a given aggregation level, but cannot be aggregated at higher levels: the political colour of a municipality—defined, for example, by the party affiliation of its mayor—cannot be aggregated with that of neighbouring municipalities, which may cover a broad spectrum. It therefore does not exist at the individual or regional level.

Conversely, it is yet more difficult to determine the parameters of the individual model from those of the aggregate model, even assuming a very simple aggregate model. In particular, the fact that information is poorer at the aggregate level than at the individual level will prevent the switch: the percentages of farmers and migrants in a given region tell us nothing about a migrant's occupation.

In consequence, we will be able to regard these two types of models—one for the social structure, the other for individual behaviours—as practically independent. Let us now introduce the time dimension, and revisit the problems encountered when trying to interlink these different approaches.

We can say that, at the macro level, we will obtain snapshots of the social structure, taken—for example—at the successive censuses examined. We must then interlink these snapshots taken in historical time to show the broad changes in the society studied during the period. For instance, the theory of demographic transition will seek to find links between the long-term changes in a country's fertility and mortality by relating them to other equally aggregate characteristics such as international migrations and the role of institutions. We may therefore describe this theory as a process that occurs at the societal level, and we can compare it with similar processes occurring in other societies. These societies may be either of the same kind (for example, developed countries) or very different in their histories (such as the developing countries as distinct from the developed countries).

At the micro level, by contrast, we are dealing with an individual process to be described within the "lived time" of the statistical individual. The period will begin with an event such as the individual's date of birth or date of entry into the labour force. It will describe the sequence of events as a function of their inter-relationships as well as of individual characteristics, which may or may not change over time: number of siblings, successive occupations of each, etc. We may also assess the effect of economic or political events on that generation's behaviour: for example, how did the Second World War influence the fertility behaviour of women born in 1920, or how did the Great Depression of the 1930s influence the occupations of workers born in 1910? Lastly, as we will possess the timelines of successive generations, we will be able to interlink their histories in order to show the changes in behaviours over time: for example, how have consensual union partnerships spread in the European countries from one generation to the next since the end of the Second World War, and which population categories have provided the momentum for their dissemination? This approach introduces another view of the evolution of a society, via a different process than the one used in the aggregate approach.

Could we then connect the two processes by introducing a dual historical temporality—or rather a social temporality and an individual temporality—that would allow a joint analysis of these two processes? This is no easy task, given the separate and even conflicting development of the two approaches, which diverge in all aspects, but their conjunction would represent a breakthrough in the social sciences. However, before outlining a scenario for such a recomposition, we must continue our examination of the levels that need to be considered.

Thus far, we have envisaged only two main levels from which to study human phenomena: society and the individual. A closer look at a society readily shows us that other intermediate levels exist between them, and that we need to position ourselves at those levels as well in order to better understand the society in which they operate and the individual behaviours they can generate. Should we not also study the time scales that these new levels will generate?

3. A PLURALITY OF AGGREGATION LEVELS AND A PLURALITY OF TIME SCALES

Progress in the social sciences has led to the use of multiple levels, creating the need to define their purposes and to examine temporalities that are multiple as well. This diversity of levels and time scales further complicates the shifts between them but, as we shall see later, it will free us from the contradictions—and the need to choose—between holism and methodological individualism.

Let us take an example from education. Between a social structure, corresponding to the national education system, and an individual level, corresponding to the personal education process, we will find intermediate levels, whose importance is far from negligible. The first such level involved is the class, to the extent that the teacher(s) and pupils in the class can play a major role in the success or failure of an individual pupil. Some teachers may focus on the class as a whole by trying, for example, to raise all pupils to the same level. Other teachers, instead, may neglect the weaker pupils to allow the best ones to over-achieve, thereby widening the gaps between them. Other levels as well may influence the pupil: the family (the child's place among his or her siblings, and parental choices concerning the child's further course of study), the school attended (in particular, whether the school is public or private), the neighbourhood, etc. We can thus identify several levels—ranked in a hierarchic order or not—that will exert diverse effects on children's behaviour.

Likewise, when demographers or population geographers study inter-regional migrations, instead of adopting an individual or national perspective on these migrations, they can use the region as intermediate level. Depending on the region, several regional characteristics can play a crucial and different role in these population flows. At the national level, we regarded average regional unemployment or wage rates as means of measuring a broader effect of unemployment or wages on inter-regional migration rates. Here, we will assess the specific effects of those same characteristics on the individual probabilities of emigrating from each region. The same is true if we examine migrations between municipalities, districts, etc., which will involve levels representing municipal divisions, district divisions, and so on. Other, non-geographic levels may also exert an influence: the individual's household may restrain migration if it includes many members with different activities in the region; by contrast, the household may trigger migration for individuals living alone and with few ties to the region.

It is easy to generalise this emergence of multiple levels in all the social sciences, and it is increasingly necessary to examine them simultaneously. Indeed, we must realise that these realities are not ontologically separate, and that it is essential to find out how the microstructures fit into the macrostructures and vice versa.

At the same time, the temporalities to be taken into account will multiply and diversify. It may not be enough to analyse the time linked to the individual's life, as intermediate time scales may play a major role. Likewise, historical time can be broken down into periods of different significance.

For instance, when demographers want to study a woman's fertility, they can analyse the woman's age and compute age-specific fertility rates. But the demographer may take the view that fertility is linked to the formation of the couple, in which case it is preferable to calculate the rates specific to the duration of the live-in partnership—a temporality that, no doubt, better reflects the woman's fertility. Again, however, for births above order one, it may be preferable to focus on the interval between births rather than the duration of the partnership, and so on. The choice between these time scales is not easy, and it would be better to examine them all simultaneously.

Moving in the other direction, it seems harder to discern a plurality of time scales under a single historical temporality. However, it is useful to introduce different periods into the latter, for example to characterise the changes in a population's fertility. It may be worth considering durations computed from key dates in the population's history that may influence its fertility. Examples include wars or economic crises; major discoveries in the field studied; the advent of the pill for the history of fertility, or major changes in the social rules concerning fertility, such as the legal restrictions on abortion in Romania in 1966.

To better understand human phenomena, therefore, we need to examine a wide diversity of levels and a great variety of time scales. The terms "micro" and "macro" become totally relative, and a level regarded as micro in an analysis can become macro in another. For instance, while the class represents a more aggregate level than the pupil, it will serve as a micro level relative to the school. This relativity of levels with respect to each other is now clearly visible. More important, however, it is essential to realise how closely interlinked these levels are, and how they can no longer be treated separately. We can no longer qualify any one of the levels as more fundamental that the others; even less can we state that it is independent of the others. We must therefore turn to the study of the inter-relationship between levels. This inter-relationship is the focus of the recomposition described in the next section.

4. TOWARDS A RECOMPOSITION AND A MULTILEVEL SYNTHESIS

After breaking down the object of the social sciences into its various levels and temporalities—which, as we have seen, can seem mutually contradictory—we must try to reconstruct an overall object that will allow a synthesis of the approaches identified here. This summary approach has been called for by many social scientists for years (Alexander *et al.*, 1987; Huber, 1991; Janssen, 1998). In this section, we shall give a very broad outline of a multilevel synthesis for use in different social sciences. To this end, we shall apply some of the concepts that were introduced in our discussion and will enable us to carry out the recomposition.

To begin with, we believe the concept of statistical individual is crucial for describing a more general process affecting the entire population. The concept allows us to link together the analyses undertaken at different aggregation levels, by accurately separating the virtual experience of these players from the virtual construct of the social sciences. There are no obstacles left to asserting that statistical individuals can be exposed to the effects of their own characteristics as well as to the structural constraints of the social system in which they live (Giddens, 1984). Such constraints are not exercised independently of individual motives and reasons—as in Durkheim's holism—but in a manner that is both enabling and restrictive. We can thus avoid the two types of fallacy described earlier: the ecological fallacy and the atomistic fallacy. The risk of ecological fallacy is removed, as the aggregate constraints will measure a construct that differs from their equivalent at the individual level. They occur not as a substitute, but as a structural constraint that can affect the behaviour of an individual subjected to it. Simultaneously, the atomistic fallacy disappears when we make proper use of the context in which the individual lives.

More profoundly, by identifying a plurality of levels, we discard the dualist approach, which pits society against the individual. Under these conditions, "it no longer makes sense to choose between *holism* and *atomism*, and, as regards the social sciences, between *holism* and *individualism*" (Franck, 1995, p. 79), for our aim now is to study how these different levels interconnect. At the same time, we want to find out how to fit a historical time scale and different individual time scales together into a single model, as indicated earlier. Multilevel analysis, therefore, effectively paves the way for a new approach in the social sciences.

The new methods to be introduced should make it possible to treat levels in a hierarchic order (pupils in classes, classes in schools, etc.) as well as more complex nestings (individuals classified by type of residential neighbourhood and type of workplace, which are in turn ranked into districts and regions). It should also be possible to generalise these contextual models—in which individual results obtained in the groups composing a given level are treated as independent—into true multilevel models where the result of an individual situated in a group can depend on the results obtained by the other members of the group. Lastly, these methods should make it possible to accommodate the multiple time scales, both historical and individual, in which the events occur.

It should be noted that the multilevel model itself, as we have outlined it, operates at the level of the statistical individual, but leaves room for the effect on the individual's behaviour of characteristics measured at different aggregation levels, as well as the interactions between individual and structural constraints. Such a model is shown in figure 1 as two dotted lines connecting the individual and aggregate characteristics to the expected result. Of course, we leave open the possibility of interactions between these characteristics—not only at a given aggregation level but especially between these levels—and the possibility of drawing on far more aggregation levels than the two depicted in the diagram.

We may legitimately ask, however, if this approach is the only solution to the problem of the recomposition of the object of the social sciences. Might it not be necessary to use different models to explain the changes in structural constraints? For example, in economics, how should we analyse the birth, functioning, and death of institutions such as the market or central planning

(Lesourne, 1991)? What, if any, interactions exist between these institutions and individual behaviours: how individual actions may break down an institution? Another valid question is whether—in view of the multiplicity of time scales to be incorporated into the analysis—several types of models should not be used to grasp the full complexity of the phenomena studied. These are some of the issues raised by multilevel models.

5. OUTLINE OF THIS VOLUME

After this general introduction, that develops the distinction between holism and individualism in the social sciences, and also discusses the link between the two approaches and the need for a multilevel analysis, a first chapter by Harvey Goldstein presents the main ingredients of such an analysis, taking examples from educational sciences. He introduces the basic notations used throughout the book and covers aspects such as the units and levels to be considered. He presents the basic linear multilevel model, and elaborates this with examples of cross-classified and multiple membership models. While this chapter is concerned mainly with educational data, almost all the issues covered apply to other disciplinary areas. The chapter provides the main tools for undertaking a multilevel analysis. In particular it proposes new ways of simultaneously modelling responses at different aggregation levels, without setting a logical priority of one over another.

The second chapter by Daniel Courgeau presents the history of demographic thinking, as an example, from the methodologist's viewpoint. He shows how, among other things, the increasing availability of detailed data has changed one's focus from the aggregate period approach, to longitudinal and individual life histories, and finally to multilevel analysis. He stresses the more general role of time and space in the social sciences, giving a wider scope than a demographic one to this history. He shows how the multilevel approach allows one to solve some of the problems encountered when using other approaches, and argues for a renewed use of the Bayesian probabilistic viewpoint.

The third chapter by Ana Diez Roux provides a stimulating discussion of the potentialities and limitations of multilevel analysis in public health and epidemiology. She discusses the challenges raised by the use of such an approach in epidemiology, in particular the danger of adopting the methods for their own sake. She also points out limitations of the present multilevel models which often ignore complex chains of causation and non-linear structural relationships, although the contemplation of these issues within a multilevel framework is currently of great interest. This cautious approach emphasises the need for using a model not as a complete picture of the real world but as an imperfect way of understanding some aspects of the world.

The fourth chapter by Mark Tranmer, David Steel, and Ed Fieldhouse focuses on the use of multilevel models in exploring small area population structures. They deal with the practical issues of mixing individual and spatial data from various sources, and present detailed examples of their approach to British data, including nested and cross-classified models. They point out the pitfalls and solutions when using geographic area data, a common approach in such fields as economy, demography, public health and human geography.

In the next chapter, Bernard Walliser presents a discussion of organisational levels and time scales in economics. This theoretical exposition gives a complete overview of the main paradigms. He shows that despite the modest role of holism in economics, this research field cannot be regarded as wholly informed by methodological individualism. He introduces useful distinctions between other methodological forms, such as weak methodological holism or individualism, autonomous or crossed methodological interactionism. He finally argues for empirical economic models to be confronted by theory.

The sixth chapter by Robert Franck deals with philosophy and epistemology, while it considers very practical issues raised by the previous chapters. First, he carries out an examination of several types of causal determination and of their impact on multilevel analysis. Then, he clarifies the nature of levels, by the aid of the philosophical concept of hylemorphism. This concept allows us to understand the emergence of systems, at a higher level, from factors acting reciprocally at the lower level. Under these conditions multilevel analysis may be enlarged to deal with the influences of factors over the emerging system, and to the influence of the emerging system over the same factors, leading to new procedures for the analysis of system functions.

The volume ends with a series of conclusions by Daniel Courgeau. He raises some more general issues on the non-experimental versus the experimental approach (Wunsch, 1994; Goldstein, 1998), on the nature of the concept of probability used (Greenland, 1998, 2000), and on the difficulty of defining relevant levels and their interconnection in the wider sense. In other words, how should we implement a fuller theory of human behaviour?

It is now up to the authors to show—for the social science area represented by each—the means of introducing such a multilevel analysis, of taking into account the various aggregation levels and complex time scales as best as possible, and of addressing the issues left unsolved (or, on the contrary, the issues raised) by this approach.

REFERENCES

Alexander, M., Giesen, B., Münch, R., & Smelser, N. J. (Eds.). (1987). *The micro-macro link*. Berkeley, Los Angeles, London: University of California Press.

Aristotle (1885). *Politics* (B. Jowett, Trans.), from http://classics.mit.edu/Aristotle/politics.html.

Aristotle (1954). *Rhetoric* (W. Rhys Roberts Trans.), from http://classics.mit.edu/Aristotle/rhetoric.html.

Berthelot, J.-M. (2001). Les sciences du social. In J.-M. Berthelot (Ed.), *Epistémologie des sciences sociales* (pp. 203-265). Paris: Presses Universitaires de France.

Berthelot, J.-M. (Ed.). (2001). *Epistémologie des sciences sociales*. Paris: Presses Universitaires de France.

Birnbaum, P.,& Leca, D. (Eds.). (1986). *Sur l'individualisme. Thèmes et méthodes*. Paris: Presses de la Fondation Nationale des Sciences Politiques.

Boudon, R. (1988). Individualisme ou holisme : un débat méthodologique fondamental. In H. Mendras & M. Verret (Eds.), *Les champs de la sociologie française* (pp. 31-45). Paris: Armand Colin.

Courgeau, D. (2002). Vers une analyse biographique multiniveau. In Christine M. (Ed.), *Actes des journées de méthodologie statistique* (pp. 375-394). Paris: INSEE méthodes 101.

Courgeau, D., & Lelièvre, E. (1986). Nuptialité et agriculture. *Population, 41*, 303-326.
Cox, D.R. (1972). Regression models and life tables (with discussion). *Journal of the Royal Statistical Society, B34*, 187-220.
Duncan, O.D., Cuzzort, R.P., & Duncan, B. (1961). *Statistical geography.* Illinois: The Free Press of Glencoe.
Duchêne, J., & Wunsch, G. (1991). Life histories, a new approach to the study of mortality. In Jozwiac, J., Kotowska, I.E. (Eds.), *Usefulness of demographic models* (pp. 111-120). Warsaw: Institute of Statistics and Demography.
Durkheim, E. (1930). *Le suicide.* Paris: PUF (original work published 1897).
Durkheim, E. (1937). *Les règles de la méthode sociologique.* Paris: PUF, (original work published 1895).
Franck, R. (1994). Les explications causale, fonctionnelle, systémique ou structurale, et dialectique sont-elles complémentaires ? In R. Franck (Ed.), *Faut-il chercher aux causes une raison ? L'explication causale dans les sciences humaines* (pp. 275-302). Paris - Lyon: Librairie Philosophique J. Vrin.
Franck, R. (1995). Mosaïques, machines, organismes et sociétés. Examen métadisciplinaire du réductionnisme, *Revue Philosophique de Louvain, 93*, 67-81.
Franck, R. (2002).Conclusion of Part IV. In R. Franck (Ed.), *The explanatory power of models. Bridging the gap between empirical and theoretical models in the social sciences* (pp. 285-294). Boston/Dordrecht/London: Kluwer Academic Publishers (Methodos Series, vol. 1).
Giddens, A. (1984). *The constitution of society.* Cambridge: Polity Press.
Goldstein, H. (1995). *Multilevel statistical models.* London: Edward Arnold.
Goldstein, H. (1998). *Model for reality: new approaches to the understanding of educational processes.* (Professorial Lecture). London: Institute of Education.
Granger, G.-G. (1967). Epistémologie économique. In Piaget, J. (Ed.), *Logique et connaissance scientifique* (pp. 1019-1055). Paris: Editions Gallimard.
Granger, G.-G. (1976). *La théorie aristotélicienne de la science.* Paris: Aubier.
Granger, G.-G. (1988). *Essai d'une philosophie du style*, Paris: Editions Odile Jacob.
Granger, G.-G. (1994). *Formes, opérations, objet.* Paris: Librairie philosophique J. Vrin.
Granger, G.-G. (2001). *Sciences et réalités.* Paris: Éditions Odile Jacob.
Greenland, S. (1998). Probability logic and probability induction. *Epidemiology, 9*, 322-332.
Greenland, S. (2000). Principles of multilevel modelling. *International Journal of Epidem*iology, *29*, 158-167.
Huber, J. (Ed.) (1991). *Macro-micro linkages in sociology.* London: Sage Publications.
Kirman, A. (1997). *Interaction and markets.* (DT-GREQAM, n° 97A02). Marseille: Groupement de Recherche en Economie.
Janssen, M. (1998). Microfoundations. In Davis, J.B., Hands, D.W., and Mäki, U. (Eds.), *Handbook of Economic Methodology* (pp. 307-310). Cheltenham: Edward Elgar.
Lesourne, J. (1991). *Economie de l'ordre et du désordre.* Paris: Economica.
McMichael, A. J. (1999). Prisoners of the proximate : loosening the constraints of epidemiology in an age of change. *American Journal of Epidemiology, 149*, 887-897.
Mill, J. S. (1843). *A system of logic, ratiocinative and inductive, being a connected view of the principles of evidence and the methods of scientific investigation.* London: Parker.
Puig, J.-P. (1981). La migration régionale de la population active. *Annales de l'Insee, 44*, 41-79.
Robinson, W.-S. (1950). Ecological correlations and the behaviour of individuals. *American Sociological Review, 15*, 351-357.
Susser, M., & Susser, E. (1996). Choosing a future for epidemiology: I Eras and paradigms. *American Journal of Public Health, 86* (5), 668-673.
Valade, B. (2001). De l'explication dans les sciences sociales: holisme et individualisme. In J.-M. Berthelot (Ed.), *Epistémologie des sciences sociales* (pp. 357-405). Paris: Presses Universitaires de France.
Walliser, B. (2001). La science économique. In J.-M. Berthelot (Ed.), *Epistémologie des sciences sociales* (pp. 117-147). Paris: Presses Universitaires de France.
Walliser, B., & Prou, C. (1988). *La science économique.* Paris: Editions du Seuil.
Walras, L. (1926). *Eléments d'économie politique pure ; ou Théorie de la richesse sociale.* Paris: R. Pichon et R. Durand-Auzias (original work published in 1874).
Wunsch, G. (1994). L'analyse causale en démographie. In R. Franck (Ed.), *Faut-il chercher aux causes une raison ? L'explication causale dans les sciences humaines* (pp. 24-40). Paris - Lyon: Librairie Philosophique J. Vrin.

Harvey GOLDSTEIN

Chapter 1

MULTILEVEL MODELLING OF EDUCATIONAL DATA

Opening. Educational science was the first social science to develop fully multilevel modelling, although it had already been long used in statistics under the form of "random-effect models" or "mixture models" (Eisenhart *et al.*, 1947). In fact, for many years, the literature on education research had been the forum for substantive discussions on the most relevant analytical unit for measuring scholastic attainment: should statistical analysis focus on the class or on the student? As Harvey Goldstein explains in this first chapter, Aitkin *et al.* (1981) came up with a genuine multilevel model inspired by an earlier study (Bennett, 1976), which recognised only students and teaching styles as the units of analysis, ignoring teacher groupings and class groupings: Aitkin and his colleagues introduced the effect of these groupings while at the same time admitting a specific student effect. They thus managed to show the important role played by the teacher: this erased the sizeable differences found between students subjected to a "formal style of teaching" and to an "informal" style in the earlier study, which also referred to a "mixed style of teaching". The choice between the class and the student ceased to be relevant. In fact, Aitkin and his co-authors argued, the effects of both aggregation levels should be examined together, so that their respective actions can be properly separated. Since that date, education researchers have accepted the need to take aggregation levels into account in order to understand the differences observed between students.

To take these analyses one step further, we must ask the following, more general question: are the inequalities observed between school-leavers greater than, equal to, or lesser than those observed when they entered the system, and should these differences be attributed to the system or to other, external reasons (Kereckhoff, 1991)? The search for a clear answer to this question leads us to envisage multilevel models far more complex than the previous one, which was hierarchical, did not examine all the aggregation levels needed to complete the analysis, and confined its study to a student's progress in a single school year.

First, it is important to realise that a ranking of levels is not always satisfactory for analysing the most general situations in which students find themselves. It is often useful to consider "cross-classifications", which involve no hierarchy. For example, when we classify students according to the school they attend and the environment in which they live, there is no reason to consider a hierarchy between these classifications. They should be treated as being at the same level, but we need to identify their effects separately. The new models offered should therefore accommodate cross-classifications.

Second, it is important to distinguish as many aggregation levels as possible in order to make sure that the dominant levels are effectively taken into consideration, and to avoid erroneous conclusions, even if we subsequently reduce that number to the most significant levels. In the example discussed above, teaching style—which can, incidentally, be broken down into more than three types—seemed important for analysing students' performance; but the introduction of another aggregation level—the teacher—sharply diminishes the style effect or even changes it in some cases. The effective way to accommodate this is to consider each student as belonging to a large number of units at different levels, leading to "multiple membership models". Naturally these must be able to separate cross-classifications from hierarchical classifications, while bringing both into play at the same time. In the end, this should make it possible to distinguish the effects of the school system from the effects of other systems or external influences.

Third, to properly introduce students' entire life histories and link their level when entering the school system to their level on leaving it, we need to adopt an event-history approach, with which we can assess the influence of past events on scholastic achievement over time. Students can change classes, teachers, schools, regions, countries, etc. To model a result obtained at a given moment, we need to take into account students' entire past histories—for example, all the schools they attended and all of their teachers. Such a model obviously requires far fuller information than that typically available to education researchers. But this information is vital to an understanding of how the school system in which students are involved, their human environment,

D. Courgeau (ed.) Methodology and Epistemology of Multilevel Analysis, 25-42.

the constraints they face, and their own personalities influence their final scholastic attainment and the structure of outflows from the school system.

In this chapter, Harvey Goldstein explores the ways of factoring in these various effects and the models that can shed new light on the dynamics of the education process. By defining the units more flexibly, we can change our way of conceptualising the effects of institutions and of individuals' environments. Likewise, we can introduce an effect of the performance or of the actions of a school in a locality on the performance and the actions of other, nearby schools—which, in a way, means adding a form of spatial autocorrelation. This also requires the introduction of new ways of understanding the education system, as these methods must allow a simultaneous modelling of responses at different aggregation levels, without setting a logical priority of one over another. For example, we can quantify the link between student performances and teacher attitudes without requiring the latter to logically precede the former (or vice versa). This ultimately leads Goldstein to examine how the new approaches affect the epistemology of education.

D. C.

1. FUNDAMENTALS: UNITS AND LEVELS

While this chapter concentrates on educational data, many of the issues are more generally relevant. This is especially the case when we consider what we mean by a "unit" and a "level".

Traditionally, pupils or students have been viewed as well-defined units, often at the lowest level of a data hierarchy. Likewise schools have typically been considered as well-defined units with students "nested" or grouped within them. Thus, we would ordinarily say that a particular student "belongs to" a particular school over a period of time. We immediately see, however, that this does not always accord with reality. For example, a student may move from one school to another during a study, or a school may change by splitting into two schools or being merged with another school. Likewise, if we consider the unit of a "class" within a school, this may vary in its form and composition frequently, and any particular student may experience several different teachers with which she or he is studying a particular subject during a year. We would regard such a student as "belonging to" or having a "multiple membership" of the set of teachers and we shall describe such structures in more detail later. The same kinds of issues arise in demographic studies (Goldstein *et al.*, 2001), health and other human sciences. In other words our definition of a "unit" has to incorporate temporal information (for what period does it exist in a particular form) and the relationships *between* units have to be specified in terms of membership at particular periods. This has clear implications for longitudinal studies, but also applies in many cases to purely cross-sectional data. Suppose, for example, that we are comparing student achievement test scores among schools at one point in time. It is well known that the use of such data to rank order schools is problematical because it fails to take account of students' prior "intake" achievements (see also Section 3). In addition, however, it assumes that the students can be assigned unequivocally to the schools they belong to at the time of the test. Typically there will be significant amounts of mobility among schools, so that many of the students will have been in their assigned schools a relatively short time and it will be unreasonable to expect those schools to have greatly influenced the student test scores.

It is important to distinguish between actual changes in the definition of a unit and merely changes in a unit's characteristics. Thus, for example, a school may change the number of students it has or its teachers, but may still be regarded as the same unit, and of course, when modelling the effects of school size or composition such changes can be taken into account. Even so, there may be borderline cases; a school may undergo reorganisation to such an extent that it changes nearly all of its staff, has a new name and perhaps new accommodation. If, at the same time, its student composition also changes with some moving to other schools and new students entering it may be more useful to consider this as a change of unit, with the new unit only coming into existence at that time. A choice in such a case will partly depend upon the research questions being asked and also upon the modelling feasibility of different approaches which I shall be discussing later.

There is another kind of unit whose definition is closely tied in with the definition of a "level". This is where a collection of lower level units belongs to a higher level unit which itself is defined solely (or partly) in terms of the particular units that belong to it. Thus, for example, a friendship group is defined solely by its members and will change when any are lost or acquired. Families and households have similar properties (Goldstein *et al.*, 2001). At any one time an individual person may belong to several friendship groups (or learning groups for example) and this can be regarded as a multiple membership structure. Because group formation can change over the period of study, it will often be the case that there will exist many more groups than there are individuals. In such a situation we may encounter modelling estimation problems in terms of separating out different effects: in terms of levels we may regard the groups as lower level units generating measurements which are "nested" within individuals, where each individual can be thought of as generating a set of friends. For example, in the case of learning groups within a classroom, if the results of a group project are being measured then the basic response is measured at the group level rather than that of the student and, so long as there is adequate movement of individuals among groups, this can be modelled as a multiple membership structure with groups at level 1 and students at level 2. This example will be discussed in more detail in Section 4. In household studies a similar situation can arise when a household characteristic, such as electricity use, is being measured over time with individuals changing households. In both these cases we can, in principle, obtain estimates of the relative contributions of groups (households) and individuals and also estimate (posterior) effects for each individual or group. The ability of such models in education to take account of group learning and performance provides a powerful tool for many situations that formerly have posed considerable analytical problems.

In order precisely to define a complex data structure of the kind I have been describing we need to specify the membership relationships among all the units involved. In fact there is just a small number of types of relationship involved and these can conveniently be set out diagrammatically for any particular structure. I shall describe how this may be done below when looking at examples.

In the next section we shall look at the specification of a basic multilevel model followed by a section on cross-classified structures, with some examples. This is followed by a section on multiple membership models, also with examples, and a final section in which I reflect on further applications and extensions.

2. THE BASIC MULTILEVEL MODEL

Before describing the basic multilevel model, it is useful to reflect on why such models are necessary. For many years, educational researchers discussed the "units of analysis" problem, one version of which has also been called the "ecological fallacy" (see also the chapter by Diez Roux). At one extreme, it is possible to study relationships among variables ignoring group structures. At the other extreme we can work solely with group, say school, averages in exploring relationships. Aitkin and Longford (1986) set out the statistical issues associated with various procedures. In an earlier analysis Aitkin *et al* (1981) reworked a well known study on teaching styles which used student level data but ignored school membership (Bennett, 1976). They showed that formerly "significant" results became non-significant when a multilevel model was used. Woodhouse and Goldstein (1989) showed how the use solely of aggregate level data based upon school means could lead to unstable and misleading conclusions.

In addition to the problem of making misleading inferences, failure to model both students and schools simultaneously makes it impossible to study the extent to which school and student characteristics interact to influence the response measurement or measurements. This can only be done within the context of a multilevel model as I shall now describe.

For simplicity consider a simple data structure where a response is measured on individual students or students in a number of schools, together with one or more explanatory variables (covariates). Instead of schools we could think of households, areas, etc. We wish to model a relationship between the individual response and the explanatory variables, taking into account the possibility that this relationship may vary across schools. The response might be a continuous variable such as a test score or survival time, or a discrete variable such as an attitude towards schooling. We shall assume in what follows that we are dealing with a continuously distributed response, and for simplicity that this has a Normal distribution. Extensions to other kinds of responses follow similar lines and these are discussed by Goldstein (1995). This is a simple 2-level structure with the schools as higher level units and students as lower level units. A simple such model can be written as follows

$$\begin{aligned} y_{ij} &= \beta_0 + \beta_1 x_{ij} + u_{0j} + e_{ij} \\ var(e_{ij}) &= \sigma_e^2 \\ var(u_{0j}) &= \sigma_{u0}^2 \end{aligned} \qquad (1)$$

where y_{ij} is the response and x_{ij} the value of a single explanatory variable (covariate) for the i-th individual in the j-th school. For example, the response might be an examination score measured on students at the age of 16 years and the explanatory variable a test score measured on the same students five years earlier at the age of 11 years (Figure 1 shows this schematically for three schools).

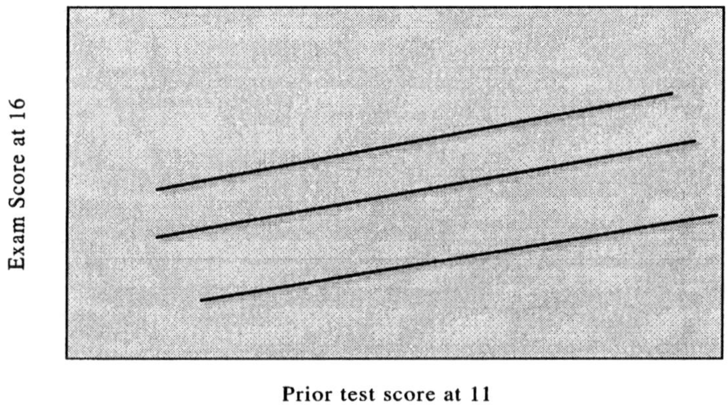

Figure 1. A simple multilevel data structure for three schools with parallel slopes

The slope coefficient β_1 is for the present assumed to be the same for all the schools while the random variable u_{0j} represents the departure of the j-th school's intercept from the overall population intercept term β_0. The first two terms on the right hand side in the first equation of (1) constitute the fixed part of the model and the last two terms describe the random variation. As mentioned we shall develop the model initially assuming that the random variables have a Normal distribution

$$u_{0j} \sim N(0, \sigma^2_{u0}) \qquad e_{ij} \sim N(0, \sigma^2_e)$$

Note that we are at liberty to "fix" one or more of the u_{0j} using an associated dummy (0,1) variable as an explanatory variable, for example if we knew that it was special and should not be considered as a member of the same population as the remainder. This is often useful for exploring "outliers" (Langford and Lewis, 1998). The key point about these random variables is that it allows us to treat the samples of units as coming from a universe or population of such units. Thus, the schools (and students) chosen are not typically the principal focus of interest; they are regarded as a random sample from a population of schools and we are concerned with making statements about that population, for example in terms of its mean and variance.

We can elaborate (1) by allowing the coefficient β_1 to vary across schools and rewrite the model in the more compact form

$$\begin{gathered} y_{ij} = \beta_{0ij} x_0 + \beta_{1j} x_{1ij} \\ \beta_{0ij} = \beta_0 + u_{0j} + e_{ij} \\ \beta_{1j} = \beta_1 + u_{1j} \\ \begin{bmatrix} u_{0j} \\ u_{1j} \end{bmatrix} \sim N(0, \Omega_u) \quad \Omega_u \begin{bmatrix} \sigma^2_{u0} & \\ \sigma_{u01} & \sigma^2_{u1} \end{bmatrix} \\ (e_{ij}) \sim N(0, \sigma^2_e), \quad x_0 = 1 \end{gathered} \tag{2}$$

This model is often referred to as a "random coefficient model" by virtue of the fact that the coefficients β_{0ij} and β_{1j} in the first equation of (2) are random quantities, each having a variance with a covariance between them. As more explanatory variables are introduced into the model, so we can choose to make their coefficients random at the school level thereby introducing further variances and covariances, and this will lead to models with complex covariance structures. One of the aims of multilevel modelling is to explore such potential structures and also to attempt to explain them in terms of further variables.

Having fitted such a model we can obtain estimates for the individual "residuals" (u_{0j}, u_{1j}, e_{ij}) at either level by estimating their expected values (or other functions of their distributions), given the data and model estimates. Thus, for example, we can estimate $E(u_{0j}, u_{1j} | Y, \beta, \theta)$ where:

$$\beta^T = \{\beta_1, \beta_2\} \quad \theta = \{\sigma^2_{u0}, \sigma_{u01}, \sigma^2_{u1}, \sigma^2_e\} \tag{3}$$

and substituting model estimates for the unknown parameters. The multilevel model is here described in non-Bayesian terms. For a full Bayesian specification of this model we would need to add prior distribution assumptions for the parameters in (3). The interested reader is referred, for example, to Rasbash *et al.* (2000) for details with worked examples. These procedures are all implemented in the software package *MlwiN* (Rasbash *et al.*, 2000) and reference will be made to other features of this package in what follows.

3. CROSS-CLASSIFIED MODELS

Suppose a student is classified as belonging sequentially to a particular combination of primary (elementary) school and secondary (high) school and we have followed a sample of such students through each school and wish to relate measurements made at the end of secondary school to those made earlier in the primary schools. The students will be identified by a *cross-classification* of primary schools and secondary schools. Note that even if we did not have prior measurements, but *did* have identification of the primary and secondary schools we could still carry out a cross-classified analysis.

Raudenbush (1993) and Rasbash and Goldstein (1994) present the general structure of a model for handling such random cross-classifications. In our example we have a cross-classified structure which can be modelled as follows:

$$y_{i(j_1j_2)} = (X\beta)_{i(j_1j_2)} + u_{j_1} + u_{j_2} + e_{i(j_1j_2)}$$
$$j_1 = 1, \ldots J_1, \quad j_2 = 1, \ldots J_2, \quad i = 1, \ldots N \tag{4}$$

in which the score of student i, belonging to the combination of primary school j_1 and secondary school j_2, is predicted by a linear "regression" function denoted by $(X\beta)_{i(j_1j_2)}$. The random part of the model is given by two level 2 residual terms, one for the primary school attended by the student (u_{j_1}) and one for the secondary school attended (u_{j_2}), together with the usual level 1 residual term for each student. We note that the latter may be further modelled to produce complex level 1 variation (Goldstein, 1995, Chapter 3), allowing for example for separate variances for males and females, etc. This applies to all our models.

As an example consider the analysis carried out by Goldstein and Sammons (1997) who fitted a series of cross-classified models to a cohort of 758 students from the age of 8 years in primary school to the age of 16 years in secondary school. There were 48 primary schools and 116 secondary schools involved. They had achievement measures at the ages of 8, 11 and 16 years and the principal aim was to separate the effect of primary school attended from that of secondary school. The results are presented in table 1 (p. 32).

Column C presents a model which includes gender and a crude measure of disadvantage (eligibility for free school meals) but no prior achievement scores, and it shows that the between primary school variation is about three times that between secondary schools. This is partly explained by the fact that secondary schools are much larger than primary schools, but the relative importance of primary schools for achievement at the end of secondary schools is nevertheless notable. Column B shows the effect of adding in achievement measures at the start of secondary schooling so that the response effectively measures adjusted achievement or "secondary school progress". Both the school level variances are reduced but the ratio is relatively unaltered. In both these analyses the level 1 (student) variance has an extra term to allow for different variances for males and females. Thus, in column C the variance between females is 0.74 whereas that between males is 0.74+2 x 0.10 = 0.94 (for technical details on how this is specified see Goldstein, 1995, Chapter 3). In Analysis A in addition the between-student variance is allowed to vary also as a function of the LRT score. Thus at an extreme, high, LRT score of 2, the variation between boys is 0.50 + 2 x 0.092 + 2 x 2 x 0.093 + 4 x 0.033 = 1.19, whereas for girls with average LRT scores it is just 0.50.

Table 1. Variance components cross-classified model for 16-year-old exam score as response

	A	*B*	*C*
Fixed			
Intercept	0.51	0.50	0.25
Males	−0.21 (0.06)	−0.19 (0.06)	−0.34 (0.07)
Free school Meal	−0.22 (0.06)	−0.23 (0.06)	−0.37 (0.08)
VR2 band	−0.39 (0.08)	−0.38 (0.08)	
VR3 band	−0.71 (0.13)	−0.71 (0.13)	
LRT score	0.31 (0.04)	0.32 (0.04)	
Random			
Level 2:			
(Primary) σ^2_{u1}	0.025 (0.013)	0.036 (0.017)	0.054 (0.024)
(Secondary) σ^2_{u2}	0.016 (0.014)	0.014 (0.014)	0.019 (0.020)
Level 1:			
σ^2_{e0}	0.500 (0.060)	0.550 (0.060)	0.740 (0.050)
σ_{e01}	0.092 (0.030)	0.060 (0.030)	0.100 (0.050)
σ_{e02}	0.093 (0.018)		
σ^2_{e2}	0.033 (0.022)		
−2Log likelihood	1848.8	1884.2	2130.3

The exam score and the LRT (Reading test) score have been transformed empirically to have $N(0,1)$ distributions. Free school meal is a binary (yes, no) variable. At level 2 the subscript 1 refers to Primary and 2 to Secondary school. At level 1 the subscript 0 refers to the intercept, 1 to males and 2 to LRT. At the age of 11 years students were allocated to a grouping based upon verbal reasoning scores: VR1 (the base category) comprises the lowest 25%, VR2 the middle 50% and VR3 the highest 25%.

When primary school is ignored the apparent variation due to secondary school attended is estimated to be more than twice the value found in the cross-classified models. The substantive importance of this for studies of schooling is that it becomes necessary to take account of achievement during periods of schooling prior to the one immediately being considered (secondary here). The researchers also carried out a bivariate response model where the 11 year achievement scores and the 16 year achievement score become responses. The simple correlation between these responses was 0.53 which reduces to 0.29 when adjustment is made for the 8 year achievements and gender (from a subsequent analysis of the data). When a cross-classified model is fitted, we can decompose this correlation into a between-(primary)-school and a between-student correlation. After adjusting for the 8 year achievement score the between-student correlation was just 0.16 and the between-primary school correlation was 0.81. This suggests that in terms of progress (that is after adjusting for the 8 year prior achievement) the moderate overall correlation of 0.29 is an average of a large correlation between the effects of primary schools on these two achievements and a much smaller correlation at the student level. This further supports the finding of the persistence of the primary school effect throughout secondary schooling.

A special case is also of some interest, where some students do not belong to any units of one "arm" of the cross-classification—an incomplete cross-classification. Consider a longitudinal study of children entering school for the first time in reception (kindergarten) classes. Some of these will have attended a form of pre school provision, say a nursery school. We wish to model achievement at the end of the reception year as a function of the effect of the school, together with that of the nursery where this was present. To do this we have a cross-classified model for one set of students and a simple hierarchical model for the other, with a common school effect. If we thought that the school effect was different for the two groups of children then we would simply fit separate effects (with different variances etc.) and the two effects would be allowed to covary at the school level.

The examples illustrate how a cross-classified model can avoid misspecification and misleading inferences as well as providing a level of detailed analysis not possible when a purely hierarchical structure is assumed. Even so, there is a further major problem with the above example. Only those students were included for analysis who had complete schooling records throughout the period and any changes in school between 8 and 11 years and between 11 and 16 years were ignored. In the next section I shall show how these problems can be overcome.

4. THE MULTIPLE MEMBERSHIP MODEL

To illustrate this model consider just the secondary schools from the above example, and suppose that we know, for each individual, the weight w_{ij_2}, associated with the j_2-th secondary school attended by student i with

$$\sum_{j_2=1}^{J_2} w_{ij_2} = 1$$

These weights, for example, may be proportional to the length of time a student is in a particular school during the course of the longitudinal study. Note that we allow the possibility that for some (perhaps most) students only one school is involved so that one of these probabilities is one and the remainder are zero. Note that when all level 1 units have a single non-zero weight of 1 we obtain the usual purely hierarchical model. We can write the following model for the case of membership of just two schools $\{1,2\}$:

$$\begin{aligned} y_{i(1,2)} &= (X\beta)_{i(1,2)} + w_{i1}u_1 + w_{i2}u_2 + e_{i(1,2)} \\ w_{i1} + w_{i2} &= 1 \end{aligned} \qquad (5a)$$

and more generally:

$$
\begin{aligned}
y_{i\{j\}} &= (X\beta)_{i\{j\}} + \sum_{h=1}^{J} w_{ih}u_h + e_{i\{j\}} \\
\sum_h w_{ih} &= 1, \quad var(u_h) = \sigma_u^2 \\
var\left(\sum_h w_{ih}u_h\right) &= \sigma_u^2 \sum_h w_{ih}^2
\end{aligned}
\tag{5b}
$$

The notation $h \in \{j\}$ means for all schools (h) that belong to the set of schools $\{j\}$.

In the particular case of membership of just two schools with equal weights we have

$$
w_{i1} = w_{i2} = 0.5 \quad var\left(\sum_h w_{ih}u_h\right) = \sigma_u^2/2
$$

In other words the contribution to the level 2 variation is just half that for a student who remains in one school, since in the former case the level 2 contribution is averaged over two (random) schools. Note that, if we ignore the multiple membership of schools and simply assign students, say, to the final school that they attend, we will underestimate the true extent of between-school variation. This is because, for those students who do attend more than one school, the true level 2 variation is less than that for students who attend a single school. In the model, however, we assume that the level 2 variation for these students is the same as that for those attending a single school, with the result that the overall level 2 variation is underestimated.

A slightly different notation to describe membership relationships is used by Browne *et al.* (2001). This is particularly useful when we have very complex structures involving mixtures of hierarchical, crossed and multiple membership classifications. Essentially it works by requiring just a single unique identification for each lowest level observation, in the present case a student. Each student then has a relationship with every other type of unit, that is in the present case, they are classified into primary and secondary schools, the model specifies which classifications are involved and the data structures specifies precisely which schools are involved for each student. Thus the cross-classified model (4) would be written as follows:

$$
\begin{aligned}
y_i &= (X\beta)_i + u^{(2)}_{secondary(i)} + u^{(3)}_{primary(i)} + e_i \\
i &= 1, \ldots N
\end{aligned}
\tag{6}
$$

where *primary(i)* and *secondary(i)* refer respectively to the primary and secondary schools attended by student *i*. The superscripts for the random variables identify the classification; where this is absent, and if there is no ambiguity, it is assumed to be the lowest level classification (1).

The multiple membership model (5b) would be written as:

$$y_i = (X\beta)_i + \sum_{h \in school(i)} w_{i,h} u_h^{(2)} + e_i$$
$$\sum_{h \in school(i)} w_{i,h} = 1, \quad var(u_h^{(2)}) = \sigma_u^2 \qquad (7)$$

Adoption of this notation for complex data structures is particularly useful for fitting such models within a Markov Chain Monte Carlo (MCMC) framework which involves repeated estimation via conditional chain sampling for each unit's random effects. As Browne *et al.* (2001) point out, MCMC procedures become necessary when structures reach certain levels of complexity. MCMC models involve generating a chain of (correlated) values sampled from the "posterior" distribution for each parameter of the model, including the random effects or residuals. At each step of the procedure a sample value for a parameter is drawn from the appropriate distribution conditional upon the observed data and the current values of all the other parameters in the model. This means that storage requirements are moderate. It also means that very complex structures can be defined simply by specifying how each parameter relates to the other parameters in the model.

Browne *et al.* (2001) also use simple diagrams for representing complex structures. Thus the cross-classified structure modelled in Table 1 can be represented as follows (Figure 2).

The single directional lines indicate a membership relation, and here students are members of just one secondary school and one primary school. Where multiple membership is involved, two parallel lines are used (Figure 3).

While the notation of (6) and (7) is powerful, we may often wish, as below, to retain the notation used in (4) and (5) since this may be more familiar and because it is easy to specify when structures are not highly complex

Equations (5) and (7) specify a 2-level model where the level 2 variation among secondary schools is modelled using the set of weights for each student

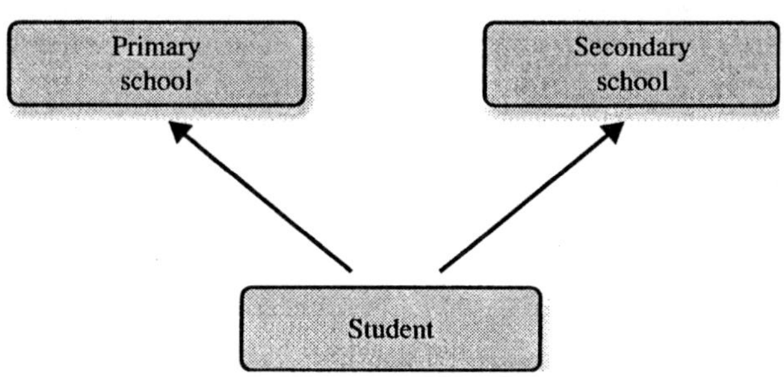

Figure 2. Diagram for the cross-classified structure modelled in Table 1

across all schools as explanatory variables. A similar formulation can be used to model the case where, for some students, there is no identification of the school(s) to which they belong. If we are able to assign a set of probabilities of membership among a subset of schools, however, then utilising the (square root) of these probabilities as weights (standardised to sum to 1) we can still carry out a valid analysis (Hill and Goldstein, 1998).

An extension of (5) is also possible and has important applications, for example in modelling spatial data. In this case we write:

$$y_{i\{j_1\}\{j_2\}} = (X\beta)_{i\{j\}} + \sum_{h \in \{j_1\}} w_{1ih} u_{1h} + \sum_{h \in \{j_2\}} w_{2ih} u_{2h} + e_{i\{j\}}$$

$$\sum_h w_{1ih} = W_1, \sum_h w_{2ih} = W_2, \quad var(u_{1h}) = \sigma^2_{u1} \quad var(u_{2h}) = \sigma^2_{u2} \qquad (8)$$

$$j = \{j_1, j_2\}$$

There are now two sets of higher level units which influence the response. In spatial models one of these sets is commonly taken to be the single area where an individual (level 1) unit lives and the other set consists of the neighbouring units that have an effect. The total weights for each set will need to be carefully chosen; in spatial models the W_1, W_2 are typically chosen each to equal 1 (see Langford *et al.*, 1999, for an example). Another application of such a model for household data is where households share facilities, for example an address. In this case the household that an individual resides in will belong to one set and the other households at the address will belong to the other set. We can readily extend (8) to the case of multiple sets—which can be thought of as a multiple cross-classification of multiple membership classification sets. This will allow us additionally to incorporate multiple spatial structures into, for example, household models.

In education we have an analogous situation to the traditional spatial correlation one. In the traditional schooling (school effectiveness) model a particular school is assumed to have an effect on student performance, attitudes etc., which is independent of any other school in the population. In practice, however, such an assumption will often be unreasonable since schools to some extent will be in "competition" with each other for a share of resources (teachers, buildings etc.) and possibly also for certain kinds of students (see Goldstein, 2000 for a discussion of this). This leads to a "spatial" type model, for example (see Langford *et al.*, 1999):

$$y_{i\{j_1\}\{j_2\}} = (X\beta)_{i\{j\}} + u_{1j_1} + \sum_{h \in \{j_2\}} w_{2ih} u_{2h} + e_{i\{j\}}$$

$$\sum_h w_{2ih} = W_2, \quad var(u_{1h}) = \sigma^2_{u1}, \quad var(u_{2h}) = \sigma^2_{u2} \qquad (9)$$

$$j = \{j_1, j_2\}$$

where the value of W_2 and the component weights will need to be carefully determined. In practice it would be advisable to carry out sensitivity analyses, trying different values for these weights. The component weights would need to take account of geographical catchment areas as well as any administrative arrangements that might affect inter-school relationships. Model (9) identifies two random effects for each school, the usual one, U_1, which is the direct effect on the students within the school and U_2, the (weighted) effect of the school on surrounding schools. Thus, we may be interested in the relative sizes of the latter among schools and also the correlation between U_1 and U_2. We can explore other topics: for example, by fitting further explanatory variables we can study the extent to which such variables "explain" the effect of each school on surrounding schools. In these ways we can address directly issues of how competition among schools operates and how the nature of the relationship between the effect of a school on the students within it and its effect on students in other schools.

We can further elaborate (9) by identifying subsets of the "spatial" effects (U_2) corresponding, for example, to different school types which might be supposed to have differing kinds of effects and we can also of course include random coefficients for any of the classifications. Note that in the fixed part of the model, $(X\beta)_{i\{j\}}$, we can incorporate characteristics measured on the schools as well as on students. We can also incorporate "spatial" effects into the fixed part of the model. For example the difference in social background between a school and the (weighted) average social background of neighbouring schools may be an important predictor of performance or behaviour, in addition to the social backgrounds of the students within a given school. If we have longitudinal data we can incorporate prior achievements of students in a given school and its neighbours, and if mobility takes place among schools then this can be incorporated by fitting a multiple membership structure for the U_1. Additionally, if we measure successive cohorts of students passing through a set of schools we can model the between-school variances as functions of time in order to obtain inferences about changing influences.

Models such as (9) can also be applied to demographic data on households, where the attitudes, opinions, consumption habits, etc. of a household, may be influenced by surrounding households. Most commonly such effects are modelled within a traditional hierarchical model where "neighbourhoods" are defined, say using administrative regions, with households nested within them. Such models, however, have the drawback of using typically arbitrary definitions of spatial units. The advantage of a multiple membership formulation is that it requires only that a suitable "distance function" determining the weights should be constructed. Of course, there may well be problems in defining such a function, since it may not be simply the Euclidean distance and there may be important problems to do with obtaining the necessary data. Nevertheless, as an approach it does have the potential for solving the spatial unit definition problem, especially with the advent of comprehensive Geographical Information Systems (GIS).

We see, therefore, that these models, in principle, enable us to provide adequately contextualised descriptions of schooling that can incorporate the social nature of institutions as described by their effects on each other. In particular these models are relevant to political and social debates about the effects of "market competition" between schools and how this affects performance and other factors, especially in terms of trends over time. Existing discussions of this issue are typically carried out at aggregate (school) level and therefore are unable to obtain valid estimates of between-school variation (see for example Gorard, 2000).

To illustrate the flexibility of these models consider again the example of modelling learning groups discussed earlier. It was pointed out that where the response was modelled at the group level we had a multiple membership model where groups "belonged" to individuals, and a model such as (7) could be used. Suppose, in addition to measuring outcomes at the group level we also have a measure of achievement or attitude at the student level. Recalling that the groups are defined as level 1 units the group response will have an individual component and this will generally be correlated with the response at the student level. We could therefore write such a model as:

$$\begin{aligned} y_{1i} &= (X_1\beta_1)_i + \sum_{j \in group(i)} w_{i,j} u_{1j}^{(2)} + e_i^{(1)} \quad \text{(group response} - i\text{)} \\ & \sum_{j \in group(i)} w_{i,j} = 1 \\ y_{2j} &= (X_2\beta_2)_j + u_{2j}^{(2)} \quad \text{(individual response} - j\text{)} \\ & cov(u_{1j}, u_{2j}) \neq 0 \end{aligned} \tag{10}$$

This is a bivariate response model with one response at each level. The first equation refers to a group response and, given suitable data with individuals belonging to different groups, can be used to estimate individual and group effects. The second equation models an individual student response and from the complete model we can directly estimate the correlation between a student's contribution to the group response and their individual response. Figure 3 shows the relationships using a double arrow for the multiple membership of groups within children and a dotted line joining the two child "effects" to indicate a bivariate response model.

We can also identify those individuals who may be discrepant, say with low contributions to the group response but high individual effect and this might be an important diagnostic for learning potential. An alternative formulation for some purposes would be to incorporate the individual level measure as a covariate in the model for the group response. If, however, we had sequential measures on individuals then we might wish to fit trend terms with random coefficients and then the full bivariate response formulation becomes necessary (see Goldstein, 1995, Chapter 6, for such a model in the purely hierarchical case). Further elaborations can be introduced, for example by modelling classes of students (containing learning groups) within teachers and/or schools and so forth.

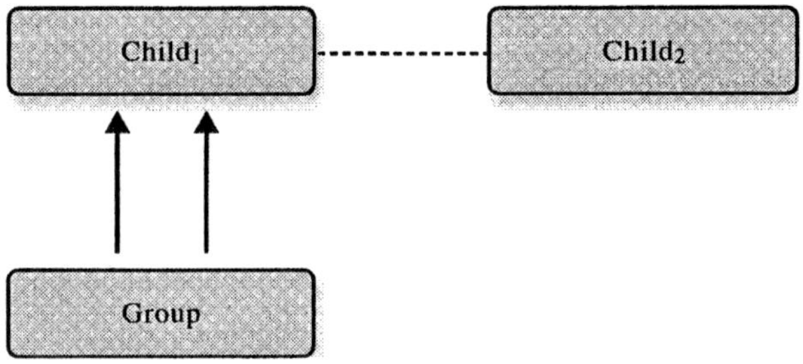

Figure 3. Diagram for a multiple membership model with a bivariate response model

It is perhaps worth mentioning that multiple membership models bear a close relationship to fuzzy sets (see for example, Manton et al, 1994, for an introduction, and Haberman, 1995, for a critique) where individual units also can belong to several groups at a time, with "membership coefficients" being equivalent to our weights. There appears to be no explicit application of fuzzy set theory, however, to general hierarchical structures.

In the final section I will explore the nature of the new kinds of knowledge that the application of such models is able to generate.

5. TYPES OF RESPONSE

We have so far considered models with a continuous (Normally distributed) univariate or multivariate response variable. Multilevel models can, however, be formulated for other response types. One of the most common is that for a binary response, for example whether or not a student passes an examination. In such a case the equivalent to (1) can be written as

$$\begin{aligned} E(y_{ij}|j) &= \pi_{ij}, y_{ij} \sim Binomial(1, \pi_{ij}) \\ y_{ij} &= \begin{cases} 0 \text{ if fail} \\ 1 \text{ if pass} \end{cases} \\ \text{logit}(\pi_{ij}) &= \log\{\pi_{ij}/(1-\pi_{ij})\} = \beta_0 + \beta_1 x_{1ij} + u_{0j} \\ var(u_{0j}) &= \sigma^2_{u0} \end{aligned} \tag{11}$$

This can then be extended in all the same ways as (1) to cross-classifications etc. This is one example of a generalised multilevel linear model and another example is where we have a count as the response variable.

An important class of models is where the response is a duration. These models are often known as survival or event history models and again the multilevel formulation involves the same kinds of generalisations as with (1).

So called parametric and semiparametric models can be fitted and Goldstein (1995, Chapter 9) gives details. A particularly useful formulation for multilevel structures is the "piecewise" model. Here the time interval is divided into small time segments and the occurrence of events noted. With a suitable specification we can then fit models using (11) together with all its generalisations.

All of these different kinds of response model assume Normal variation at higher levels. This implies that we can create multivariate response models where we have a mixture of different kinds of responses. For example, we may measure the duration of tasks undertaken by children as well as their scores on a test and the responses of a group to which they belong. In principle all of these can be incorporated into a single linked model.

Finally, we can have models with underlying latent structures (see McDonald and Goldstein, 1989). These may be factor analysis models with different factor structures at each level or classification or more general structural relation models where the factors are related to each other.

6. FINAL THOUGHTS ABOUT NEW INSIGHTS

It is worth making the general point that all of these complex models require adequate, and generally large, data sources. Obtaining such data often will be costly and time consuming. Thus, as well as posing methodological challenges in terms of formulation and estimation there is the overwhelming prior condition that suitable data are available.

It would be agreed generally that the reality of education and learning involves complex processes and interactions. This does not preclude providing useful information in terms of simplified models or even simple summaries. Nevertheless, within the context of statistical modelling, I would argue that unless we can formulate models (based on appropriate data) that approach the real underlying complexity our descriptions of these processes will be incomplete and that this will hinder adequate causal explanations and understandings. For example, the models described in this paper may be suitable for the analysis of ethnographic data collected from student observations in ways that can preserve the detail with which the data are collected. Such data will often incorporate details of interactions among students and groups of students within a classroom in an attempt to understand the ways in which peer group influences may work. We may be able to begin to model such data using the spatial models and group response models that have been described. A simple example would be observations made on the tasks children are engaged on and the length of time they spend on these. Traditionally, such measurements would be assumed to be independent from child to child, i.e. the length of time spent by one child does not affect the length of time spent by a nearby child. This, however, is debateable and a spatial type model would be useful here. Furthermore, where such data are collected over a long time period, with changing group or spatial structures, the multiple membership models can be used to characterise these. By embedding such data within a formal modelling framework we can extend the range of existing analyses and construct the foundation for secure generalisations and in this way help to secure a link, that is a common framework, between existing quantitative and qualitative research traditions. As we explore deeper levels of complexity so we would expect to generate new theoretical insights and the process of developing the models themselves will often suggest new directions for data collection and theory development.

A further important class of models are those known as "meta analyses". These seek to combine results from several studies in order to achieve a more reliable inference. Thus, in the simplest case, each study is a level 2 unit and individuals within a study are level 1 units. A 2-level model for such studies can allow overall variability as well as variability in relation to particular coefficients. Thus, for example, if each study is concerned with the effect of class size on achievement we can see whether the relationship with class size varies from study to study, as well as estimating the average effect. We can also incorporate studies where data are available only at aggregate level, rather than at individual level. This is particularly important since many published studies quote only aggregate results. Goldstein et al (2000) discuss how such studies can be incorporated into a general multilevel framework. This is done using a device similar to that used in (10) where we have two equations, one of which models a level 2 response and one models a level 1 response. The level 1 response equation has a level 2 random effect as does the level 2 response equation. By allowing the level 2 random effects to be correlated we link the two equations and this linking allows efficient estimation of all the parameters.

While this chapter has been concerned largely with education, with some reference to demography, almost all the issues covered apply to other areas for example health, and collaboration between such disciplinary areas will be fruitful. Finally, there is a wealth of further information about applications and current developments that can be found on the website of the London based Multilevel models project (http://multilevel.ioe.ac.uk/).

REFERENCES

Aitkin, M., Anderson, D., & Hinde, J. (1981). Statistical modelling of data on teaching styles. *Journal of the Royal Statistical Association, 144*, 419-461.

Aitkin, M., Bonnet, S. N., & Hesketh, J. (1981). Teaching Styles and Pupil Progress: a reanalysis. *British Journal of Educational Psychology, 51*, 170-186.

Aitkin, M., & Longford, N. (1986). Statistical modelling in school Effectiveness studies. *Journal of the Royal Statistical Society, A. 149*, 1-43.

Bennett, S. N. (1976). *Teaching styles and pupil progress*. London: Open Books:

Browne, W. J., Goldstein, H., &Rasbash, J. (2001). Multiple membership multiple classification (MMMC) models. *Statistical Modelling, 1,* 103-124.

Eisenhart, C., Hastay, M. W., & Wallis, W. A. (Eds.). (1947). *Techniques of statistical analysis by the Statistical Research Group of Colombia University.* New York: McGraw-Hill.

Goldstein, H. (1995). *Multilevel Statistical Models*. London: Edward Arnold. New York: Wiley.

Goldstein, H., & Woodhouse, G. (2000). School effectiveness research and Educational Policy. *Oxford Review of Education, 2,* 353-363.

Goldstein, H., Rabash, J., Browne, W, Woodhouse, G., & Poulain, M. (2000). Multilevel models in the study of dynamic household structures. *European Journal of Population, 16*, 373-387.

Goldstein, H., & Sammons, P. (1997). The influence of secondary and junior schools on sixteen year examination performance: a cross-classified multilevel analysis. *School effectiveness and school improvement, 8,* 219-230.

Goldstein, H., Yang, M., Omar, R., Turner, R., *et al.* (2000). Meta analysis using multilevel models with an application to the study of class size effects. *Journal of the Royal Statistical Society, Series C* 49, 399-412.

Gorard, S. (2000). *Education and Social Justice*. Cardiff: University of Wales Press:

Haberman, S (1995). Review of Statistical applications using fuzzy sets. *Journal of the American Statistical Association., 90,* 1131-1133.

Hill, P. W., & Goldstein, H. (1998), Multilevel modelling of educational data with cross-classification and missing identification of units. *Journal of Educational and Behavioural statistics, 23,* 117-128.

Kereckhoff, A. C. (1991). Creating inequality in the schools: A structural perspective. In Huber J. (ed.) *Macro-Micro Linkages in Sociology.* Newbury Park, London, New Delhi: Sage Publications.

Langford, I., & Lewis, T. (1998), Outliers in multilevel data. *Journal of the Royal Statistical Society. A. 161,* 121-160.

Langford, I., Leyland, A., Rasbash, J., & Goldstein, H. (1999). Multilevel modelling of the geographical distribution of diseases. *Journal of the Royal Statistical Society, C. 48,* 253-268.

Manton, R. G., Woodbury, M. A., & Tolley, H. D. (1994). *Statistical applications using fuzzy sets.* New York: Wiley.

McDonald, R. P., & Goldstein, H. (1989). Balanced versus unbalanced designs for linear structural relations in two-level data. *British Journal of mathematical and statistical psychology, 42,* 215-232.

Rasbash, J., & Goldstein, H. (1994). Efficient analysis of mixed hierarchical and cross-classified random structures using a multilevel model. *Journal of Educational and Behavioural statistics 19,* 337-50.

Rasbash, J., Browne, W., Goldstein, H., Yang, M., *et al.* (2000), *A user's guide to MlwiN (Second Edition).* London: Institute of Education.

Raudenbush, S. W. (1993). A crossed random effects model for unbalanced data with applications in cross-sectional and longitudinal research. *Journal of Educational Statistics, 18,* 321-349.

Woodhouse, G., Yang, M., Goldstein, H., & Rasbash, J. (1996). Adjusting for measurement error in multilevel analysis. *Journal of the Royal Statistical Society, A. 159,* 201-12.

Woodhouse, G., & Goldstein, H. (1989). Educational Performance Indicators and LEA league tables. *Oxford Review of Education, 14,* 301-319.

Daniel COURGEAU

Chapter 2

FROM THE MACRO-MICRO OPPOSITION TO MULTILEVEL ANALYSIS IN DEMOGRAPHY

Opening. If educational science, examined in the previous chapter, was the first social science to develop a fully multilevel approach, one must also bear in mind that it is one of the most recently constituted social sciences. It was only in the late 1960s (Travers, 1969) that education emerged from the prevailing earlier discipline of pedagogy, whose focus was on the adjustment of teaching practices rather than on studying the processes linking teacher to student—the goal of education as a social science (Filloux, 2001). Demography, in contrast, has a far longer history. It traces its origins back to the "political arithmetic" of the late seventeenth century, illustrated by the work of John Graunt (1662/1977); in the nineteenth century, it pulled away from the other social sciences derived from the same source. The present chapter adopts a long-term perspective in order to discern the links between those historical stages and the aggregation levels—and to show the place of multilevel analysis in demography's evolution over the centuries.

We will show the privileged position of analysis at the aggregate level—most often, an individual country—from the inception of demography to the mid-twentieth century. This analysis was informed by methodological holism, which produced (1) population censuses, performed at regular intervals to obtain an instantaneous view of the population, and (2) comprehensive measurements of the events experienced by its members. There was no room for the individual in the analyses and tables derived from these censuses, which were attached to civil-registration statistics: the analyses and tables showed relationships external to the life of individuals, who expressed the constraints laid down by the society in which they lived. These constraints can remain identical for long periods; when they change, they can do so very gradually, adjusting to new economic or social conditions, or rapidly in periods of crisis such as a war or an economic recession. This effect occurs in a historical time-frame, which justifies the use of period analysis, and in a homogeneous national space, which justifies the analysis on aggregate data.

The lagged effects of World War II—on marriage, for example—cast doubt on the effects identified by period analysis. The use of fictitious cohorts displaying the behaviours observed in a given period led demographers to postulate the existence of a fictitious cohort that—in such demographic-recovery periods—would make a life-long effort to catch up on a lag it never actually experienced (Henry, 1966). Likewise, the effects of period events may impact the lives of individuals much later than at the time of their occurrence—hence the need to develop an other approach accommodating those effects.

Cohort analysis initially enabled demographers to introduce the time lived by individuals and to illustrate more clearly the effect of wars or economic crises on the deferral of the events studied to better times. The implementation of such an approach, however, required very restrictive hypotheses: the homogeneity of the population studied and independence between events. These hypotheses allowed the use of individual data from civil-registration records in aggregate form to compile cohort tables. However, survey data, using much more abundant and detailed information than the civil-registration records, showed that the hypotheses did not hold up and needed to be waived.

Event-history analysis offered a solution to these difficulties, by examining the entire life of a sample of individuals: demographers could now analyse the interferences between the events experienced by individuals and the effects of individual characteristics on the events. The focus of the analysis thus shifted from society as a whole to the individual, situated in a heterogeneous society and experiencing interdependent events. This led to methodological individualism. However, the analysis centred not on the individual in all his or her complexity, but on a statistical individual, subjected to a specific process by the events and characteristics examined.

Whereas the aggregate level analysis demonstrated processes at work at the population level, the individual level analysis showed the mechanisms underlying individual behaviour. But are the two approaches entirely antagonistic? Might it not be possible to interlink them in order to improve our knowledge of human behaviour? Somewhat later than education, demography tried to gather individual data and aggregate data into a single model: Mason *et al.* (1983) and Wong

D. Courgeau (ed.) Methodology and Epistemology of Multilevel Analysis, 43-91.

and Mason (1985) conducted multilevel analyses—of fertility and contraception respectively—through a simultaneous study at the individual and aggregate levels: the aggregate levels consisted of the individuals' countries of residence. The authors used data from the World Fertility Surveys performed in several developing countries. Such analyses were later extended to a variety of segmentations (villages, ethnic groups, regions, etc.) and to fuller models than the logistic regressions used in these early examples. We will show how this led to the introduction of multilevel event history models, which are still under development and continue to raise many issues examined here in detail.

D. C.

1. INTRODUCTION

Although the word *demography* first appeared in print in the nineteenth century in Guillard's *Eléments de statistique humaine, ou démographie comparée* (1855), its origins can be traced back to what in the seventeenth century was known as *political arithmetic*, a term introduced by Petty in the 1670s (Dupâquier, 1983) and the title of his book published in 1690. The earliest application of thorough going statistical methods to the study of populations was in fact the work of Graunt (1662/1977), where for the first time the information contained in the Bills of Mortality was treated as a source for measuring the population of a country or region. This was a revolutionary idea at a time when the events of human existence such as birth, illness and death were believed to be the prerogative of god and hence not admitting of scientific inquiry.

Let us take a closer look at how Graunt envisaged this political arithmetic. In common with most of the natural sciences at the time, the approach was essentially descriptive, the purpose being to produce accurate measurements of a state's population and of the various phenomena responsible for keeping it at a given level. It is important to appreciate that no reliable census of the population existed at this time, so that the only means of estimating the population of a city, let alone a country, was by making highly speculative calculations. Contemporary estimates of the population of London, for example, varied between two million and six million. The first task was thus to produce a more reliable estimate of this population based on the sources available at the time (the Bills of Mortality and the Bills of Baptism) and with a careful and critical examination of their quality. Working with what he judged to be the most credible hypotheses, Graunt demonstrated that the population of London was close to 380 000 and not the millions previously thought.

As the above shows, although essentially descriptive in approach the new science found it necessary from the outset to propound hypotheses about the populations and events that formed its field of inquiry. The idea that prevailed in the eighteenth century was that a kingdom's population stayed more or less unchanging through history, and although epidemics, wars and natural catastrophes and so forth caused localized and short-term variations, these were quickly made good by the return of prosperity and the concomitant increase in births. By working on larger and larger populations, compensations would operate, revealing greater regularity and effacing these localized variations. In *The Divine Order* (1741/1979), Süssmilch interpreted this regularity as the action of Providence, a view that well illustrates the importance of the religious outlook in the early development of political arithmetic. Later on, however, rationalist thinkers suggested that human phenomena might be subject to laws as strict as those which had been discovered in the natural sciences.

The existence and assumed form of these laws provide the starting point for our discussion. The lack of censuses in the seventeenth and eighteenth centuries obliged the early analysts to make hypotheses about the relationships which existed, at a given point in time, between the events observed (births, marriages and deaths) and the populations in which they occurred. A question that began to be explored was that of the variation in a population consequent on the births and deaths it experiences. When Euler (1760) said that he had assumed that the total number living in one place remains the same, or that it increases or decreases uniformly, he was in effect anticipating the concepts of stationary or stable populations that were not formalized until the start of the twentieth century (Lotka, 1939).

In the nineteenth century, the main impetus for the study of populations came from Quetelet with his theory of the "average man", but it was the sociologist Durkheim who did most to elaborate a theory for the quantitative analysis of human behaviour, based on clearly stated hypotheses and the method of concomitant variations. The same methodology was in fact presented fifty years later in Landry's (1945) treatise on demography, although the latter contains no reference to this famous precursor. This method implies adoption of a period approach, which is examined in the first part of this chapter. The main source for this approach are population censuses, which provide "snapshots" of the population under observation at nearly regular intervals.

Although the distinction between "historical time" and "individual time" was not at first clearly understood, some analysts had already made use of sources which followed individuals over their lifetime, such as data concerning tontines or annuities (Deparcieux, 1746). Later on, it began to be suggested that the period perspective employed by most authors might not be the only one possible (Delaporte, 1941). It was after the Second World War that demographers showed how this approach, based on hypotheses which completely ignored individuals' experience of time, produced results whose interpretation was problematic. Their solution was to develop methods of longitudinal analysis that could follow individuals over their entire lifetime and for which civil registration materials and population registers were the most important sources. So as to observe the various phenomena in isolation, this new paradigm treated them as mutually independent and occurring in populations that were assumed to be homogeneous. This approach is explored in the second part of this chapter.

These hypotheses of independence and homogeneity were challenged, however, by the growing volume of survey results that provided more detailed information than population registers and civil registration sources. A need was increasingly felt for methods that could handle the interdependence of phenomena and the heterogeneity of populations. This change came at the beginning of the 1980s with the introduction of event history analysis. These techniques employed more complex mathematics and probability theory than had previously been used. The third part of this article is given over to exploring the theoretical notions that lie behind these methods.

However, this approach is itself overly focused on the individual and neglects the influence on individual behaviour of the social context and its associated constraints and rules. A new theory was needed, one that retained the vantage point of the individual, in contrast to the period approach, yet that introduced multiple levels of aggregation so as to take account of the constraints which underpin individual behaviour. This methodological innovation is what is known as multilevel analysis. The fourth part of this chapter attempts to set out the conditions that must be met for this technique to be valid.

A general discussion of the various paradigms that have been proposed is the framework for examining their respective contributions and for considering the position held by the multilevel approach in the development of hypotheses in demography. The point to stress here is that demography does not possess a collection of perspectives and orientations that are fixed for all time; they are in fact specific to the society in which the researcher lives and are thus subject to change over time (Singleton, 1999). Our task, therefore, is to define carefully the different paradigmatic choices, identifying their specific features and assessing their fundamental premises.

2. THE AGGREGATE PERIOD APPROACH

Notwithstanding the great diversity in outlook and interests of those working in the field of political arithmetic up to the mid-nineteenth century, and in demography until the mid-twentieth century, we propose to show here that they had a certain number of intellectual positions and postulates in common. It is suggested that in consequence the whole of this long period can be identified with a single paradigm. This involves identifying the ideas and principles that underline this research, by demonstrating the unity which lies behind the apparent diversity of the authors and the research undertaken.

2.1. From divine order to secular order

The early authors discovered that the Bills of Mortality and Bills of Baptism could be used to count deaths by cause, births and so forth, and that from these figures firm conclusions could be produced. Graunt's (1662/1977) comment that he did not know what first led him to begin his completely unplanned work with the Bills of Mortality is clear evidence that contemporaries saw no interest in collating these weekly statements in tabular form. Yet such tables were to yield rich results, since providing care was taken to check the quality of the data, they made it possible to quantify with greater accuracy a large number of earlier approximations which now appeared far removed from reality.

Once this discovery had been made, it could be asserted that the events experienced by man could, like other natural phenomena, be subjected to quantitative study. This is what Petty (1690/1963) had in mind when he wrote:

> The Method I take to do this is not yet very usual: for instead of using only comparative and superlative Words, and intellectual Arguments, I have taken the course (as a Specimen of the Political Arithmetic I have long aimed at) to express myself in Terms of Number, Weight, or Measure; to use only Arguments of Sense, and to consider only such Causes as visible Foundations in Nature; leaving those that depend upon the mutable Minds, Opinions, Appetites of particular Men, to the Consideration of others (p. 7).

Although the result of his estimations contained numerous errors and approximations, Petty's comment in effect laid out what was to form the foundations of the social sciences.

The primary aim of these early authors was to count the population so as to have a more precise idea of the actual figures, for comparison with earlier estimates that lacked any statistical basis. Many of these authors drew up a list of very similar questions for which they attempted to find answers (e.g. Graunt (1662/1977), Süssmilch (1741/1979), Moheau (1778/1994)), such as, what is the size of the population? how many men and women are there? how many are married and unmarried? and so forth.

But the sources available to these early authors meant that sooner rather than later they had to resort to making hypotheses about the production of these figures for use in their estimations. For example, when they wanted to estimate the population of a city or a country, they had only the numbers of deaths, births and other incomplete figures relating to these units. Consequently the relationships that existed between populations, deaths, births and so on had to be expressed as hypotheses, which could then be applied to the enumerated quantities in order to deduce the total population. This concept of the "multiplier" used in these calculations was employed by many authors, and did not become redundant until the introduction of exhaustive population censuses in the late-eighteenth and early-nineteenth centuries meant that these hypotheses were no longer needed.

This technique presented a number of problems, as is illustrated by the argument that opposed Moheau and Condorcet (see Condorcet, 1776-1789/1994: pp. 130-141). Moheau (1778/1994) estimated the total population of France using observations for eight *Généralités* (administrative regions) in different parts of the country and for which population enumerations and birth statistics were available. The ratio between the number of births and the number of inhabitants was not constant across the regions but varied between 27.5 and 23.25. Taking the births registered for France as a whole and an average value for the multiplier of approximately 25.5, Moheau produced a figure of 23 500 000 for the total population. Condorcet attacked this estimation, stating:

> If, on the basis of observations made on a certain number of men, I want to determine with accuracy what the situation is in a large country, my experiment must be conducted on men drawn from that country's different climates and types of air, from its different social orders and conditions of existence (p. 132).

In other words to obtain a valid estimate it is necessary to take a representative sample of the country's population, a criterion that Moheau's observations do not respect.

This criticism had far-reaching implications in that it opened the way for the study of population to go beyond simple enumeration to analysis. A satisfactory solution to the problem exposed by Condorcet required use of what would later be referred to as regression methods in order to determine relationships between births, populations and the characteristics of the different regions of a country. This leads us to consider the use of statistics and probability theory in the scientific study of population.

It is in fact crucial to realize that political arithmetic was born just a few years after the correspondence between Pascal and Fermat (1651/1986) in which they laid the bases of probability theory of. These concepts were employed in the very first works of political arithmetic. For example, Graunt (1662) reported that he bet equal odds that a man picked at random would live another ten years; and Deparcieux (1746) wrote an *Essai sur les probabilités de la durée de la vie Humaine* [*Essay on the probabilities of the length of human life*]. The emergence of probability theory opened the way for an entirely new way of considering human phenomena. Previously, because the timing of these phenomena could not be predicted it was thought that their occurrence could have no rational explanation. Each individual was believed to have a unique destiny that could be interrupted at any time. Consequently it appeared futile and unnecessary to try to find laws that implied a certainty of occurrence, comparable to those already known to govern the workings of physical phenomena. In other words, calculations about a man's death were excluded, whereas the laws governing the trajectory of a falling stone, which under fixed initial conditions will always be the same, had been formulated.

A full account cannot be given here of the bases of probability calculation (see for example: Matalon,1967; Suppes, 1981), which is a vast field of inquiry. Attention is instead focused on how the basic hypotheses of probability and statistics have been applied in the social sciences. The important point to appreciate is that the two disciplines developed at the same time and that progress in probability theory was paralleled by progress in the social sciences.

As an example let us consider the study of mortality. It is not hard to see that these applications were conducted from the "objectivist" perspective. The law of large numbers propounded by Bernouilli (1713) states that the value of the ratio between the number of events observed and the total number of individuals exposed to the risk, approaches the theoretical probability as the number of individuals observed approaches infinity, the assumption being made that this population is homogeneous. A probability of dying can thus be considered as closer to the corresponding probability the larger the population being observed. This is why uncertainty is justified when small populations are being observed and indicates the desirability of working on complete data. Süssmilch (1741/1979) stated that the inexactitudes of small figures disappear when the numbers being compared are large, thereby showing his commitment to the objectivist approach. This is also the reason why censuses and an exhaustive system of civil registration became accepted during the nineteenth century as the indispensable source for the study of society.

2.2. Towards a statistical period analysis

Let us now consider the type of inference that is required in order to move beyond simple description to explanation and an authentic analysis of phenomena. Establishing whether or not the phenomenon being studied is influenced by a particular factor raises the question of how to define and measure this factor, and of how to identify the relationship between the phenomenon being studied and those which may explain it. We begin by considering the problems of measurement.

As was seen earlier, in the perspective adopted here measures have to be aggregated to estimate the probabilities of different events. This means that the probability of a given event can be determined by working either on an entire population or on a large enough number of sub-populations. But if the aim is then to relate this event to another event or to another characteristic, this is impossible when considering the whole population, since two marginal probabilities tell us nothing about any link that may exist between them. Such a relationship can only be identified when working on sub-populations. To take a simple example—that will be referred to throughout this chapter—if we know only the migration probabilities for the whole population and the proportion of farmers in that population, no relationship can be established between these two quantities. One solution is to divide this population into a large number of sub-populations and to estimate the same quantities for each. The migration probabilities can then be calculated for farmers and for the rest of the population, under certain hypotheses which, as will be seen shortly, may vary.

This way of reasoning was obviously not present when this approach first developed, but it did underlie early efforts to identify relationships between demographic phenomena. The work of Süsmilch (1741/1979) was already moving in this direction. When comparing urban and rural mortality in different countries, he concluded: "The difference between the towns and the villages must be traced to the forms of nourishment, the manners and the customs" (p. 335), thus implying that different phenomena could be inter-related. Likewise, rather later, Quetelet (1869/1997) when introducing his theory of the average man affirmed that

> man is under the influence of causes of which most are regular and recurrent. By means of a sustained study, it is possible to determine these causes and their mode of action, as well as the laws they give rise to, though to succeed in this, very large groups must be studied, so as to eliminate from the observations all that is merely accidental or individual. Probability calculation shows that, all things being equal, one comes closer to the truth or to the laws one is trying to define, the larger the number of individuals on which observations are based (p. 33).

Of the various applications of this approach, we give here an example that Quetelet borrowed from Sadler (1830). Examining the link between fertility and nuptiality in a given country, he divides the country into departments (France) or provinces (Belgium). For each of these units he then calculates the proportion of marriages and the number of legitimate children per marriage. A comparison of these two quantities leads him to observe that "the places which have the greatest number of marriages each year are those where the fertility of marriages is lowest, by a form of compensation which prevents a country from having too rapid a growth of population"(Quetelet, 1869/1997, p. 80). It is clearly a correlation that he observes between these aggregated quantities, and no attempt is made to show that one is the cause of the other. A correlation of this kind carries no causal implication and may be due to a third factor, without any causal relationship existing between the first two.

In my view it was Durkheim (1895/1937, 1897/1930) who gave the clearest statement of the objectives of this social science and of the means for their realization, at the same time as offering a critique of his predecessors' approach, and in particular of Quetelet's "average man". The latter theory can provide explanations of human behaviour, if it is accepted that it depends solely on the country in which it occurs and on the correlations that exist between the various social facts in the society. But the raison d'être of this behaviour is not explained and the underlying causes have to be sought elsewhere.

Durkheim's starting point is that social facts are independent of their function in society and that without being changed they can be employed for different purposes. This function is the priority for study, whereas identifying the usefulness of a social fact is of secondary importance. However, this function cannot be considered without taking account of the various constituent elements present in the society being studied, such as the religious, domestic and political groups, and how these are associated. Social phenomena must therefore vary according to the forms of this association and the organization of these constituent parts of society. The function of a social fact can thus be identified by relating it to other social facts, though the social system itself is the basis of this explanation (Franck, 1994).

In these conditions how can it be proved that one phenomenon is the cause of another? Ethical considerations preclude use of authentic experimentation in most of the social sciences. Some form of comparative method has therefore to be used, and of these the most effective is the method of concomitant variations, as proposed by Durkheim (1895/1937). The idea behind this is to see whether the variations exhibited by the phenomena in a sufficient number of cases are evidence of interdependency between them. Thus when Durkheim observed that the proportion of suicides in different provinces of Prussia varied with the percentage of Protestants (Durkehim, 1897/1930), he concluded that suicide was inversely proportional to the degree of integration of religious society, since in his view the Protestant church was "a less strongly integrated church than the Catholic church" (p. 159). This method is the same as that proposed by Landry (1945), for whom understanding of a temporal or spatial variation required identification of the relationship of concomitance between the phenomena being studied. It amounts to what in present-day vocabulary would be described as a regression analysis between the percentage of suicides and the percentage of Protestants living in different regions. A simple example, that has already been referred to, can be used to give this model a more precise formulation.

For this purpose we work with Norwegian data[1] relating to the generation born in 1948, which gives each individual's occupation at the 1970 census. Individuals are identified who have changed region in the following three years, distinguishing between farmers and the rest of the population. If m_a and $m_{\bar{a}}$ are the migration probabilities of farmers and non-farmers, which are required to keep the same level in every region of the country, it can easily be shown (Courgeau, 2002) that the migration rate for region, $m_{.j}$, will be a linear function of the proportion of farmers in each region, $a_{.j}$ (see figure 1):

$$m_{.j} = a_{.j}m_a + (1 - a_{.j})m_{\bar{a}} = a_{.j}(m_a - m_{\bar{a}}) + m_{\bar{a}} \tag{1}$$

Figure 1 gives the increase in the estimated migration rates with the proportion of farmers and the extrapolation of these results shows the migration probability of farmers to be five times higher than that of non-farmers (0.60 as against 0.12), if the hypothesis that these probabilities are independent of the regions is verified.

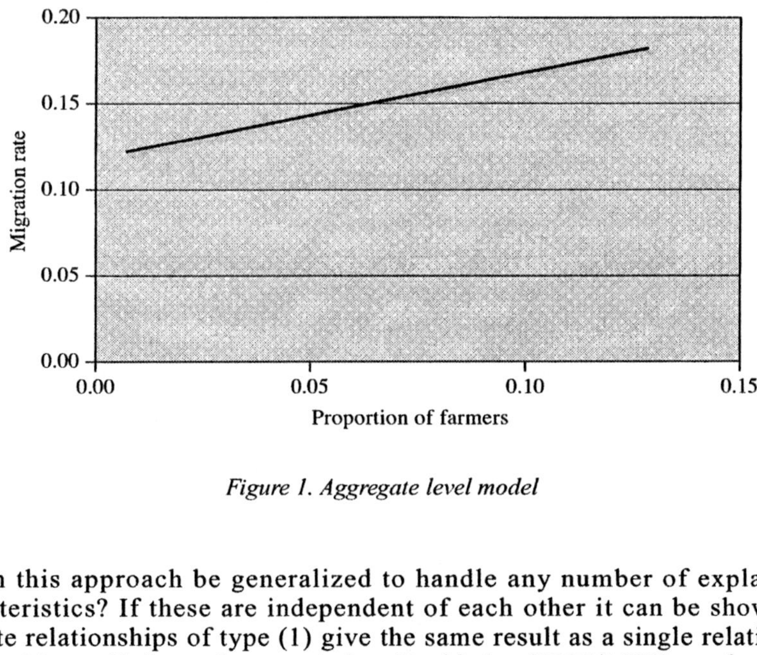

Figure 1. Aggregate level model

Can this approach be generalized to handle any number of explanatory characteristics? If these are independent of each other it can be shown that separate relationships of type (1) give the same result as a single relationship that combines all these characteristics. Durkheim (1895/1937) used separate analyses of various characteristics to show that suicide was inversely proportional to the levels of religious, domestic and political integration prevailing in the society. The same result could have been obtained by examining all these characteristics simultaneously, if the hypothesis of independence in their effects is verified. If this hypothesis is violated, however, the relationship between the phenomenon being studied and the explanatory characteristics cannot be estimated accurately, when we have only the marginal percentages for individuals presenting these various characteristcs (Courgeau, 1999b).

We also need to consider how time is incorporated in such an analysis. For the early authors, who suspected the existence of laws as strict as those governing the physical world, human phenomena could not be time-dependent as such but merely experienced short-term variations that were quickly followed by a return to equilibrium. This is what Halley (1693) had in mind when he spoke of "the mortality of mankind". However, observation of increasingly large populations revealed this hypothesis to be untenable and showed that populations could in fact experience very long periods of continuous growth or contraction, for example. Notwithstanding this fact, observation of a population at a given point in time, by means of a census, is not affected by such a variation. The great strength of this approach is that by basing analysis on "snapshot" views of a population it does not initially have to consider its changes over time. These can be analysed later by comparison of two or several "snapshots" taken at different points of time.

This approach is at the origin of what demographers refer to as cross-sectional or period analysis, and which was used almost exclusively until the end of the Second World War. It makes the assumption that behaviour in any given period depends on the events of an economic (e.g. economic crises, periods of full-employment), political (e.g. wars, revolutions) or more generally social nature (e.g. changes in the integration of social groups, in values) occurring at the same time. On the other hand, it also makes the assumption that the past, the lived experience of generations, has no influence on present behaviour.

2.3. Recent developments of this approach

Given the difficulties of estimating the populations of different countries in the seventeenth and eighteenth century, before the introduction of censuses, it is clear that any attempt at estimation of long-term change in the population would have been futile. Moreover, as already noted, in the early days of political arithmetic the dominant hypothesis was that of a constant population. Before long, however, observation had shown that demographic phenomena could not realistically be treated as constant over long periods and that these variations could be interpreted in relation to each other.

These observations were at the origin of *demographic transition* theory, which has provided an analytic context for the comparison of the snapshot views produced by successive censuses. A partial formulation of this theory had already been given by Landry (1909/1982) and a definitive statement was produced by Notestein in 1945. Although it cannot be described in full here the essentials of the theory as they relate to the period approach in demography need to be identified. A more comprehensive account can be found in Burch (1999).

Demographic transition theory aspired to offer a universal explanatory framework for relating long-term demographic change to the various economic, sociological, ecological and psychological changes occurring in the world over the same period. The theory was closely associated with the cross-sectional approach since it sought to explain changes in conditions at a point in time by reference to characteristics that were also specific to one point in time. However, inasmuch as it introduced results from a range of social sciences it did represent a broadening of perspective.

The demographic indicators used in the model were extremely simple —rates of mortality and fertility and of international immigration and emigration—and were usually single country level though larger groups were also employed. Slightly more sophisticated indicators were sometimes used but they were always period measures: child mortality rates, life expectancy, total fertility rate, and so forth. The explanatory factors were intended to characterize different turning points in the history of a country, such as agricultural and industrial revolutions, diffusion of new norms, and cultural changes.

This theory was developed from an initial schema which presented industrialization and urbanization as the main driving forces in this transition (Davis, 1945). The changes wrought by these two major phenomena brought about a decline in mortality, which, with some lag, was responsible for a reduction in fertility, consequent on larger family size due to the survival of more children and the higher cost of child-rearing. This explanation is in fact not always empirically substantiated—in some countries a mortality decline has not preceded a reduction in fertility, and the change has occurred in the opposite direction (Coale, 1973), thus contradicting the universality of the sequence.

Zelinsky (1973) argued that this transition had to be situated in geographical space and demonstrated that expanding the list of phenomena to include spatial diffusion in the analysis helped make sense of the "mobility transition" which occurred in parallel to the "fertility transition". This spatial approach was completed by Cleland (1985) whose "ideational theory" explains the differences in the timing of the transition in different countries by reference to information diffusion and the establishment of new social norms concerning fertility control.

Economists have also contributed to the debate over this transition. Becker (1960) and Schultz (1973) have emphasized the role of three characteristics in explaining couples' decisions: the relative cost of children compared with other goods; couples' income levels; and their preferences over the choice between bringing up children and other forms of consumption. Easterlin (1961) postulated that women from large birth cohorts tend to have fewer children than those from smaller birth cohorts, thereby causing cyclical variations in period fertility. A more detailed formalization of this approach (Easterlin and Crimmins, 1985) has eventually led to a new economic model, with the addition of a number of sociological determinants: "the supply of children", denoting the number of children the parents would have in the absence of conscious birth control; "the demand for children", corresponding to the stated desired number of children; and "the costs of fertility control" which are psychic, social and monetary. However, attempts to fit this model to empirical data have not been wholly convincing (Wachter and Lee, 1989).

Lesthaeghe (1983) has suggested in addition to economic considerations a shift in personal values in favour of individualism and self-fulfilment, attributed to the rise of secularism and materialism in society. For his part,

Caldwell (1982) speaks of the "emotional nucleation of family", whereby the money, goods and services that used to go to parents now go to children, a process he refers to as an intergenerational reversal of "wealth flows".

More generally, these theories have contributed to a systemic approach to population change. In common with those already outlined, this method attempts to establish links between facts occurring in very disparate domains at a given time and from them deduce the evolution of the system at the next instant. The complexity of the system results in recourse to simulation models. Unfortunately such models often impose a simplification of the relationships between the different elements of the system and this can quickly lead to outcomes very different from those actually observed.

Lastly, Bonneuil (1997) has applied viability theory to introduce a random component into these deterministic models. As in the previous examples, it is assumed that the evolution of a group can be represented by a small number of characteristics. This group is subject to a certain number of constraints. The trajectories which allow its survival are thus not insignificant and will be determined by the various controls which the group can act upon. The author uses the theory to calculate which among all the possible trajectories produce viable outcomes, and to identify the periods of stagnation and of jumps between norms. Applied to changes in Swedish fertility since 1930 (Bonneuil, 1994), this model has outperformed the Easterlin hypothesis in predicting the sharp changes in population behaviour associated with the Second World War.

The different theories presented above may describe changes affecting demographic phenomena in some parts of the world yet fail to explain the behaviour observed in others. The question thus arises of their legitimacy, since they postulate a purely holistic approach to the evolution of humanity. Is it the case that the transitions occurring in different countries have the same causes? Is a decline in mortality a prerequisite for the reduction in fertility? Would we not expect the changes to differ widely depending on when and where in the world they occurred? The countries which had their transition at the end of the nineteenth century are not in the same position at all as those which had it the end of the twentieth century.

As can be seen, these theories are based on the same hypotheses as the period analyses: changes affecting populations are related to the conditions in which they live. The validity of the theories thus depends on the solidity of these hypotheses. It is time now to examine the paradigm which links all these results together.

2.4. An underlying paradigm

This paradigm, never clearly stated by the early authors, can be deduced from the presentation given above. Broadly construed, a paradigm dictates what constitutes legitimate activity in the scientific domain that it governs (Kuhn, 1972). While such a paradigm is by its nature hard to define with precision, its form can be delimited by principles that are sufficiently general. Thus in the present case it can be said that social facts exist independently of the individuals whose lives they regulate. They are shaped by the economic, political, religious, social and other characteristics of the society, and the result is a form of causality that originates not in the individual but in society itself and whose effects are felt by the population as a whole. From this interpretation follows the form of data collection, namely the comprehensive recording at regular intervals of information on the characteristics of the population and its physical and social environment. This approach can thus be described as a *holism*, in that it explains change in a society by reference to its overall structure and not to individual free will.

Development of this paradigm can be traced to the period of consolidation of political arithmetic, when data from registers began to be analysed in a cross-sectional perspective, and it was reinforced from the start of the nineteenth century with the creation of official national statistical services and the introduction of censuses. These supplied "snapshot" views of the population in its totality and recorded numerous characteristics of individuals and households. Combined with civil registration data, also treated in a cross-sectional perspective, they were the raw material for a comprehensive study of the mortality, fertility and nuptiality of populations at a given point in time. Where population registers also existed or where censuses contained a question about the previous place of residence, the country's internal migrations could be analysed in the same way.

The analytical method elaborated by Durkheim was perfectly suited to this approach. Indeed, he acknowledged the value of statistics for isolating social facts (Durkheim, 1895/1937):

> They are in effect expressed in numerical form, with real accuracy, by the rates of nuptiality, births, suicides, that is by the number obtained by dividing the total annual average of marriages, births, and deliberate deaths, by the number of men of an age to marry, procreate, and commit suicide (pp. 9-10).

These rates are too simple to give an accurate reflection of the phenomena being studied but although more sophisticated period measures can of course be elaborated the principle remains the same.

Other tools for the analysis of these period statistics, some of which had been prefigured by the political arithmeticians, were developed in the course of the nineteenth century and the first half of the twentieth century. The shortcomings of concepts such as the birth rate and the ratio of baptisms to marriage, for measuring the fertility of populations were soon recognized. New indexes were devised, requiring new questions to be included in the censuses or civil registration system. For example, the method elaborated by Körösi (1896) for construction of cross-sectional fertility functions by the age of spouses gave a more complex but more realistic measurement of fertility. A number of summary indexes were also developed, such as the total legitimate fertility rate and the cumulated marriage frequency—the problems associated with their use will be discussed later. Other refinements were proposed, such as the introduction of women's age at marriage for legitimate fertility, the sex and birth order of children, the religion and occupation of the parents, etc. An excellent synthesis is provided by Landry's *Traité de démographie* (1945).

Indices of this kind can be used with regression methods that relate them to each other and, more importantly, to various aggregate characteristics of the zones inhabited by the individuals. Such regression models still find applications today. Puig (1981), for example, relates emigration and immigration rates for the French regions to selected aggregate characteristics of these regions (e.g. average income, unemployment rate). He states clearly that these characteristics had been selected according to a preconceived explanatory schema of individual migratory behaviour, applying hypotheses identical to those framed by Durkheim nearly one hundred years earlier.

2.5. Problems encountered in the application of this paradigm

This paradigm predominated almost unchallenged until the end of the Second World War. Exceptions had first been noted during the early days of political arithmetic. The relationship between the value of annuities and the mortality of the population led some authors to adopt a longitudinal rather than cross-sectional analysis of mortality. Following the example of earlier authors, such as Jean De Wit in 1671 (Dupâquier, 1985), Deparcieux (1746) constructed life tables of annuity holders for 1689 and 1696, observed up to the start of 1742, by their age when the annuity was purchased. But this use of a longitudinal approach was not incompatible with the period approach, since the underlying hypothesis was that of a stationary population.

It was however the use of summary indices constructed on the basis of period life tables that generated a renewed interest in this longitudinal approach. Elaborated to provide answers to entirely legitimate questions, these indices sometimes produced results that were hard to interpret and even logically inconsistent with what they were supposed to be measuring. For example, when estimating a survival probability at a particular age, the complements to one of the period mortality probabilities from birth to the age in question can be combined. But the result obviously cannot refer to any real generation, since it measures the effect of mortality conditions at a particular point in time (e.g. epidemic, harsh winter) on a synthetic cohort. Comparison of such an estimate between different populations or sub-populations of the same country, observed at the same time, is thus not as straightforward an operation as it first appears. In particular, it is important "that the generations do not start the year to be studied with particular experiences which largely condition their mortality in the course of the year" (Pressat, 1966, p. 137). What is being attempted here is a use of cross-sectional analysis to obtain results for generations, although the analysis is actually on a synthetic generation that does not correspond to any real generation.

Still more serious difficulties are encountered when studying phenomena such as fertility or nuptiality, where periods of postponement are followed by periods of recovery, as after an economic crisis or a war, for example. As Henry (1966) explains:

> in the course of a period of recovery, behaviour is influenced by the earlier delay. Attributing to a synthetic cohort a set of indices observed during a period of recovery in fact amounts to postulating the existence of a generation which, during its entire existence, is trying to make up ground that it had never lost (p. 468).

This explains why the period sum of first marriage rates by age, which measures the quantum of nuptiality and which in a real cohort must always be less than unity, can take a value much higher than unity in a synthetic cohort. The figure stands above 1.5 in 1946 for France, just after the Second World War. For a more detailed discussion on this topic see Keilman (1986) and (2001), van Imhoff and Keilman (2000).

In addition, the assumption that behaviour is influenced only by the economic, political and social conditions prevailing at that particular time has raised a growing number of questions. For example, the demographic problems caused by wartime conditions are problems not just at the time but affect the generations experiencing them over the very long term. More generally, greater weight needs to be given to the effect of fundamental factors which are much more closely linked to generations, who, as Ryder (1965) observes, share a common historical location and have lived the same experiences at the same ages. Period factors are in fact experienced at very different stages of life depending on the generation and may well also have different consequences. For example, for a young person an economic crisis may be an opportunity to experience different kinds of employment, between which he or she can later chose on the basis of experience, whereas for an older person it is more likely to produce successive periods of unemployment from which it will be hard to escape.

Another consideration is that while the use of aggregate data was legitimate under the previous paradigm, this may not be the case for individual level data. Using new methods, such as logistic regression, models can be estimated based on individual characteristics. But the results obtained are not necessarily consistent with those obtained with aggregate data. For instance, the positive association observed earlier between the percentage of farmers and the percentage of migrants merely shows that the highest probability of migration is associated with a high proportion of farmers, but we do not know if it is in fact the farmers or the non-farmers who migrate most from these regions. It is perfectly conceivable that the presence of a high percentage of farmers, by limiting employment opportunities in other occupations, means that non-farmers are forced to migrate to find better employment, whereas farmers themselves do not have a greater reason to migrate out of these areas.

Such a problem was highlighted some fifty years ago (Robinson, 1950). When the results obtained with aggregate data are not identical to those obtained with individual data, this produces what is known as the *ecological fallacy* . For example, it is often found that the correlations between two characteristics measured by binary variables for individuals and by proportions for regions give different results. Indeed, they may even be of opposite signs, thus leading to completely misleading results if we try to make individual level inferences.

3. COHORT ANALYSIS

From the end of the Second World War, questions such as those described above encouraged demographers to reconsider the assumptions on which their analyses were based. Behind this change was the idea that the multiple problems associated with the period approach might be overcome by a cohort analysis which gave a more realistic account of individuals' own experiences over time.

3.1. The introduction of lived time

Period analysis examined relations between events and characteristics considered simultaneously. Time had only a secondary role in the analysis, when it was necessary to move from one date to the next. The innovation involves placing biographical time, that is, the time actually lived by members of the population, at the centre of the analysis. Attention will then focus on the change over time of a *generation*, born in the same calendar year in a country, or of a *cohort* that experienced a defining event at a specific point in time. The behaviour observed corresponds to the various demographic phenomena (deaths, births, marriage, migration, etc.) that will occur in the lifetime of the members of this generation.

Adoption of this perspective means that the various phenomena will appear inextricably linked to each other—a death can prevent a marriage, a birth may occur before or after a migration, and so forth. Faced with this complexity, the demographer can adopt a simplifying approach to facilitate analysis, by assuming that the various phenomena are independent of each other. In this way the effect of other phenomena, considered to be interfering events, could be eliminated, thereby isolating the phenomenon being studied in the *pure state* (Henry, 1972).

Let us see how the demographer proceeds in order to obtain these events in their pure state, for example first marriages. For this we will follow the argument developed by Henry (1972):

> a premature death prevents unmarried people from marrying; this is the origin of the interference of mortality on nuptiality. To eliminate this we need to know how the people who died unmarried before age 50 would have married if they had lived. Since this is not known a hypothesis has to be made: it is assumed that those dying unmarried at a certain age *a* would have married, had they lived beyond age *a*, as did those who were not dead at this age (p. 77).

A hypothesis of independence between marriage and mortality is thus made here, and an equivalent hypothesis has to be made for international migration. Once these hypotheses have been made, a marriage probability can be calculated from the population observed, which will be the same as that calculated if we had been working with a population not exposed to mortality and migration. If we use the term "quantum" to denote the proportion of individuals in such a cohort who ever experience a vital event, these indices allow the quantum of nuptiality up to age 50 to be estimated. If we use the term "tempo" for the timing of this event during the life course, their distribution in time will give its tempo.

These notions of quantum and tempo can be used to obtain a correct analysis of the occurrence of all types of demographic phenomena. For example, the quantum for mortality thus calculated will necessarily be equal to unity, since everyone is mortal, while its timing will show if child mortality is very high, how mortality varies with age of individuals, and so on. It is possible to work with order-specific fertility and define the quantum and tempo of each birth; one can also look at fertility for all birth orders combined and calculate the completed fertility and age-specific rates, to see their timing, and so on.

The results from such an analysis, based as it is on observation of a real generation or cohort, are free from some of the problems noted earlier for period analysis. For example, the quantum of nuptiality (first marriage) will always be less or equal to unity. The impact on nuptiality of a war or any other historical event can now be clearly evaluated and measure the course of the subsequent recovery, according to the ages at which the generation experienced these events.

This analysis makes the assumption that the population being studied is homogeneous. The key question is: How can the heterogeneity of the population be included so as to get a more realistic picture? Heterogeneity is harder to integrate in a longitudinal perspective than when working with period data. In the latter case, a region can be represented simply by each of its characteristics at the time of a census (proportion of shopkeepers, farmers, individuals with a given income, and so forth), which can be related to certain of its demographic characteristics (e.g. percentages of deaths, births) measured in the following year, for example. By contrast, when working in a longitudinal perspective the question arises of which characteristics to take into account, since they will be changing continuously over time. In addition, a continuous indicator of changes in, for example, occupation or income, is no longer available, because the civil registration data that are used to measure demographic events over time do not supply sufficiently detailed information about these characteristics.

The solution envisaged by differential longitudinal analysis is to examine the occurrence of a particular phenomenon in groups defined by various characteristics (e.g. occupation, labour market status). In this case, however, there are losses from observation through mortality and international emigration but also because of exits from the group being studied. And there will also be entrances by individuals who take up the profession being studied, for example. These individuals will usually not be measured over the whole time and, more importantly, the hypothesis of independence between studied and interfering phenomena cannot usually be considered to be verified.

3.2. Extension to multistate models

This approach which analysed phenomena in isolation from each other was extended in the 1960s and 1970s by the introduction of models with the capacity to handle two or more demographic phenomena simultaneously while retaining the condition of independence between them. Schoen and Nelson (1974) introduced a model to analyse the transitions between marriage, divorce and mortality. Similarly, the multiregional models developed by Rogers (1973) introduce regional mortality and fertility by age as well as migrations between the different regions, also broken down by age. These provide the basis for multiregional population projections in which several demographic phenomena are treated simultaneously. This leads to the construction of Markovian models with a large number of states, in which the probability of experiencing an event is independent of the individual's past history and depends only upon his or her state immediately before its occurrence.

The condition of independence between the different phenomena appears harder to satisfy when working on regional data than in the national context. It implies, for example, that an individual's probability of dying must immediately become the same as that of the zone to which he or she has moved. Yet individuals who have lived in regions where, for example, alcoholism-related mortality is very high and who themselves may be alcoholics, are unlikely to adopt a new pattern of behaviour as soon as they migrate to a region with lower alcoholism. In the same way, female migrants from abroad or indeed from a region with lower fertility than the destination zone may not adopt the latter's fertility level immediately. It has been shown that female migrants to France from the developing countries adopt the fertility behaviour of French women, not immediately but only after a delay of varying length. Equally, different regional fertility levels are likely to be reflected in longer or shorter periods of adaptation.

The probability of migrating from one region to another can of course depend on the age of the individual but is required to be independent of the length of stay in the initial region, of the earlier stages of the itinerary and of the length of these stages. This means that the individual's probability of returning to a region they had previously inhabited is the same as if they had never lived there. There is abundant evidence, however, that return migrations are much more common than migrations to third and not previously inhabited destinations (Courgeau, 1982).

Finally, these models can only include migration rates from the different regions to other regions calculated in relation to the initial populations; they cannot include the populations of the destination regions. Yet it is known that inter-regional migration flows often depend on both the starting populations and the arrival populations. The elaboration of models incorporating both of these populations produces solutions that are no longer linear as in all the previous cases (Courgeau, 1991). In contrast to the previous Markovian model which produces projections with an ultimate stable growth ratio and distribution, these new models produce solutions that are completely distinct over the long-term: solutions that are cyclical and in some cases even "chaotic".

In conclusion, all these models show that the conditions in which longitudinal analysis is valid can be highly restrictive. We must now state its paradigm more explicitly in order to identify these conditions and the limits of their validity.

3.3. Paradigm of longitudinal analysis

The aim of this analysis is to isolate the various demographic phenomena in the *pure state*, thereby freeing them of interfering phenomena and allowing comparisons between countries or regions. Its paradigm can be approached by the following postulate: the demographer can study only the occurrence of one single event over of the life of a generation or cohort, in a sub-population "that retains *all its characteristics and the same characteristics* as long as the phenomenon is present" (Blayo, 1995, p. 1504). We have already seen that this population is considered to be *homogeneous*, but for the analysis to be correct a further condition is that the interfering phenomena be *independent* of the phenomenon being studied (Henry, 1959). These two conditions are always present in the multistate models, where they are applied to each of the sub-populations being analysed: the events that a sub-population may experience occur independently of each other, in conditions that are specific to the region the individuals inhabit.

Under these hypotheses, data from civil registration and population registers can be used to obtain clear information about the demography of generations or cohorts defined by initial events such as marriage for studying legitimate fertility or a birth for studying the transition to the next birth. Census data can also be used to measure, for example, the frequency of celibacy or the proportion unmarried at different ages in different generations. The fundamental hypothesis of independence between the nuptiality and mortality of unmarried people, allows these estimations to be made. When migration also occurs, the hypothesis of independence between nuptiality and migrations seems less credible and caution is needed when interpreting census observations on the proportion unmarried.

Behaviour which appears so strongly influenced by short-term events in a cross-sectional analysis exhibits much greater regularity when considered at the level of generations. The curve of fertility variations fluctuates wildly when period analysis is used but appears much clearer in a longitudinal perspective, evolving smoothly from one generation to the next. Starting from seven children per women born before 1760, it falls continuously until the generations born in 1896, where it reaches a value of less than two children, followed by a recovery up to the generations born in 1930, when it stands at 2.6 children, followed by a steady decline to 2.1 children for the generations born in 1948, with finally a levelling out leading to 2.0 children forecast for the generations currently aged 40, that is those born in 1960.

This paradigm makes possible the analysis of civil registration data, by measuring the *quantum* of various phenomena (e.g. proportion never-married at age 50 in a particular generation, parity progression ratios) and the *tempo* of these same phenomena (e.g. distribution of age at first marriage for the first marriages in this generation before age 50, age-specific birth rates). Comparisons can be made of the behaviour of different generations or cohorts in the same country or between different countries. The demography textbooks associated with this approach treat phenomena such as fertility, mortality, migration, in separate chapters, since they are isolated in the pure state (Pressat, 1966; Henry, 1972).

Henry (1959) gave a clear statement of the conditions necessary for a correct application of this longitudinal analysis:

> The use of probabilities assumes that the cohorts are homogeneous, either for the event being studied or for the interfering event, or that there is no correlation between the two risks, that corresponding to the event being studied and that from the interfering event.
>
> This condition is still not sufficient to justify use of differed observation, at least not without correction of its results; it also requires that the risk due to the interfering event is not modified by the occurrence of the studied event.

> Given the multiple differences between people, we can be certain that no human group is homogeneous; everyday observation and reflection lead us also to the view that usually there is not independence between the risks (p. 31).

These conditions are fully consistent with the proposed paradigm. The author of the preceding comments, which actually establish very strict conditions for the validity of the longitudinal approach, indicated that in practice the approximate procedures employed to perform such an analysis are acceptable:

> The answer would appear to be affirmative for fertility interfering with mortality. We have also given an example where at first sight it did not appear justified to treat a group as if it was homogeneous, and where, nonetheless, acceptable results were obtained (Henry, 1959, p. 31).

These analyses thus appeared to be acceptable, even though the underlying paradigm was not fully respected. It was when surveys providing more detailed information than the civil registration and census data began to be used that the limitations of this approach really became apparent.

3.4. Problems in the application of this paradigm

The first point to note is that the focus of this analysis is not individual life-courses observed over time, but rather a population into and out of which some individuals are moving. It is in this population, which is assumed to remain homogeneous over time, that the quantum and tempo of a phenomenon are calculated. Such an approach in effect denies any specificity to individual lives, and instead considers only the occurrence of an event in a population which as a whole remains identical over time because it is made up of units that are interchangeable. When this analysis divides the population into subgroups between which there is migration, each of these must again be homogeneous. This approach is in fact a *holism*, albeit different from the previous one, being concerned only with comparisons between homogeneous groups and ignoring the existence of their component individuals.

The events governing entrance to and exit from the target population must occur under precise conditions. The interfering events, such as mortality and emigration, which prevent some individuals from experiencing the studied phenomenon, and the competing events, such as unmarried cohabitation, which is in competition with marriage, must be independent of the studied phenomenon. If they are not, an obvious selection bias will remove from the population at risk some individuals having specific characteristics, and introduce other individuals who will modify the composition of the group. Since many demographic events occur within a short span of the life-course, they are competing with the studied phenomenon: a longitudinal analysis on the lines proposed means considering that the event is independent of the others, or abandoning the analysis because it is impossible.

A further difficulty is that because this paradigm only allows the study of one single event, it is impossible to study losses from observation due to the occurrence of a competing event. Cause-specific mortality studies are thus completely excluded, unless the various causes are assumed to be independent of each other. In fact, it is obvious that eradicating one cause of mortality will affect the probabilities of dying from other causes, and this in a way that is virtually impossible to predict as long as the first cause still exists. In the same way, moves out of the unmarried state through either cohabitation or marriage cannot be studied, since the unrealistic assumption has to be made that these are independent phenomena. Finally, it is "also why a study should not be conducted on a population which can be entered through several different events" (Blayo, 1995, p. 1507). In all this adds up to a great many cases where the postulate rules out all possibility of analysis.

Another set of problems is associated with the hypothesis of homogeneity. This was not a source of difficulty when analysis was carried out using civil registration data—for the simple reason that the hypothesis could not be verified. Civil registration data is valuable because of its exhaustivity, yet in consequence it supplies little very detailed information about the population being studied. For example, it tells us whether a birth is legitimate or not and about its parity, but it contains little about the life history of the couple on which to base a more detailed analysis of fertility. However, it is obvious that the population being studied is in many respects heterogeneous.

Period studies (Roussel, 1971) have shown that nuptiality in 1968 was much lower among farmers and farm labourers than among other occupational groups. There is thus a clear interest in studying this more specific sub-population, which is more homogeneous than the initial general population. But a new phenomenon then has to be taken into account, namely the departure from farming of the unmarried individuals. This will involve far more individuals than mortality or internal migration, and occurs at the ages when most marriages take place. Furthermore, it is hard to imagine that if these individuals had remained in farming their nuptiality would have been the same as those who actually did remain in farming. Even before they left farming they are likely to have formed a subgroup with a nuptiality different from that of the initial population. Moreover, within this group it is quite possible that farmers will have a marriage behaviour very different from that of farm labourers, and also a different likelihood of leaving the farming population. In this case the marriage probabilities, calculated on the sub-population of those who stayed in farming, are unreliable since the condition of homogeneity is not verified.

The classical approach is then to divide this sub-population into an ever-growing number of sub-sub-populations, in an attempt to guarantee homogeneity in respect of the phenomenon studied. As Henry (1959) remarked:

> To determine exactly the practical significance of heterogeneity of human groups, differential demographic research needs to go down to the level of individual physical and psychological characteristics, so as to study both the dispersion and correlation of demographic indices within the crudely defined groups considered so far (p. 25).

These sub-populations could be distinguished by place of residence—the probability of marriage for a farmer from the rich plains of the Beauce will certainly be different from that of a farmer from the rugged uplands of the Ariège—and by income, educational level, for example. Yet in this case we will end up with groups with so few members that they will be too small to sustain longitudinal analysis. Moreover, it is impossible to be sure that all the factors of heterogeneity in the population have been taken into account. There always remains an unobserved heterogeneity, whose effect on the probabilities will be completely unknown, which, as will be seen shortly, is not the case with event history analysis.

Finally, analysis is further complicated by the possibility that individuals have of moving between groups. This can be illustrated using the earlier example of how migration among Norwegians is influenced by the fact of being a farmer. Applying longitudinal analysis to this case, it can be seen that in the course of their lives individuals can not only migrate but also change occupation. An individual who starts out as a farmer can change occupation, become unemployed or leave the labour market. Being a farmer is thus not a stable state through time, and the Norwegian population register does not provide a continuous observation of this occupation. Occupation is known only by means of censuses, which are only held at ten-year intervals. In this case, therefore, it is not possible to perform a longitudinal analysis of migration by farmers. But even if these changes were subject to continuous registration, there is no longer any reason to assume that the hypothesis of independence between entering and leaving farming is verified, as could still be assumed for the interaction of mortality and nuptiality. In this case, the longitudinal analysis, based on this hypothesis of independence, is not valid.

The conclusion would thus seem to be that a strict application of this paradigm to real demographic problems amounts to denying any possibility of serious longitudinal analysis of demographic events. It requires the target population to be sub-divided to such an extent that the calculations lose all precision. In addition, it is so restrictive as regards the events being studied that it effectively rules out entire sectors of demographic analysis (analysis of competing events, of interactions between events, of events occurring in a population subject to entrance and exit).

Given these multiple difficulties, it is reasonable to ask whether there is not a need to change the hypotheses underpinning the analysis, and provide a firmer basis for the arguments developed.

4. EVENT HISTORY ANALYSIS

More than thirty years after the introduction of longitudinal analysis, the beginning of the 1980s saw the development of a new approach in demography. This took the form not of further refinement of the methods of differential longitudinal analysis, the difficulties with which have been outlined above, but of a generalization of logistic regression methods, initially in cross-sectional perspective and subsequently in a longitudinal approach (Cox, 1972). We begin by examining the changes that made possible this analysis of individual level events and how, by introducing time into analysis it offered a solution to the problems indicated above, before going on to set out the paradigm on which it rests.

4.1. Introducing individual behaviour

The first point is that the analysis of individual behaviour was not a possibility with either cross-sectional or longitudinal analysis. Both approaches, as has been seen, considered population from an essentially aggregate standpoint. The new approach innovated, firstly, by considering the phenomena studied as individual.

In the period analysis of aggregate data, examined earlier, and by working on a certain number of sub-populations, the probability of experiencing an event was related to the probability of experiencing another event or of having certain characteristics. In this case, it was enough to know the marginal distributions of the events studied to be able, under given hypotheses, to estimate the relationship. The next step is to try to estimate the joint distribution of all the combinations of variables at the individual level, thus establishing a different kind of relationship between the occurrence of an event and the characteristics of an individual. Naturally this requires much more detailed data than an aggregate level analysis, but the advantage is that it makes possible a clearer estimation of individual effects. In this way we reach a logistic analysis, which prefigures an event history analysis.

Let us take another look at the example examined earlier of the effect of the proportion of farmers on the rate of inter-regional migration in Norway (Courgeau, 2002). An aggregate level analysis produced a positive association: the more farmers in a region, the higher the probability of migration out of it. Working now with individual level data, these probabilities can be estimated in another way, by a logit model, for example, which in this simple case is equivalent to estimating separately the migration probabilities of farmers and non-farmers. The probability for the individual i present in region j of migrating ($\mu_{ij} = 1$) depending on whether he is a farmer ($a_{ij} = 1$) or not ($a_{ij} = 0$) can be written in the following form, which is independent of the region of residence j:

$$P(\mu_{ij} = 1 | a_{ij}) = (1 + \exp-[\alpha_0 + \alpha_1 a_{ij}])^{-1}$$

Once the parameters of this formula have been estimated, it is straightforward to calculate the migration probabilities of farmers and non-farmers (see figure 2, p. 66) and the estimates of migration rates for each region (Courgeau, 2002).

This gives an opposite result to the previous one—the probability of migrating for farmers (0.09) is now more than a third less than that for the other occupations (0.15)—and the estimate of the regional migration rate with this model will decrease wile its proportion of farmers increases. The individual behaviour brought to light here contradicts the results obtained using aggregate level data and which also estimate migration probabilities. Another look is thus necessary at the hypotheses that underpin these two approaches, which are mutually incompatible. This problem cannot be resolved until later, when the paradigm for the event history approach has been more precisely stated. For the moment let us continue to examine this approach.

This analysis can easily be generalized to include any number of individual characteristics in order to explain a given behaviour. The problems of dependence between these characteristics are not the same in this case as in aggregate analysis. Indeed, if two characteristics are not independent of each

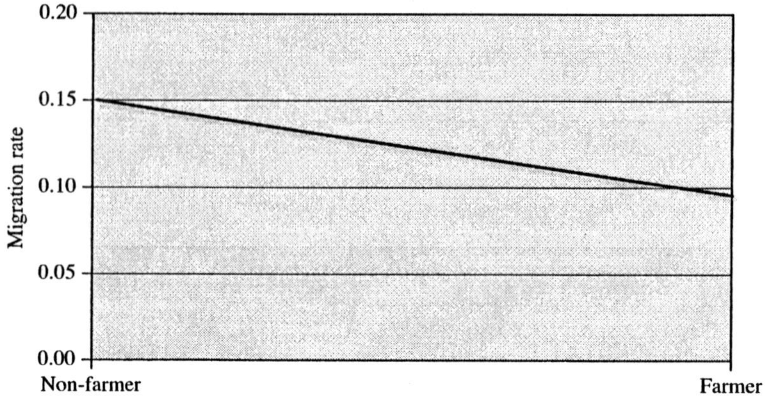

Figure 2. Logit Model

other, this approach allows us to consider separately the individuals who have separately one of these characteristics but not the other and the individuals who possess both characteristics simultaneously. A logit model can still be used to explain the behaviour of these different groups.

This approach, whereby the events experienced by individuals over a short period of time are explained by their characteristics at the start of the period, presents a number of drawbacks. The first concerns the considerable information loss caused by aggregating events that occur over a period, in this case three years, and excluding their exact date of occurrence. Also excluded is the date of arrival in the region of residence in 1970, thus preventing measurement of an effect of duration of stay on the migration probability. Nor does it let us observe a time-dependent effect of the initial characteristics. The second drawback is that these characteristics are fixed at their measurement in 1970, and cannot vary over time. Once again, there is no reason to suppose a move out of farming will not modify the migration probabilities of individuals. Unfortunately this variation cannot be introduced in a logit model.

4.2. Introducing time-dependent regressions

We indicated earlier that an analysis with exhaustive longitudinal data could not be as detailed as one using cross-sectional data from combined census and civil registration sources. Further progress thus appears to be conditional on breaking out of the rigid straight-jacket of these administrative records. At the same time, however, when the information becomes too voluminous and detailed, its collection has to be in a non-exhaustive form. The solution to this double constraint lies with the gathering of individual life history surveys.

Use of surveys means that questionnaires can be designed to provide answers to precise questions. It is therefore possible, bearing in mind the difficulties associated with longitudinal analysis, to collect more comprehensive information about the lives of the individuals being surveyed. We can then establish whether the effect of so-called interfering phenomena is really independent of the phenomena being studied and, if it is not, elaborate new analytical methods for measuring clearly its effects.

These surveys must therefore record the maximum of events in the subjects' lives, including the timing of their occurrence and the intervals between them, so that the interdependencies between them can be explored fully. The surveys must also record as much information as possible about the respondents' characteristics and personal environments for inclusion in the analysis of behaviour. Two types of survey, each with its own advantages and disadvantages, are suitable for observing these various events and states.

The first is the *prospective* survey in which the members of a sample are observed over their entire lifetime. Depending on the specific aims of the survey, it can begin at the birth of these individuals or at any other stage of their existence (at marriage, for example, in order to study their legitimate fertility, union dissolution, remarriage, etc.). The respondents can be re-interviewed annually so as to have a small number of events or characteristics to record. This produces extremely accurate reporting of the timing of the events. By contrast, many analysts are deterred by the time that has to elapse between the start of observation and analysis of the data, which can only take place after a sufficiently long period of time. In addition, subject loss in the course of the research, mainly due to moves to unknown destinations and to refusals to participate further, can be a source of bias in the results. The best example of such a survey is that carried out by Cribier and Kych (1999) on a sample of just-retired people.

Investigators often prefer to carry out a *retrospective* survey in which all the relevant events of interest and individual characteristics are recorded in a single round. The survey can be used immediately and there is no problem of subject loss in the course of the survey. On the other hand, such surveys are time-consuming and expensive to conduct (Courgeau, 1999a). It can be noted that there is a risk of bias due to selection by survival of the respondents, which is usually negligible (Lyberg, 1983). Reporting errors of timing, and omission of events by the respondents can also be a problem. We had the opportunity to evaluate these recall errors in Belgium, a country which possesses population registers. We were able to show that errors arose over the dating of events (Poulain *et al.*, 1991) but that their logical sequence was remembered correctly (Courgeau, 1991).

Whichever type of survey is used, some of the intervals between events will not be observed fully. Observations may be interrupted (censored) either by the date of the survey, in the case of a retrospective survey, or by the ending of the observation, in the case of a prospective survey, unless it is continued until all the respondents are dead. It is in fact possible to use this information, which tells us that the individual has not experienced the event being studied before the observation.

The first analyses were concerned with observation of a single phenomenon that was to be explained by various individual characteristics. Menken and Trussel (1981) analysed marriage dissolution in relation to various socio-demographic characteristics of the respondents. Subsequent studies explored more complex interactions between a variety of demographic events, while taking into account the heterogeneity of the population being examined.

The aim here is merely to present the general procedure involved, not to examine the methods of analysis in detail, and those interested are referred to works with a more mathematical (Andersen *et al.*, 1993) or demographic content (Courgeau and Lelièvre, 1989, 1992). The example we will consider now is the interaction between nuptiality and leaving farming (Courgeau and Lelièvre, 1985), working with the generations born between 1911 and 1936 and resident in France in 1981. This is because the two phenomena studied, migration and leaving farming, cannot be observed through time in the Norwegian example used above.

The principle of this method is to estimate the instantaneous hazard rates for nuptiality, for the same age, depending on whether the individual is still in farming or has left. Symmetrically, the instantaneous hazard rates for leaving agriculture are estimated for still single and already married individuals, still for the same age. If T_i^m and T_i^a are two random variables, corresponding to the date of marriage and the date of leaving farming of individual i, the instantaneous hazard rate of nuptiality can be written, if the exit from farming has not occurred before time t:

$$h_i^{am}(t) = \lim_{\Delta t \to 0} P(T_i^m < t + \Delta t | T_i^m \geq t, T_i^a \geq t) \tag{3}$$

and the instantaneous hazard rate of nuptiality, if the departure from farming has occurred before t:

$$h_i^{\bar{a}m}(t) = \lim_{\Delta t \to 0} P(T_i^m < t + \Delta t | T_i^m \geq t, T_i^a = u) \qquad u < t \tag{4}$$

A symmetrical formulation is given for the hazard rates of leaving farming depending on whether the individuals are not yet married or married. Estimation of these hazard rates is by the maximum likelihood method, which uses data about the individuals experiencing the various events, the populations at risk, and the right censored intervals at the survey date.

These four sets of hazard rates give a preliminary indication of the interdependence between these various events, even before the other characteristics have been taken into account. If marriage of men who began their working lives in farming is appreciably more frequent after their departure from farming, whereas their change of occupation is not dependent on their marital status, this means that there is a *local dependence* (Schweder, 1970) of marriage on the exit from farming. This is what is actually observed in France for the male generations born between 1911 and 1935 - their working life takes precedence over their family life, with the former determining the latter, whereas the latter has no effect on the former. Conversely, for women there is a local dependence in the opposite direction—marriage has the effect of strongly "anchoring" them in the farming sector, whereas leaving farming does not modify their probability of marriage.

This concept of local dependence is much closer to the concept of causality—even if strictly speaking causality can never be established in the human sciences—than the correlations measured in period analysis. Because it introduces time, it indicates that the occurrence of one phenomenon can bring about a change in the probabilities of experiencing another. A correlation, by contrast, gives no indication of causality, since the two phenomena may depend on a third, unmeasured phenomenon, and yet be independent of each other.

It is of course possible to observe a *reciprocal dependence* between two phenomena, as is the case for the interactions between fertility and migration to metropolitan areas (Courgeau, 1987). A *total independence* between these events is also possible though this case appears much rarer. However, it is exactly one of the preconditions for application of the methods of longitudinal analysis, requiring independence between events, which is thus called into question.

More complex dependencies can also be identified. For example, in the study of interactions between fertility and migration to metropolitan areas (Courgeau, 1987), a large reduction in fertility after the birth of one child is observed among women who migrate. The question thus arises of whether this is evidence of an adaptation to the behaviour of the destination area, whereby the women who migrate adopt the low fertility of city-dwellers, or of a selection, if the women who migrate are those whose fertility is already different from the women in the initial area. The women who migrated to the metropolitan areas timed their fertility before migration differently from that of women who remained in non-metropolitan areas. Moreover their timing was the same as that of women who had already moved to these areas. What is revealed here is an *a priori dependence* of fertility on future migration, which is responsible for this selection within the original population.

Likewise, migration to areas of high fertility is observed to have a positive effect on the chance of having a second and third child. Using research of the same kind as above, it is possible this time to show an authentic adaptation of fertility behaviour among women who migrate to less urbanized areas. This is because their initial fertility behaviour is no different from that of the women who remain in the metropolitan areas, but becomes identical after migration to that of women who have not moved from the less urbanized regions.

Nonparametric analysis can be used to show how dependencies change with age. Thus, for example, young women born between 1911 and 1936, who have had a first child and gone back to work, are more likely to have a second child than those who have not returned to work. After age 30, however, the pattern is reversed, and it is the older women who are less likely to have a second child than those who have not returned to work (Lelièvre, 1987).

Finally, a generalized Cox model can be used to examine the effect on these behaviours of various individual characteristics, some of these being subject to modification once individuals have experienced one of the events.

For the nuptiality of farmers with a certain number of characteristics this model can be written in the form of a column vector Z:

$$h_i^{am}(t|Z_i(t)) = h_0^{am}(t)\exp[\beta Z_i(t)] \tag{5}$$

where $h_0^{am}(t)$ is a baseline hazard rate independent of the characteristics $Z_i(t)$, which may or may not be time-dependent, and β is a row vector of parameters to be estimated. As indicated above, it will be possible to take account of the interactions between these characteristics.

Estimation of these effects is possible by means of maximizing the partial likelihood. In the case of women leaving farming, the fact of having many brothers and sisters is observed to hasten their departure, whether or not they are married, whereas the fact of being the eldest child or of having a father who is a farmer, keeps women in this sector as long as they are unmarried. Once they are married, however, these characteristics no longer influence their departure from farming. In addition, the characteristics of the husband can then also be introduced. Thus having a farmer for a husband greatly increases the likelihood for a woman of staying in farming, presumably because of the possibility of combining the two farms to create one larger and more profitable holding.

The foregoing examples suggest that event history analyses can produce more firmly based conclusions than those obtained with longitudinal analysis. This approach had been used in different social sciences such as sociology (Tuma and Hannan, 1984), economics (Lancaster, 1990), epidemiology (Commenges, 1999; Keiding, 1999) and so on.

In the next section we examine the paradigm which underlies these methods and assess its advantages compared with those of period and longitudinal analyses, as well as the drawbacks it nonetheless presents relative to the issues of demographic research.

4.4. A paradigm for event history analysis

The focus of interest is no longer the study of homogeneous sub-populations but a set of individual trajectories between a large number of states. The unit of analysis is no longer the event but the individual life history, considered as a complex stochastic process. The aim is no longer to isolate each phenomenon in the pure state but, on the contrary, to see how an event in an existence can influence the rest of the individual's life, and how certain characteristics can induce one individual to behave differently to another.

In this case, the paradigm can be approached by the following proposition: throughout his or her life an individual follows a complex itinerary, which at any given moment depends on the life-course to date and on the information acquired in the past (Courgeau and Lelièvre, 1997). This approach is unequivocally *individualist*. It postulates that a person's behaviour is to be explained by reference to his or her past life history, and not by looking to society for the reason for these actions. It is therefore diametrically opposed to the aggregated period approach which, as was seen, is a methodological holism.

The first principle is that a group of individuals belonging to a particular generation or cohort is tracked through time. The main way that an individual can be lost to observation is by leaving the sample at the date of the survey, or of the study if the prospective technique is being used. Insofar as there is no reason for these dates to be linked in any way with the individual's life, the condition of independence is fully satisfied: the observation is said to be non-informative and these losses from observation can be allowed for when estimating the hazard rates. This it can be seen how the change of perspective overcomes the problem of interfering events.

On the other hand, however, selection bias can occur, especially in retrospective surveys, since only the individuals who survive and are in the country at the time of the survey can be interviewed. In this case, it is often necessary to work on the assumption that the losses from the population under observation are not selective, unless population register data is available to adjust for this bias (Hoem, 1985). Such selection bias is reduced, however, if the event being studied does not occur in an elderly population or one particularly concerned by emigration.

Analysis can be done on sub-populations that have experienced the same initial event, such as entrance to the farming population, for example, and then study the occurrence of an event such as marriage. If these individuals experience so-called "interfering" events (exit from farming), they do not move out of observation but can change their behaviour in respect of marriage. This can be tested by comparing the behaviour of farmers of the same age or with that of the population which had never been farmers. By this means, as was shown earlier, we can establish whether selection has occurred or, on the contrary, if behaviour has been adapted.

Whereas in classical longitudinal analysis there was no need to distinguish between interfering events and competing or concurrent events, these now have to be examined separately. As has just been shown, an interfering phenomenon—that we prefer here to call "interacting phenomenon"—modifies the probability of the studied event occurring. Conversely, what are described as competing or concurrent events are the different modalities of an event which has the same final outcome: e.g. cause-specific mortality, union formation by marriage or by cohabitation.

It is important to be clear that the aim is not to find out what mortality from a particular cause would be if other causes were assumed to be eliminated, or the marriage probabilities if there was no cohabitation. Such questions are beyond the scope of the statistics with which we are working, and the answers proposed by some social scientists should be treated with extreme caution. Our objective is rather to show how these various causes act simultaneously, to examine how exit from the never-married state occurs by either marriage or cohabitation, without attempting to distinguish these effects. In these conditions it is no longer possible to define a quantum for the transitions into these different states but merely to compare the relative probabilities and timing of the different transitions.

We are thus equipped to examine how an event, be it of a family, economic or other nature, experienced by an individual whose past trajectory is known, will modify the probability of other events happening to him or her. For example, we might wish to examine how marriage influences professional career, spatial mobility, and the occurrence of events such as the birth of a child or the break from the family of origin. This corresponds exactly to what we have described as the analysis of interacting demographic phenomena, and is clearly consistent with the proposed paradigm.

An analysis along these lines assumes an initial population that is homogeneous in terms of the process being studied, that is, at the start of the analysis the individuals are in the same state in relation to the process. But the population becomes increasingly heterogeneous with the passage of time, as it experiences the different interacting events. This hypothesis of homogeneity used in the first stage of the analysis in order to unravel the interactions between phenomena, must necessarily be discarded in a second stage. There is in fact no reason that the individuals of the initial population should be identical, and the time-dependent regression methods employed in a second stage enable us to explore their initial heterogeneity and that which is introduced over time.

Any understanding of an individual's behaviour must take account of his or her social origins and past history. Behaviour is assumed to be not innate but to change over the course of the individual's lifetime in response to what is experienced and learned with time. Two individuals born into families initially very close in terms of, for example, social background, religious beliefs, occupation, but who followed completely different career paths, can be expected to have increasingly divergent behaviour in respect of the various demographic phenomena.

In this way we arrive at an analysis of population heterogeneity, using a dynamic approach rather than a static approach as in period analysis. Regression analysis, used in cross-sectional analysis to relate aggregate behaviour to the characteristics of populations that are also aggregate, now has to be extended to the analysis of individual characteristics. When an individual is born, the range of possible life courses is large. But these different trajectories are far from being of equal probability. The life history of an individual can therefore be defined as the result of a complex stochastic process, occurring over the time lived by the individual.

These processes have been studied by probability specialists and statisticians using the theory of martingales (Dellacherie and Meyer, 1980), stochastic integration (Dellacherie, 1980) and counting processes (Brémaud and Jacod, 1977). These methods cannot be presented here and the interested reader is referred to the excellent synthesis by Anderson *et al.* (1993). All that is given here are the main aspects of this approach, to illustrate its potential for making the best use of the proposed paradigm.

An individual's life course is modelled as interacting stochastic processes occurring within a given generation or cohort (Willekens,1999, 2001). These individuals can experience a certain number of demographic events which cause them to change state. The order in which these events are experienced is of course not specified and may vary widely. But it is also obvious that the probability of experiencing one of these events at any given time will be related to the prior history of the individual (events experienced, the order and timing of their occurrence) and to characteristics that are time-invariant (e.g. social and geographical origins, number of siblings) or time-dependent (e.g. economic crises, wars).

These transitions are studied using an essentially semiparametric model, in which the effect of the characteristics of interest for the research is modelled parametrically but no assumption is made about the form of the distribution of the duration of stay in each of the states studied. This model is dynamic in that it can model the instantaneous hazard rates of the various events being studied, in relation to the different populations exposed to the risk. It also offers the possibility of introducing time-dependent characteristics, thus allowing a truly dynamic model of the change in stochastic processes over time to be estimated. These changes are related primarily to individual events and characteristics.

Another important property of these models is their capacity to introduce the effects of interaction between individual characteristics. For example, if an individual's migration at a given time depends on the fact of being a farmer and of being married, a difference in behaviour may be observed between unmarried farmers and the rest of the population, and between married farmers and the rest of the population. This interaction effect can be taken into account by also including the product of the binary variables that correspond to the two characteristics and estimating the model which includes the three variables. This logistic model can of course be generalized as an event history model, into which is introduced this same interaction between characteristics, which will now be time-dependent.

Finally, this model is largely exempt from a number of problems. Loss of subjects from observation at the time of the survey, for example, can be fully estimated, as can the occurrence of competing events, or the existence of unobserved heterogeneity. The last point is very important for the validity of the analysis and is worth examining in more detail.

When carrying out an analysis it is clear that not all the factors which influence the process being studied will be included, either because they have not been captured by the survey or because they are believed, mistakenly, to have no effect. This is referred to as unobserved heterogeneity and it can invalidate results obtained from the observed data only. When regression models are used to analyse period data, incorporating this unobserved heterogeneity is known to have no effect on the estimated parameters if it is independent of the observed variables. Unfortunately this is no longer the case when we use a semiparametric model that incorporates time.

However, the effect of non-observed characteristics on parameters estimated with observed characteristics has been successfully modeled by Bretagnolle and Huber-Carol (1988). They showed that when the omitted characteristic is independent of the observed characteristics, its omission does not change the sign of the estimated parameters. On the other hand, it does reduce the absolute value of the parameters. This means that if the effect of a characteristic appears fully significant when the other characteristic is omitted, introducing it into the model will merely reinforce the effect of the first characteristic. On the other hand a characteristic with no significant effect on the phenomenon being studied could acquire a completely significant effect when the unobserved characteristic is introduced.

These results are very important since they allow us to be certain about the direction of the effects observed to be significant, and of their degree of significance, whereas we do not know if all the characteristics affecting the durations of stay have been introduced into the model. In the presentation of longitudinal analysis we saw how this problem compromised the validity of the approach. The procedure mentioned above give us a means of verifying its effect on the results of an event history analysis.

4.5. Risk of the atomistic fallacy

Factors of a demographic or non-demographic nature can now be identified and their influence on individual behaviour subjected to very detailed analysis. In most cases, however, this behaviour is explained in terms of the characteristics of the individual. The danger here is of committing the *atomistic fallacy,* since no attention is paid to the context in which human behaviour actually occurs. This context can be defined as the family environment in which the individual lives, or more generally as a "contact circle" of varying size organized around the individual and based on the neighbourhood or commune, for example. In fact this context does have an influence on individual behaviours and it seems fallacious to consider individuals in isolation from the constraints imposed by the society and milieu in which they live.

The danger of this fallacy—which can be compared with the ecological fallacy—was first identified by sociologists (Lazarsfeld and Menzel, 1961). They showed the need for careful definition of various types of groups, communities, organizations and, more generally, other groups of individuals. These can be composed of members who are comparable in respect of the studied behaviour and must be described by a certain number of properties. What appears as a group in one study can be treated in another study as a member of a more general grouping. This property is very important since it shows the relative nature of the individual that the event history approach treats as the principal unit. Used carefully it should make it possible to move beyond the individualism-holism dichotomy.

How this can be done is considered in the next section.

5. CONTEXTUAL AND MULTILEVEL ANALYSIS

For the investigator wishing to avoid the atomistic fallacy the solution is to work at several levels of aggregation simultaneously. Such an approach can take two forms that will be explored successively. One is to introduce the effect of aggregated characteristics in the individual level model being used; the other is to try to take into account the various levels of aggregation available for analysis.

5.1. From contextual analysis...

The conditions that have to be satisfied in order for a model estimated on individual data to be identical to an equivalent model calculated on aggregate data have been specified for linear regressions (Firebaugh, 1978) and for logistic regressions and event history models (Baccaïni and Courgeau 1996). It is shown that once the fact of the individual having the explanatory characteristic (being a farmer, for example) has been controlled for, the corresponding aggregate characteristic (the percentage of farmers, for example) no longer influences the probability of experiencing the event studied (migrating, for example). In this case, the aggregate and individual level models are perfectly equivalent. The problem is that this is seldom what is actually observed, as we have established with the Norwegian example.

The simplest solution is to introduce data measured at several levels of aggregation to explain a behaviour which is still individual. We can then see the difference between this approach, in which aggregate characteristics are used to explain an individual behaviour, and the aggregate approach in which an aggregate-level behaviour is explained by characteristics that are themselves defined at the aggregate level.

In this way the risk of ecological fallacy is eliminated, since the construction measured by the aggregate characteristic will be different from that measured by its equivalent at the individual level. It no longer operates as a substitute but as a characteristic of the sub-population with an influence on the behaviour of an individual belonging to it. Simultaneously, the atomistic fallacy is eliminated by the inclusion of the context in which the individual lives. One may wonder, however, if the introduction of aggregate level characteristics is really adequate to model this context. We will see later that it is necessary to move further towards a genuinely multilevel analysis.

Returning to the example of migration among Norwegian farmers, application of a contextual model can include the fact that the individual is a farmer and the percentage of farmers in the region of residence, $a_{.j}$. This model can be written:

$$P(\mu_{ij} = 1 \mid a_{ij}, a_{.j}) = (1 + \exp-[\alpha_0 + \alpha_2 a_{.j} + (\alpha_1 + \alpha_3 a_{.j})a_{ij}])^{-1} \qquad (6)$$

The results it produces, given in figure 3 (p. 76), can be used to harmonize the contradictory results obtained earlier: the fact of being a farmer still strongly reduces the probability of migrating, while the fact of living in a region with a large percentage of farmers increases the chances of migrating for both farmers and non-farmers (Courgeau 2002). This time, however, the reason for the emigration rates increasing as the percentage of farmers increases is completely different. In the analysis on aggregate data, it is the stability of the migration probabilities of farmers and other occupations—at different values—that explains, through the calculations of the percentages of farmers, why the regions with more farmers are those with higher rates of migration. In the present model it is the variation of these migration probabilities according to the percentage of farmers which explains the same result. This

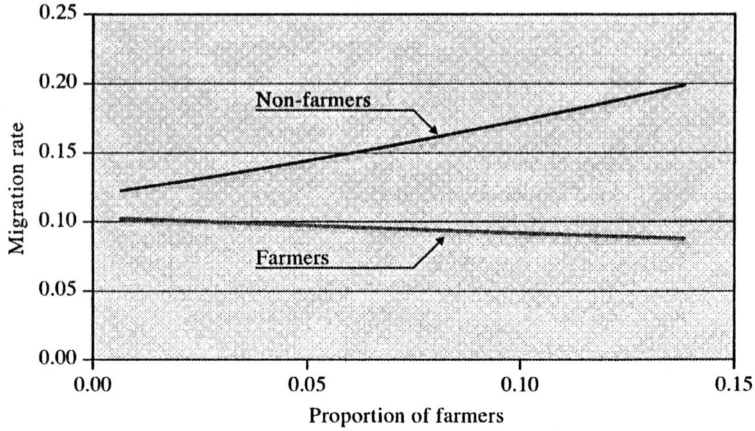

Figure 3. Contextual logit Model

shows us that this higher migration probability relates primarily to non-farmers, since the migration probabilities of farmers are not significantly modified by the percentage of farmers. This model supports the hypothesis we put forward earlier: a high proportion of farmers in a zone increases the probability of migration for those in other occupations. This could be explained by a relative shortage in these regions of non-agricultural employment which encourages those in other occupations to emigrate more than farmers when looking for a new job.

It is interesting to see now that the characteristics which are introduced may be of very different types. Although the characteristics to be analysed will always be treated as individual, they may be period characteristics and thus analysed using a logit-type model, but they can also be life history characteristics and analysed as such. The explanatory characteristics can be much more diverse.

Initially we could introduce individual characteristics, measured just before the occurrence of the event in the case of a logit model, or measured over time in the case of an event history model. Then, for a given level of aggregation, some of these individual characteristics could be simply aggregated so as to estimate the percentages or averages for a given region, such as its percentage of farmers, or the average number of children per family, for example. More complex analytical procedures could be used: as well as the average number of children, the standard deviation of this number could be included, or the correlation between this number and income at each level of aggregation.

The structural characteristics are the properties of each of the units at a given level of aggregation. They are obtained by quantification of certain relationships existing between members of these units. If we consider a household for example, its structural characteristics are the number of children it contains, the proportion of its members not related to the head of the household (live-in staff, for example), and so on. Other characteristics are more general and concern the units in their entirety: number of hospital beds or population density, for example. These do not correspond to any individual characteristic, but they can be aggregated at various levels. Thus the number of hospital beds in a region is the sum of the number of beds in each of the departments that make up the region, and its density is the sum of the densities weighted according to the population of each department. Other collective characteristics are well defined for a given level of aggregation but cannot be aggregated at higher levels. The electoral orientation of a commune, as defined by the party affiliation of its mayor, for example, cannot be aggregated with those of neighbouring communes which may range over a wide spectrum. This characteristic does not exist at either the individual level, or the departmental and regional levels.

The use of contextual models imposes very restrictive conditions on the formulation of the logarithm of relative risks (log-odds) in relation to the characteristics. In particular, the behaviours of individuals within a group are treated as independent of each other. In practice, it is more likely that the risk faced by an individual in a given group will depend on the risks faced by the individuals in the same group. Failure to include this within-group dependence usually produces bias in the estimations of the variances of the contextual effects, resulting in confidence intervals that are too narrow. Also, these "log-odds" for individuals in different groups cannot vary freely but have restrictive constraints imposed by the model being used (Loriaux, 1989). In the previous case, for instance, if the migration probabilities of non-farmers ($a_{ij} = 0$) and farmers ($a_{ij} = 1$) in each region are linked by segments of line, it can be shown that all these lines will pass through a common point (Courgeau 2001).

In view of these constraints, it becomes necessary to formulate the proposed model in its full complexity, which brings us to authentic multilevel models.

5.2. ... to a multilevel analysis

For a clearer idea of what we intend to do, it is useful to review what was said earlier in the discussion of longitudinal analysis, concerning the effect of different characteristics on demographic behaviour. It was shown that subdivision into more homogeneous sub-populations, according to different regions or different characteristics, meant that the numbers exposed to the risk quickly fell to very low levels. The results from such an analysis are too unstable for significant relationships to be identified. In these conditions the large number of random variations (noise) are likely to mask any interesting result.

This problem was overcome using the methods of linear or, more usually in demography, logistic regression, which identify the relevant results of the analysis. The introduction of time into Cox-type models has made it possible to study the heterogeneity of the population and obtain results that are completely significant even when large numbers of characteristics are introduced. However, this method implies making new hypotheses, whose validity must be tested using tests whose power, unfortunately, is so low that they provide no adequate basis for rejecting the model even if the error component is very large. The contextual models which generalize these methods by introducing regions or groups of different individuals, offer no solution to the difficulties outlined above. In these conditions the best approach may be to look for a compromise between a model which does not constrain its estimators but fails to produce a significant estimation, and a model that sets excessive constraints but whose validity cannot be tested.

In our view the solution to this two-fold problem lies with multilevel models. These introduce random effects into the previous individual or contextual models, thus allowing the regression methods considered to be generalized.

Let us have another look at the example of Norwegian migrations. First of all we have the possibility of estimating a logistic model by region, suitable for measuring the effect of a characteristic, in this case that of being a farmer, on the migration probability:

$$P(\mu_{ij} = 1 \mid i \in j, a_{ij}) = (1 + \exp-[\alpha_{0j} + \alpha_{1j} a_{ij}])^{-1} \qquad (7)$$

This is the first stage of the analysis, in which the whole set of regional parameters (for 19 regions there are 38 parameters) are estimated. But when a large number of regions is included or the parameters are numerous, these parameters resemble random noise when plotted and are subject to a very large error that prevents any firm conclusions from being reached. The solution envisaged involves placing constraints on these parameters to obtain more accurate results. If it is assumed, for example, that they are distributed randomly around their mean value, estimated by models (6) and (7), we can then write:

$$\alpha_{0j} = \alpha_0 + \alpha_2 a_{.j} + u_{0j} \qquad \text{and} \qquad \alpha_{1j} = \alpha_1 + \alpha_3 a_{.j} + u_{1j}$$

where u_{0j} and u_{1j} are random values of expectation zero. Attention can thus be limited to the variances and covariances between these random values:

$$var(u_{0j}) = \sigma^2_{u0} \qquad var(u_{1j}) = \sigma^2_{u1} \qquad cov(u_{0j}, u_{1j}) = \sigma_{u01}$$

The full model can now be written in condensed form:

$$P(\mu_{ij} = 1 \mid a_{ij}, a_{.j}) = (1 + \exp-[\alpha_0 + \alpha_2 a_{.j} + u_{0j} + (\alpha_1 + \alpha_3 a_{.j} + u_{1j}) a_{ij}])^{-1} \qquad (8)$$

Now we need to estimate only 7 parameters, compared with the 38 previous ones.

Remaining with the Norwegian example, let us see in table 1 what light these models shed on migration behaviour. If the aggregated characteristics of the regions are not introduced (simple model), the individual level parameters remain almost the same as those estimated without including regional effects in the previous logit model, both for farmers and for other occupations (Courgeau, 2002). By contrast, significant effects appear for the regional random variables, showing a very diverse behaviour for inhabitants of the different regions. When the proportions of farmers of the regions are introduced (model with aggregate characteristic), as in the contextual model estimated earlier, their effect appears entirely significant and identical to that observed with a single level of aggregation. By contrast, at the level of the regional random variables, a sharp reduction of one half is observed for non-farmers, showing clearly that introduction of the regional percentages for farmers has an influence on this variance, whereas for farmers the effect remains as high as before. However, the fact that the regional variance remains significant shows that the aggregate characteristics do not explain everything. This model, while confirming the results of the previous contextual model, is nonetheless more complete.

Tableau 1. Multilevel analysis parameters and their standard error in parentheses

Parameter	*Multilevel Model*	
Fixed:	Simple	With aggregate characteristic
α_0 (non-farmer)	−1,710 (0,070)	−2,067 (0,119)
α_1 (farmer)	−2,306 (0,133)	−2.017 (0,340)
α_2 (proportion of farmers)		5,420 (1,209)
α_3 (farmer × % farmers)		−8,691 (3.238)
Random:		
$\sigma^2_{u_0}$ (non-farmer)	0,088 (0,032)	0,047 (0,024)
$\sigma_{u_{01}}$ (covariance)	0,054 (0,044)	0,085 (0,042)
$\sigma^2_{u_1}$ (farmer)	0,167 (0,135)	0,181 (0,119)

A multilevel model, because it uses all the available information, avoids any arbitrariness in the choice of characteristics for inclusion in the model and in the means of selecting the variables to be used. Consequently the variances and covariances between characteristics present at a given level of aggregation will no longer be bound by the restrictive conditions that apply when a contextual model is used.

A similar approach is now used in different social sciences as educational sciences (Goldstein, 1995), epidemiology (Greenland, 1998; Morgenstern, 1998), human geography (Jones, 1997), and so forth.

More generally, such a model is suitable for showing how differences between rates estimated for groups can be explained by differences in the distribution of various individual characteristics. A first level might consider the individual risks within each group with regard to a large number of characteristics of these same individuals. A second, more aggregated level, is then used to predict the first level coefficients for various characteristics, not only aggregate but also particular to the groups. The underlying hypothesis is that the coefficients of the groups are random samples of a more general population of such parameters. By combining the results obtained for each level, it is possible to predict the probability of an event's occurrence, for a given individual, in relation to his or her individual characteristics, and the characteristics of the various groups and their interactions.

Multilevel event history models can also be set up by introducing random variables both in the baseline hazards and in the effect of the various characteristics of a generalized Cox-type model. Using the previous example of nuptiality among farmers (model (5)), we add the effects of regions j (regional percentages with the individual characteristic, $Z_{.j}(t)$, or other regional characteristics, $Y_j(t)$, leading to estimate probabilities of the following type:

$$h_{ij}^{am}(t|Z_{ij}(t)) = h_0^{am}(t)\exp[(\beta + \gamma Z_{.j}(t) + u_j)Z_{ij}(t) + \delta Y_j(t) + v_j + w_{ij}] \qquad (9)$$

We see that with this model we can write $h_{0j}^{am}(t) = h_0^{am}(t)\exp(\delta Y_j(t) + v_j)$, which introduces the underlying regional baseline hazards, that depend on regional characteristics. In the same way, the effect of each characteristic can now depend on the region. Finally, an unobserved individual heterogeneity is introduced by the parameter w_{ij}.

Models of this kind facilitate the study of several processes taking place simultaneously. Thus, for example, fertility in different regions of a country can be studied at the same time as the migrations occurring between these regions. In this way we can see if a change in the fertility behaviour of migrants takes place and to measure the time needed to adapt to the fertility of the region of immigration, if this is the case, or conversely to see if there is not a selection of migrants from in the initial population.

The statistical models necessary for handling this data are now well developed (Goldstein, 1995). However, it has to be noted that *multilevel event history* models still require major extensions before they can be applied to complex situations. On the other hand, they offer the possibility of being able to introduce any number of levels, regardless of how they are organized in relation to each other.

The simplest and most widely used structure is hierarchical. For example, individuals live in communes, which are themselves in departments, and so on. Each level is formed by the grouping together of all the units of the preceding level. The division adopted may be administrative, as in the example just given, or of a completely different type: workshops, factories, companies, production sectors, and so one.

More complicated relationships between the levels can be envisaged. Individuals can be distributed between towns classified by ascending size order but also between administrative, industrial and tourist centres, for example. In this case there is a cross-classification, according to whether the towns are classified by size or by function. It is of course possible to have relationships that combine hierarchical and cross-classifications. For example, individuals may be classified by type of residential neighbourhood and by the type of place of work (cross-classification), which are themselves subject to a hierarchical classification of departments and regions.

New forms of surveys are required for carrying out analysis on these lines. Such surveys need to distinguish carefully between the various groups to be considered and must be capable of producing aggregated measurements. Individual characteristics can of course always be aggregated, but as was shown earlier there are other group characteristics which cannot be obtained in this way. These must therefore be measured, independently of the survey conducted on the members of the group. This data-gathering exercise is likely to be particularly time-consuming and complicated for the purpose of multilevel event history analysis. Information has to be collected on the variations of these characteristics over time.

5.3. Towards a more comprehensive paradigm

This new approach does not imply a dramatic change in the paradigm used for event history analysis since the focus of analysis remains at the individual level. Rather, by introducing the effects of groups or regions on individual behaviour it extends and completes that paradigm.

Within the new paradigm the behaviour of an individual is still considered to depend on his or her past history, but the perspective is broadened to recognize that this behaviour can also depend on the external constraints that weigh on the individual, and of which he or she may or may not be aware. In this way it becomes possible to examine the "unintended side effects" of individual actions with initial aims completely different from the results obtained (Boudon, 1977). These effects are a product of the milieu in which the individual lives and can be identified by means of multilevel methods. Similarly, individuals may be unaware of the constraints that society places on its members, though these may influence their behaviour without their knowledge. Finally, individuals may be fully aware of these constraints and act accordingly, so as to resist their influence, to avoid them, or even use them to their own advantage.

With this approach it is possible to study individual biographies situated in a multidimensional space. This context can be defined not merely in the conventional physical terms, making a distinction between regions and towns, for example, but could also be socially-defined, introducing the networks of relations between individuals, or economically-defined, taking account of the companies and public utilities, for example, where these individuals are employed, or of any other functional space.

This paradigm also opens the way for a new statistical perspective on human behaviour. The "subjective" position elaborated by Bayes in 1763 introduces a larger dimension to this approach. Starting from the "prior" probability of a particular event, this method uses new empirical information from observation in order to calculate a "posterior" probability for the same event. The application of such a formulation was vigorously rejected by the proponents of an "objective" viewpoint, for whom the notion of "prior" probability was completely meaningless since the probability was that of a one-off event. The "objectivists" worked to develop methods of inference that were compatible with this conception of probabilities and avoided recourse to Bayes's theorem. The multilevel approach is a powerful stimulus for a renewed use of the Bayesian conception of probability.

Model (7) produces estimations for a large number of coefficients, in the present case 38 for 19 regions, some of which may be determined on small numbers and thus have a very high variance. As was indicated, it is hard to reach any firm conclusions from this first stage. For this reason we go back to model (6), which this time requires estimation of only four coefficients, and attempt to make a synthesis of these two models, leading to the introduction of four fixed parameters and two random variables for which only the variances and covariances are estimated, representing seven quantities in all (model (8)). However, the residuals can be estimated, making it possible to situate the regions in relation to each other and to identify those in an extreme position in relation to the others, by estimating a confidence interval for each region. This is what is commonly referred to as an empirical-Bayes estimator, in which the "prior" distribution is estimated from empirical data as is the "posterior" distribution (Lee, 1997). It is of course possible to go further and introduce at a third level an authentic "prior" estimation, thereby producing a model operating on more fully Bayesian principles leading to a Bayes empirical-Bayes estimation (Greenland, 2000).

By its simultaneous introduction of individual characteristics and aggregate characteristics at different levels, this provides both a synthesis of and an improvement on the three previous approaches. It introduces the aggregated characteristics, and is therefore able to explain the results obtained with a period model, though using different hypotheses, as was seen. It incorporates the individual characteristics, and therefore produces results comparable to those obtained with event history models. Finally, by its improved capacity to take into account the diversity of behaviour at different levels of aggregation, it provides a solution to the problems encountered in longitudinal analysis, where the sub-division of categories and places quickly renders analysis impractical.

5.4. Unanswered questions

A rapid review was given earlier of the various types of divisions or groupings that can be used in analysis: sociological and anthropological (e.g. family, "contact circle", clan), geographical and administrative (e.g. communes, cantons, departments, regions, countries), religious (e.g. parishioners of a Catholic church, or a Protestant church, animists), and many others. Some of these divisions are obvious candidates for use in analysis (such as the family or the workshop), since the potential influence of these groups on individual behaviour is already well established, but the use of others can be less obvious.

First of all, if, as is theoretically possible, a large number of levels of aggregation are introduced, there is a danger of duplication between some of the levels. For example, if local government divisions were being used, duplication might well occur between the division by communes (of which there are roughly 36 000 in France) and by cantons (roughly 3000 in France). Use of multilevel analysis should supply an answer to these questions, since the random variables corresponding to one level of aggregation can disappear when another is introduced that takes account of these variables correctly. Another point is that some divisions may be entirely appropriate for studying one phenomenon but not another. Thus for example the regional division that we used in Norway is clearly suitable for the analysis of inter-regional migrations; but it would be inappropriate for studying migrations at a more detailed level.

Further advance in this field requires a very thorough examination for each type of study of the various possible levels of aggregation. It would also be useful to see if combining zones gives results as good as those obtained using a larger number, and with no loss of information. A broad investigation to assess the validity of existing divisions and the creation of new and more relevant divisions is needed and as yet remains to be undertaken.

From another point of view, this analysis, in which individual behaviour is explained by reference to both individual and aggregated characteristics, may fail to explain evolution in the rules which apply at higher levels of aggregation. It is important to understand that these rules result from the transmission between individuals in the same group of behaviour which is similar at a certain point in time but which can change over time. There is thus a two-fold problem for analysis: that of the change in these groups over time, and that of the changes in the different behaviours.

How are appropriate groups formed? What are the factors responsible for their survival or demise? And what are the mechanisms which explain their evolution? These are all questions which require answers and which to date have received little attention. Studies do of course exist on the rise and fall of great cultures in the past, but analysis of cohesion and change in smaller-scale groups is still in its infancy. Research in this direction must be continued in order to place multilevel analysis on firmer foundations.

Another problem concerns an investigation of how particular types of behaviour come into being, are modified or disappear. Little work has been done on this genesis of social behaviour, although the various demographic transition theories attempted to provide general explanations. Thus, for example, in the case of the developed countries, the emergence and spread of cohabitation as an alternative to marriage in the 1960s has still not been satisfactorily explained. The explanation is doubtless that it was a form of behaviour better adapted than traditional marriage to the prevailing conditions at the time and for this reason was able to spread in these countries. Attention needs to focus on how isolated individual actions, occurring in a given community, can produce an awareness of a problem that affects society as a whole and stimulate an acceptable solution; then examine how these new behaviours are diffused and prompt the introduction of policies (such as the civil solidarity pact or PACS recently introduced in France, giving legal recognition to couples of either sex, for example), taken at a higher level of aggregation. These measures will in turn, of course, influence individual conduct, producing new actions to counter their negative side-effects, and so on and so forth.

Finally, more attention needs to be given to the social structure of the groups being considered. Existing multilevel models do introduce a correlation between the behaviour of the members of a particular group, but this correlation applies without distinction to each couple of individuals in this group. For some groups, usually of small size, it could be worthwhile to consider the interactions existing between some members, for example the spouses in a family. These interactions can be examined by means of "models of shocks" (Lelièvre *et al.*, 1997). However, many difficulties remain to be overcome before these models can be fully implemented.

6. CONCLUSION

After this historical review, it is now time to broaden the debate over the different approaches presented here by raising a number of more fundamental questions about the hypotheses that underpin demography. As we have indicated, the prerequisite for the emergence of the discipline was the development of the bases of probability theory. Our discussion will thus focus on the application of this theory to human populations and on the ways of interpreting the results obtained.

Let us remember, first of all, that for ethical reasons there can be no experimental research in demography. The demographer therefore has to work on populations that possess certain characteristics and whose behaviour is observed at a particular point in time, or over all or at least part of their lifetime. The question to be answered is: does this provides the material for deducing, not a theory of causality in the social sciences (Wunsch, 1988; Duchêne *et al.*, 1989; Franck, 1994; Courgeau, 2000), which is not the object of discussion in this article, but rather an empirical theory of human behaviour, such as can be verified by means of this observation? In these conditions it is easy to understand the important role played by the methods of observation in this verification and in the development of new empirical theories.

A first theory assumes that an individual's membership of a certain number of groups influences the occurrence of various demographic events. For the analysis to be meaningful, the existence and relevance of these groups has to be assumed. If they are defined by a property or by a founding event, their existence is not problematic: the members of a particular profession, married individuals, inhabitants of a geographical unit, followers of a religion, for example, constitute clearly defined groups, membership of which may change over time. There is, however, an important difference between these groups: some are actually relevant to the analysis, whereas others are used to break down the population for the purpose of testing the relationship that is being studied.

In period analysis, the relevant groups are those defined by demographic, religious, economic and similar criteria, whereas the geographical or administrative groups are used to reveal the relationship between the event being studied and the various social groups. The underlying assumption in such an analysis is that an individual's membership of a particular geographical unit has no effect on his or her behaviour, other than that induced by the different social composition of each unit. Moreover, since the analysis uses period data, the movements into and out of these groups will not distort the results. This leads to using data from censuses or other cross-sectional sources.

However, as has been seen, this theory runs into difficulties because it fails to take into account the time lived by individuals. This was the idea behind adoption of a longitudinal perspective that could introduce the events occurring in their lifetime (e.g. wars, economic crises) and explore their effect on this life as a whole. Such a theory has to set extremely strict conditions of homogeneity for the populations being studied and of independence between the various phenomena under examination. This is the reason for using data from civil registration or other exhaustive longitudinal sources. However, if the aim is to analyse the effect on the phenomenon of belonging to a group, the movements into and out of it can no longer be omitted. Unfortunately these are not usually recorded in the civil registration statistics; and even if they were, the conditions of homogeneity of the group would no longer be satisfied, nor the conditions of independence between the event being studied and the movement into or out of the group. An entire sector of demographic analysis of populations is thus ruled out.

Escaping from this impasse requires this fragmented view of independent events to be abandoned. The solution is to consider human existence as a process that is dependent on the individual's entire past history. This becomes possible with event history analysis. An individual's membership of a group is no longer defined once and for all, but can vary from one moment to the next—either the individual will be able to move from one group to another, or the membership of a group will be defined as a time-dependent variable. In this way the occurrence of any number of demographic events can be studied simultaneously, with all the interactions that may exist between them. This makes it possible to examine the effect of a large number of characteristics which may or may not be time-dependent.

New questions then arise, however. Are the individuals questioned, who possess certain characteristics, all exposed to the same risk of experiencing the event being studied? An initial hypothesis is to consider each observed trajectory as the realization of an individual random process, whose probability is specific to each individual. In this case, however, because only one realization of the process, an individual trajectory, is available, the probability of this process cannot be determined. A second hypothesis is required in order to move the analysis forward: this is the assumption that the group observed follows an underlying stochastic process, whose probability structure it is possible to identify from the set of trajectories followed. It is important not to confuse the person surveyed and the statistical individual who follows this process. No hypothesis is made about the personal processes, which are by nature evanescent, but the process followed by the statistical individual can be analysed.

Other problems also arise from the fact that this approach no longer has to consider the various geographical or administrative entities in which the individuals are located. Although these were useful in the period approach for examining the effect of demographic or economic characteristics, for example, they appear to be of no interest for an event history analysis. Yet an examination of some results obtained with this analysis appear in contradiction with those obtained by the period approach, even though they concern the same populations.

An extension of this event history analysis thus seems necessary to produce a synthesis of these contradictory results. Such a synthesis can be achieved with the multilevel event history approach. It no longer treats the differences between regions or between any other territorial division as random variables devoid of interest, but actually tries to identify and if necessary explain them by aggregate or other characteristics. These aggregate characteristics are thus brought into the analysis, but the underlying hypotheses employed are different. Instead of affecting individual probabilities in a uniform way, as in the period approach, these characteristics will on the contrary modulate the probabilities according to the regions in which the individuals live.

This multilevel approach thus accommodates the various earlier observations with each other, at the same as clearly setting out the hypotheses on which it is based: it seeks to explain a behaviour at the individual level by introducing various levels of aggregation with some of their characteristics. In contrast to the aggregate approach, which was supposed to reveal the virtually unchanging bases of social organization as passed down in more or less final form from preceding generations (Durkheim, 1897/1930), this approach not only no longer postulates stability in social organization, but on the contrary actually facilitates understanding of its rapid changes over time. If a sufficient number of generations are used in the analysis, the modifications can be identified in the effects of individuals or aggregated characteristics on one or several behaviours under study. In this way the existence and pace of these changes can be verified and measured at various levels of aggregation.

It is possible to produce a table with these different approaches, according to the fact that they introduce or not space and time and, for the time points of view, according to the fact that they are with or without explicit characteristics. The following table gives eight patterns of analysis. We have already presented in this paper the major part of these patterns, except the one made between national and regional period analysis. As a matter of fact, it is not necessary to add such a distiction as the methods used to undertake national or regional period analysis are nearly similar.

Time →	Absent		Present	
Space ↓	Without explicit characteristics	With explicit characteristics	Without explicit characteristics	With explicit characteristics
Absent	National period analysis	Demographic transition analysis	Cohort analysis	Event history analysis
Present	Regional period analysis	Regional regression analysis	Multistate analysis	Multilevel analysis

Might it be possible to go further still and show the genesis of these changes in behaviour and track their diffusion in a context that is social as well as geographical? Imagine that we have a survey involving a large number of generations, with which we can observe the emergence and development of a new behaviour, such as cohabitation in the generations born after the Second World War. Because observation is of individuals living in a large number of geographical regions and social groups, it will be possible to identify where this behaviour first appeared and to try to find out what is particular about these zones and why it has appeared here. Attention would then turn to the next affected zones and to how they differed from those where this behaviour was still not present despite their proximity, and so on and so forth. Such detailed case studies are an opportunity to link the quantitative multilevel approach to approaches of a more qualitative nature, and to allow a more precise identification of the mechanisms at work.

By way of conclusion it can be said that while raising numerous and as yet unresolved questions, this approach constitutes a major advance in demography, since it provides a statistical basis for a synthesizing analytical instrument that is both more rigorous and more flexible than all the others described in this article. Its rich potential for application has only begun to be developed, but in our opinion it holds the key to an improved understanding of human behaviour.

NOTE

[1] The Norwegian statistical services allowed me to use the files produced from the population register and created by Kjetil Sørlie and Øysten Kravdal.

REFERENCES

Andersen, P., Borgan, O., Gill, R., & Keiding, N. (1993). *Statistical models based on counting processes*. New York: Springer-Verlag.

Baccaïni, B., & Courgeau D. (1996). Approche individuelle et approche agrégée: utilisation du registre de population norvégien pour l'étude des migrations In J. P. Bocquet-Appel, D. Courgeau, & D. Pumain (Eds.), *Analyse spatiale de données biodémographiques* (pp. 79-104). Paris: John-Libbey/INED.

Bayes, T.R. (1763). An essay towards solving a problem in the doctrines of chance. *Philosophical Transactions Royal Society London*, *53*, 370-418.

Becker, G.S. (1960). An economic analysis of fertility. In *Demographic and economic change in developed counties: A conference of the Universities-National Bureau Committee for economic research*. Princeton: Princeton University Press.

Bernoulli, J. I (1713). *Ars conjectandi*. Bâle: Impensis Thurnisiorum Fratrum.

Blayo, C. (1995). La condition d'homogénéité en analyse démographique et en analyse statistique des biographies. *Population*, *50*, 1501-1518.

Bonneuil, N. (1994). Capital accumulation, inertia of consumption and norms of reproduction. *Journal of Population Economics*, *7*, 49-62.

Bonneuil, N. (1997). Jeux, équilibres et régulation des populations sous contrainte de viabilité. Une lecture de l'œuvre de l'anthropologue Fredrik Barth. In Courgeau (Ed.) *Nouvelles approches méthodologiques en sciences sociales. Population, 52*, 947-976 ((1998), Games, equilibria and population regulation under viability constraints: An interpretation of the work of the anthropologist Fredrik Barth. In Courgeau (Ed.) *New methodological approaches in the social sciences. Population : an English Selection, 10*, 151-179).

Boudon, R. (1977). *Effets pervers et ordre social.* Paris: Presses Universitaires de France.

Brémaud, P., & Jacod, J. (1977). Processus ponctuels et martingales: résultats récents sur la modélisation et le filtrage. *Advanced Applied Probabilities, 9*, 362-416.

Bretagnole, J., & Huber-Carol, C. (1988). Effects of omitting covariates in Cox's model for survival data. *Scandinavian Journal of Statistics, 15*, 125-138.

Burch, T.K. (1999). Something ventured, something gained: Progress towards a unified theory of fertility decline. In D. Tabutin, C. Gourbin, G. Masuy-Strobant & B. Schoumaker (Eds.), *Théories, paradigmes et courants explicatifs en démographie, Chaire Quetelet 1997* (pp. 253-278). Louvain-la-Neuve: Academia-Bruylant/L'Harmattan.

Caldwell, J.C. (1982). *Theory of fertility decline.* London: Academic Press.

Cleland, J. (1985). Marital fertility decline in developing countries: Theories and the evidence. In J. Cleland and J. Hobcraft (Eds.), *Reproductive change in developing countries: Insights from the World Fertility Survey* (pp. 223-252). Oxford: Oxford University Press.

Coale, A. J. (1973). The demographic transition reconsidered. In *International Population Conference, Liège, Vol. 1* (pp. 53-72). Liège: IUSSP.

Commenges, D. (1999). Multistate models in epidemiology. *Lifetime Data Analysis, 5*, 315-327.

Condorcet (1994). *Arithmétique politique. Textes rares ou inédits (1767-1789),* Édition critique commentée par Bernard Bru et Pierre Crépel. Paris: INED/PUF.

Courgeau, D., (1982). Premiers migrants, migrants secondaires et retours (France 1968-1975). *Population, 37*, 1189-1193.

Courgeau, D. (1987). Constitution de la famille et urbanisation. *Population, 42*, 57-82 ((1989). Family Formation and Urbanization. *Population: An English Selection, 1*, 123-146).

Courgeau, D. (1991). Perspectives avec migrations. *Population, 46*, 1513-1530.

Courgeau, D. (1999a). L'enquête " Triple biographie : familiale, professionnelle et migratoire ". In Groupe de réflexion sur l'approche biographique *Biographies d'enquêtes,* Collection: Méthodes et savoirs (pp..59-74). Paris: PUF diffusion/INED,

Courgeau, D. (1999b). De l'intétêt des analyses multi-niveaux pour l'explication en démographie. In D. Tabutin, C. Gourbin, G. Masuy-Strobant, & B. Schoumaker (Eds.) *Théories, paradigmes et courants explicatifs en démographie, Chaire Quetelet 1997* (pp. 93-116). Louvain-la-Neuve: Academia-Bruylant/L'Harmattan.

Courgeau, D. (2000). Réflexions sur la causalité en sciences sociales. *Recherches et prévisions, 60*, 49-60.

Courgeau, D. (2001). Individus et contextes dans l'analyse des comportements selon l'approche multiniveau. In G. Caselli, J. Vallin, G. Wunsch (Eds.) *Démographie: analyse et synthèse. I La dynamique des populations* (pp. 519-536). Paris: Editions de l'INED.

Courgeau, D. (2002). Vers une analyse biographique multiniveau, In Christine M. (Ed.) *Actes des Journées de Méthodologie Statistique* (pp. 375-394). Paris: INSEE méthodes 101.

Courgeau, D., & Baccaïni, B. (1997). Analyse multi-niveaux en sciences sociales. In Courgeau (Ed.) *Nouvelles approches méthodologiques en sciences sociales* (pp. 831-864). *Population, 52*, (1998), Multilevel analysis in the social sciences, in Courgeau (Ed.) *New methodological approaches in the social sciences* (pp. 39-71). *Population : an English Selection, 10*).

Courgeau, D., & Lelièvre, E. (1985). Nuptialité et agriculture. *Population, 41*, 303-326.

Courgeau, D., & Lelièvre E. (1989). *Analyse démographique des biographies*. Paris: Éditions de l'INED.

Courgeau, D., & Lelièvre, E. (1992). *Event history analysis in demography.* Oxford: Clarendon Press.

Courgeau, D., & Lelièvre, E. (1996). Changement de paradigme en démographie. *Population, 51*, 645-654 ((1997). Changing paradigm in demography. *Population: an English Selection*, 9, 1-10).

Cox, D. (1972). Regression models and life tables (with discussion). *Journal of the Royal Statistical Society, B34*, 269-276.

Cribier, F., & Kych, A. (1999). Un ensemble d'enquêtes auprès de deux cohortes de retraités parisiens. In Groupe de réflexion sur l'approche biographique : *Biographies d'enquêtes, Méthodes et savoirs* (pp. 75-103). Paris: PUF diffusion/INED,.

Davis, K. (1945). The world demographic transition. *Annals of the American Academy of Political and Social science, 237*, 1-11.

Delaporte, P. (1941). *Evolution de la mortalité en Europe depuis les origines des statistiques de l'état civil.* Paris.

Dellacherie, C. (1980). Un survol de l'intégrale stochastique. *Stochastic Processes Applications, 10,* 115-144.

Dellacherie, C., & Meyer, P.A. (1980) *Probabilités et potentiels: théorie des martingales.* Paris: Hermann.

Deparcieux, A. (1746). *Essai sur les probabilités de la durée de la vie humaine.* Paris: Guérin frères.

Duchêne, J., Wunsch, G., & Vilquin, E. (Eds.). (1989). *L'explication en sciences sociales: la recherche des causes en démographie.* Bruxelles: Éditions Ciaco.

Dupâquier, J. (1985). Le mémoire de Jean de Witt sur la valeur des rentes viagères. *Annales de démographie historique,* 355-394.

Dupâquier, J. (1996). *L'invention de la table de mortalité.* Paris: PUF.

Dupâquier, J. & Dupâquier, M. (1985). *L'histoire de la démographie.* Paris: Librairie Académique Perrin.

Durkheim, E. (1930). *Le suicide.* Paris: PUF (original work published 1897).

Durkheim, E. (1937). *Les règles de la méthode sociologique.* Paris: PUF (original work published 1895).

Easterlin, R.A. (1961). The American baby-boom in historical perspective. *American Economic Review, 51,* 860-911.

Easterlin, R.A., & Crimmins, E.N. (1985). *The fertility revolution: A demand-supply analysis.* Chicago: University of Chicago Press.

Euler, L. (1760). Recherches générales sur la mortalité et la multiplication du genre humain, *Mémoires de l'Académie Royale des Sciences et Belles-Lettres de Berlin, VII,* 144-175.

Filloux, J.C. (2001). *Epistémologie, éthique et sciences de l'éducation.* Paris: L'Harmattan.

Firebaugh, G. (1978). A rule for inferring individual-level relationships from aggregate data. *American Sociological Review, 43,* 557-572.

Franck, R. (Ed.). (1994). *Faut-il chercher aux causes une raison? L'explication dans les sciences humaines.* Paris-Lyon: Librairie Philosophique Vrin.

Goldstein, H. (1995). *Multilevel statistical models.* London: Arnold.

Graunt, J. (1662). *Natural and political observations upon the bills of mortality... of the city of London.* Tho. Roycroft: London ((1977) *Observations naturelles et politiques*, translated by Vilquin E., Paris: INED).

Greenland, S. (2000). Principles of multilevel modelling. *International Journal of epidemiology, 29,*. 158-167.

Greenland, S. (1998). Hierarchical regression. In K. Rothman and S. Greenland (Eds.), *Modern Epidemiology* (pp. 427-432). Philadelphia: Lippincott-Raven.

Guillard, A. (1855). *Éléments de statistique humaine ou démographie comparée.* Paris: Guillaumin.

Halley, E. (1693). An estimate of the degrees of the mortality of mankind drawn from curious tables of the births and funerals at the city of Breslaw. *Philosophical Transactions, XVII,* 596-610.

Henry, L. (1959). D'un problème fondamental d'analyse démographique. *Population, 13,* 9-32.

Henry, L. (1966). Analyse et mesure des phénomènes démographiques par cohorte. *Population, 20,* 465-482.

Henry, L. (1972). *Démographie: Analyse et modèles.* Paris: Larousse.

Hoem, J. (1985). Weighting, misclassification and other issues in the analysis of survey samples of life histories. In Heckman and Singer (Eds.), *Longitudinal analysis of labour market data* (pp. 249-293). Cambridge: Cambridge University Press.

van Imhoff, E., & Keilman, N. (2000). On the quantum and tempo of fertility: comment. *Population and Development Review, 26,* 549-553.

Jones, K. (1997). Multilevel approaches to modelling contextuality: from nuisance to substance in the analysis of voting behaviour. In G.P. Westert and R.N. Verhoeff (Eds.), *Places and people: multilevel modelling in geographical research* (pp.19-43). Utrecht: Nederlandse Geografische studies 227.

Keiding, N. (1999). Event history analysis and inference from observational epidemiology. *Statistics in Medicine, 18,* 2353-2363.

Keilman, N. (1986). Analysing nuptiality:The multidimensional method and the French school. In *Population and family in the low fertility countries* (pp. 91-113). Den Haag/Brussels: Nidi/ CBGS publicaties 16.

Keilman, N. (2001). La translation démographique: les indicateurs du moment aux indicateurs de génération et réciproquement. In G. Caselli, J. Vallin, & G. Wunsch (Eds.), *Démographie: Analyse te synthèse. I La dynamique des populations* (pp. 359-378). Paris: Ined.

Körösi, J. (1896). An estimate of the degrees of legitimate natality as derived from a table of natality compiled by the author from his observations made at Budapest. *Philosophical Transactions, (Royal Society of London), series B, 186*, 781-875.

Krieger, N. (2000). Epidemiology and social sciences: towards a critical reengagement in the 21st century. *Epidemiologic Reviews, 22*, 155-163.

Kuhn, T.S. (1972). *La structure des révolutions scientifiques.* Paris: Flamarion.

Lancaster, T. (1990). *The econometric analysis of transition data.* Cambridge: Cambridge University Press,.

Landry, A. (1982). Les trois théories principales de la population. In A. Landry, *La révolution démographique.* Paris: Ined (original work published 1909).

Landry, A. (1945). *Traité de démographie.* Paris: Payot.

Lazarsfeld, P.-F., & Menzel, H. (1961). On the relation between individual and collective properties. In Etzioni (Ed.), *Complex organizations* (pp. 422-440). New York: Holt, Reinhart, and Winston.

Lee, P.M. (1997). *Bayesian statistics. An introduction.* Second edition. London: Arnold.

Lelièvre, E. (1987). Activité professionnelle etfécondité: les choix et les déterminations des femmes françaises entre 1930 et 1960. *Cahiers Québéquois de Démographie, 16*, 207-236.

Lelièvre, E., Bonvalet, C., & Bry, X. (1997). Analyse biographique des groupes. Les avancées d'une recherche en cours. In D. Courgeau (Ed.), *Nouvelles approches méthodologiques en sciences sociales. Population, 52*, 803-830 ((1998), Event history analysis of groups. The findings of an on-going project. In Courgeau (Ed.), *New methodological approaches in the social sciences. Population: an English Selection, 10*, 11-37).

Lesthaeghe, R. (1983). A century of demographic and cultural change in Western Europe: An exploration of underlying dimensions. *Population and Development Review, 9*, 411-435.

Loriaux, M. (1989). L'analyse contextuelle: renouveau théorique ou impasse méthodologique. In J. Duchêne, G. Wunsch, E. Vilquin (Eds.), *L'explication en sciences sociales. La recherche des causes en démographie, Chaire Quetelet '87* (pp. 333-368). Bruxelles: Ciaco Editeur.

Lotka, A. (1939). *Théorie analytique des associations biologiques, Deuxième partie.* Paris: Hermann et Cie.

Lyberg, I. (1983). The effect of sampling and nonresponse on estimates of transitions intensities: some empirical results from the 1981 Swedish Fertility Survey. *Stockholm Research Reports in Demography, 14.*

Mason, K. O. (1997). Explaining fertility transitions. *Demography, 34*, 443-454.

Mason, W.M., Wong, G.W., & Entwistle, B. (1983). Contextual analysis through the multilevel linear model. In S. Leinhart (ed.), *Sociological Methodology 1983-1984* (pp. 72-103). San Francisco: Jossey-Bass.

Matalon, B. (1967). Epistémologie des probabilités. In Piaget J. (Ed.), *Logique et connaissance scientifique* (pp. 526-553). Paris: Éditions Gallimard.

Menken, J., & Trussel, J. (1981). Proportional hazards life table models: An illustrative analysis of socio-demographic influences on marriage dissolution in the United States. *Demography, 18*, 181-200.

Moheau, J.-B. (1994). *Recherches et considérations sur la population de la France.* Paris: Editions de l'Institut National d'Etudes Démographiques (original work published 1778).

Morgenstern, H. (1998). Multilevel analyses and design. In K. Rothman and S. Greenland (Eds.), *Modern Epidemiology* (pp. 478-480). Philadelphia: Lippincott-Raven.

Notestein, F. (1945). Population - The long view. In Schulz (Ed.) , *Food in the world.* Chicago: University of Chicago Press.

Pascal, B. (1986). Traité du triangle arithmétique. In Edwards A.W.F. (Ed.), *Pascal arithmetic triangle.* London: Charles Griffin, (original work published 1651).

Petty, W. (1690). *Political arithmetick.* London: Robert Clavel & Hen. Mortlock. Retrieved February 6, 2003, from: http://socserv2.socsci.mcmaster.ca/~econ/ugcm/3113/petty/poliarith.html.

Piaget, J. (Ed.). (1967). *Logique et connaissance scientifique.* Paris: Éditions Gallimard.

Popper, K. R. (1973). *La logique de la découverte scientifique.* Paris: Éditions Payot (original work published 1935).

Poulain, M., Riandey, B., & Firdion, J.M. (1991). Enquête biographique et registre belge de population: une confrontation des données. *Population, 46*, 65-88 ((1992) Data from a life history survey and the Belgian Population Register: a comparison. *Population: An English Selection, 4*, 77-96).

Pressat, R. (1966). *Principes d'analyse.* Paris: Éditions de l'INED.

Puig, J. P. (1981). La migration régionale de la population active. *Annales de l'INSEE, 44*, 41-79.

Quetelet, A. (1997). *Physique sociale ou essai sur le développement des facultés de l'homme.* Bruxelles: Académie Royale de Belgique (original work published 1869).

Robinson, W. S. (1950). Ecological correlations and the behavior of individuals. *American Sociological Review, 15*, 351-357.

Rogers, A. (1973). The multiregional life table. *The Journal of Mathematical Sociology, 3*, 127-137.

Roussel, L. (1971). La nuptialité en France. Précocité et intensité suivant les régions et les catégories socio-professionnelles. *Population, 26*, 1029-1056.

Ryder, N. B. (1965). The cohort as a concept in the study of social change. *American Sociological Review, 30*, 843-861.

Sadler, M.T. (1830). *The law of population: a treatise, in six books, in disproof of the superfecundity of human beings, and developing the real principle of their increase.* London.

Schoen, R., & Nelson, V.E. (1974). Marriage, divorce, and mortality: a life table analysis. *Demography, 11*, 267-290.

Schultz, T.W. (1973). New economic approaches to fertility: Proceedings of a Conference, June 8-9, 1972. *Journal of political economy, 81*, (2, Part II).

Schweder, T. (1970). Composable Markov processes. *Journal of Applied Probabilities, 7*, 400-410.

Singleton, M. (1999). Les sens et les non-sens d'un nominalisme démographique. In D.Tabutin, C. Gourbin, G. Masuy-Strobant, & B. Schoumaker (Eds.), *Théories, paradigmes et courants explicatifs en démographie, Chaire Quetelet 1997* (pp.15-39). Louvain-la-Neuve / Paris: Academia-Bruylant / L'Harmattan.

Suppes, P. (1981). *Logique du probable.* Paris: Flamarion.

Süssmilch, J.P. (1979). *L'Ordre Divin dans les changements du genre humain*, translated by Hecht J. INED: Paris, (original work published 1741).

Travers, R. (1969). *An introduction to educational research.* New York: Mac Millan.

Tuma, N. B., & Hannan, M. T. (1984). *Social dynamics. Models and methods.* Orlando, Florida: Academic Press.

Wachter, K.W., & Lee, R.D. (1989). US births and limit cycle models. *Demography, 26*, 99-115.

Willekens, F.J. (1999). The life course: models and analysis. In L. van Vissen, & P. Dykstra (Eds.), *Population issues. An interdisciplinary review* (pp. 23-52). New York: Kluwer Academic / Plenum Publishers.

Willekens, F.J. (2001). Theoretical and technical orientations towards longitudinal research in the social sciences. *Canadian Studies in Population*, Special issue on longitudinal methodology, *28*, 189-217.

Wong, G.W., & Mason, W.M. (1985). The hierarchical logistic regression model for multilevel analysis. *Journal of the American Statistical Association, 80*, 513-524.

Wunsch, G. (1988). *Causal theory and causal modelling.* Leuven: Leuven University Press.

Zelinsky, W. (1971). The hypothesis of the mobility transition. *Geographical Review, 61*, 219-249.

Ana V. DIEZ ROUX

Chapter 3

POTENTIALITIES AND LIMITATIONS OF MULTILEVEL ANALYSIS IN PUBLIC HEALTH AND EPIDEMIOLOGY[1]

Opening. Like demography, discussed in the previous chapter, epidemiology traces its origins back to the investigations of John Graunt in the seventeenth century. But the two disciplines soon diverged because of their different objectives: demography seeks to understand how populations evolve in time and space, by interconnecting the phenomena that determine their size and composition, whereas epidemiology tries to understand the history of public-health problems affecting those populations and to combat them. As a result, epidemiology has evolved differently from demography over the centuries. In particular, it has used new aggregation levels and posed new questions, which this contribution will now examine.

The starting point at the aggregate level is, however, identical. The "sanitary statistics" that prevailed up to the mid-nineteenth century—along with their paradigm, "miasma"—were effectively situated at the aggregate level, where the sanitary conditions of populations were seen as the main causes of morbidity and mortality in those populations—far more so than any specific diseases. This led to improvements in sewage systems, drinking-water supply, sanitation systems, and so on.

But microbiological discoveries, particularly by Pasteur, revealed the existence of agents responsible for the transmission of diseases and spelled the end of the "sanitary" era. They heralded the era of "infectious-disease epidemiology" with its new paradigm: "germ theory". The goal now was not to detect the effects of sanitary conditions, but to discover disease-causing germs, to curb their spread by means of vaccines, and to cure their effects through chemotherapy and antibiotics. The theory's operating level shifted to the germ, which scientists needed to identify and study in order to combat it. This approach prevailed until the mid-twentieth century. It led to the eradication of several diseases through vaccination and to the development of antibiotics—although economic development and social change, as well, played a significant role in the process.

During this period, however, when the main infectious agents were apparently identified, new chronic diseases—of unknown origin—took centre stage: peptic ulcer disease, coronary heart disease, and lung cancer. "Germ theory" was incapable of supplying the resources to battle them. The new "chronic-disease epidemiology", with its conventional biomedical paradigm, was free to flourish. It operated at the individual level, generating studies on "case control" and on cohorts monitored over long periods. The multicausal nature of public-health problems was emphasised, and the studies revealed the various causes of chronic diseases, whose origins were initially a mystery.

Ana Diez Roux shows us that this paradigm, as well, has been challenged in the late twentieth century. We must now take a broader view of epidemiology, with the aim of integrating the different earlier approaches into a more general model. The model must accordingly take simultaneous account of social factors (sanitary, sociological, and psychological conditions) and biological factors (genes, viruses, germs, individual risk factors, etc.). Moreover, these factors must be defined at multiple aggregation levels in order to incorporate advances in epidemiology: molecule, gene, virus, or germ level, individual level, social level, etc.

Ana Diez Roux examines how an epidemiology that tries to transcend the dichotomies in the "social/biological" and "groups/individuals" categories can help us understand not only the whole but also the parts—not only populations but the individuals in them. We are indeed witnessing the establishment of a paradigm of complex, hierarchical systems that may contain non-linear relationships. In these conditions, we may ask if the multilevel approach fully satisfies these expectations, or whether it is merely an analytical strategy providing a partial response to the need to examine factors in an overall context.

This chapter examines the possible reasons for using multilevel analysis in epidemiology, and discusses the theoretical and methodological issues raised by that use. What remedies does it

D. Courgeau (ed.) Methodology and Epistemology of Multilevel Analysis, 93-119.

offer for the fallacies generated by the previous approaches: ecological fallacy, atomistic fallacy, psychologistic fallacy, and sociologistic fallacy? How does it integrate the aggregation levels described earlier? Does it allow us to develop more satisfactory strategies than the classical methods for analysing complex, dynamic systems, in interaction with their past? The answers to all these questions will give us a clearer view of the goals, potential, and limits of multilevel analysis in epidemiology.

D. C.

1. INTRODUCTION

Throughout history different types of factors have been emphasised as potential "causes" of disease (Susser and Susser, 1996a; Catalano, 1979; Tesh, 1990). In the early 19th century, disease was presumed to arise from foul emanations from soil, water and air (the miasmatic theory of disease causation), and emphasis was placed on the role of broadly defined ecological and environmental factors in disease aetiology. With the advent of the germ theory and the associated unicausal theory of disease causation, infectious organisms became the relevant "environmental" factors. Other aspects of the environment were important only to the extent that they were conducive to the reproduction or transmission of the "true biological cause". In the mid 20th century, the growing importance of chronic diseases led to the search for new causal factors, and research focused on the behavioural and biological characteristics of individuals as risk factors for disease. The study of the causes of disease thus shifted from the environment as a whole, to specific factors within the environment (biological organisms) and finally to the behaviours and biological characteristics of individuals. Concomitantly, the model of disease causation changed from a rather vague holistic determination, to the unicausal model of the germ theory, and finally to the multicausal model (the "web of causation") largely dominant in epidemiology today in which a variety of individual level biological and behavioural risk factors are presumed to interact in the causation of specific diseases (Krieger, 1994).

Over the past few years there has been an ongoing debate within epidemiology regarding the future of the field (Vandenbroucke, 1990; Krieger, 1994; Taubes, 1995; Charlton, 1996; Pearce, 1996; Schwartz *et al.*, 1999; Susser and Susser, 1996b; Susser, 1998; Poole and Rothman, 1998; Diez Roux, 1999; McMichael, 1999). Discussion of the origins and limitations the current epidemiological approach have been a key part of this debate. Much of the debate has centred around the critique of what is perceived to be the dominant paradigm in epidemiology over the past few decades: so-called "risk factor epidemiology", i.e. an epidemiology centred around identifying the "independent" contributions of individual level factors (usually biomedical or behavioural factors) to disease risk. The critique of risk factor epidemiology has had two distinct origins. On one hand it has been argued that epidemiology has severed its connections to biological and clinical science and hence has lost its ability to completely understand the causes of disease. On the other hand, it has been argued that risk factor epidemiology has divorced disease from its social origins, reducing the causes of disease to biological or behavioural characteristics and isolating individual level characteristics (e.g. health-related behaviours) from the social contexts which promote their development and maintenance.

A key element of the current discussion pertains to the ways in which populations and population level factors are conceptualised and incorporated into epidemiological models of disease causation and empirical analyses. The concept of "populations" (as opposed to "individuals") has been key in epidemiology throughout its history. Indeed, epidemiology is often defined as the study of "patterns of disease occurrence in human populations and the factors that influence these patterns" (Lilienfeld and Stolley, 1994). Its object of study, "disease in populations" is often thus distinguished from the object of study of clinical medicine: "disease in individuals". Despite these general statements, however, the concrete ways in which the "population dimension" should be included in epidemiological models and empirical analyses has been rarely articulated or developed in mainstream epidemiology. In fact, the enormous methodological development and sophistication of epidemiology over the past decades has been marked by increasing "individualization", the notion that the risk of disease depends exclusively on individual level characteristics. This notion has been reflected in the behavioural model of disease (in which disease stems from the choices and behaviours of individuals, isolated from their social contexts), and reappears today in the genetic model (in which disease is strongly influenced by an individual's unique genetic makeup). In fact, much of today's epidemiology conceptualises populations merely as aggregates of individuals (useful from a statistical point of view), rather than as groups of interacting individuals with social relationships and social organisations, and with group level properties that may partly influence risk of disease (Pearce, 1996; Loomis and Wing, 1990; Almeida, 1992).

This process of "individualisation" of disease risk (i.e. attributing disease causation to characteristics of individuals rather than to environmental or social influences affecting populations) has also had methodological correlates. The underlying assumption that all disease determinants are best conceptualised (and consequently best measured) at the individual level has been accompanied by an emphasis on study designs where the units of analysis are individuals and where much effort is invested in the measurement of individual level characteristics, particularly behavioural and biological factors. group level variables are used only as (often unsatisfactory) proxies for individual level data when the latter are unavailable. Interest centres in the examination of inter-individual variability and the individual level factors associated with it. Group-to-group variability (and the factors associated with it) is of little interest per se, except to the extent that it can be used to draw inferences regarding inter-individual variability. Thus, although there has been abundant discussion in the epidemiological literature of the fallacy inherent in using group level associations (ecological studies) to draw inferences regarding individual level relationships (i.e. the ecological fallacy) (Morgenstern, 1982, 1995; Piantadosi *et al.*, 1988; Greenland, 1992), there has been little discussion of the potential substantive problem of ignoring group level variables in understanding the causes of disease in individuals.

Even during the dominant period of the individual level risk factor paradigm, however, there have been periodic calls for restoring the population dimension to epidemiology. Rose, for example, cogently argued that population level factors are crucial for understanding the causes of disease and for the development of disease prevention strategies (Rose, 1985). He emphasised the need to examine factors that influence differences in disease rates across populations ("the causes of incidence") rather than only factors that determine who does or does not get the disease within a population ("causes of cases" in Rose's terminology). The role of group level factors (such as the prevalence of disease itself in the group or population to which a person belongs) has long been considered a key factor in understanding the distribution of infectious diseases (Halloran, 1998). The call for including population or group level factors in explaining the causes of ill-health has been reinvigorated today in part because of the recent increase in interest in the social determinants of disease. Because social facts often refer to groups or populations or to how individuals are related to each other within groups, the loss of the population-dimension has been perceived as particularly problematic by epidemiologists interested in the social determinants of disease. There has been growing interest in factors such as income inequality (Kennedy *et al.*, 1996; Kaplan *et al.*, 1996; Daly *et al.*, 1998), social capital and social cohesion (Kawachi, 1999), and neighbourhood or community characteristics (Pickett and Pearl, 2001; Robert, 1999) which are best conceptualised as group, rather than individual level properties. Recent discussions and critiques of epidemiology have also called for a new paradigm that incorporates factors at multiple levels (from genes to societies) in studying the cases of disease. Krieger has articulated the need for an "ecosocial epidemiological theory" that "embraces population level thinking and rejects the underlying assumptions of biomedical individualism without discarding biology"(Krieger, 1994, p. 896). Susser and Susser have called for a new paradigm in epidemiology, the Chinese box or ecoepidemiology paradigm which incorporates molecular, individual, and societal dimensions, as well as interactions across these levels, in the understanding of disease (Susser and Susser, 1996b). These trends have sparked renewed interest in population level factors, in group level or ecological variables, and in the implications of the presence of multiple levels for study design, analysis, and the interpretation of study results.

Multilevel analysis has emerged in the field of epidemiology within this context. It has initially generated great expectation because of the possibility of including both characteristics of groups (or populations) and characteristics of individuals simultaneously in epidemiological analyses. This chapter will (1) review the implications of the presence of factors defined at multiple levels for epidemiology and the rationale for the inclusion of group level variables in conceptual models and empirical analyses; (2) summarise the potentialities of multilevel analysis in this regard and how it differs from analytical approaches commonly used, and (3) discuss the challenges faced by epidemiologists in their use of multilevel analysis to study the causes of disease. The chapter will focus on the use of multilevel analysis to simultaneously examine groups and individuals within them because this use is the most innovative in public health and is strongly related to critiques of the dominant epidemiological paradigm. Other applications of multilevel analysis (for example, in longitudinal data analysis) are only briefly mentioned.

2. THE PRESENCE OF MULTIPLE LEVELS: CONCEPTUAL AND METHODOLOGICAL IMPLICATIONS

As noted above, there has been renewed interest in the notion that group level variables (sometimes also termed ecological or macro variables) may provide information which is not always captured by individual level data (Susser, 1994a, 1994b; Schwartz, 1994; Koopman and Lynch, 1999), and in rethinking the ways in which these group level constructs can be examined in epidemiological analyses. More broadly, there has been growing recognition of the need to consider multiple levels of organisation (e.g. from molecules to society) in studying the determinants of health and disease. Many of the issues that arise when dealing with individuals nested within groups derive from the presence of multiple levels of organisation and nested data structures generally. Thus, they are also present when dealing with groups nested within larger groups (e.g. states nested within countries), persons nested within families, or multiple measurements on individuals over time (in this case the "group" is the individual him or herself, and the "individuals" are the measurement occasions). In fact, although infrequently recognised, the need to deal with multiple levels of organisation is the norm, rather than the exception in epidemiology.

The presence of multiple levels has several implications. First, the units of analysis (or observations for which independent and dependent variables are measured) can be defined at different levels. The unit of analysis selected determines the level at which variability is examined. For example, a study with individuals as the units of analysis (i.e. where each observation is an individual for whom independent and dependent variables are measured) can investigate the causes of inter-individual variation in the outcome. A study with groups as the units of analysis, can investigate the causes of inter-group variation in the outcome. A study involving repeat observations on individuals over time in which measurement occasions are the unit of analysis can investigate the causes of variability in the outcome across measurement occasions. As we will see, the use of units of analysis at one level to infer things about the causes of variability at another level leads to a series of methodological problems.

The second implication of the presence of multiple levels is that both independent and dependent variables can be conceptualised and measured at different levels. Constructs pertaining to a higher level may be important in understanding variability at a lower level, and vice versa, constructs defined at a lower level may be important in understanding variability at a higher level. For example, characteristics of the groups to which individuals belong may be important in explaining interindividual variability, and characteristics of individuals comprising the groups may be important in explaining inter-group variability.

2.1. Common study designs in epidemiology

Epidemiology has traditionally distinguished two types of studies based on the units of analysis: ecological studies and studies of individuals. Ecological studies are studies in which groups are the units of analysis: both the dependent and the independent variables are measured for groups, and group level factors associated with group-to-group variability in the dependent variable are examined. Common ecological studies in public health involve measuring rates of disease for different areas, and relating these rates to area socioenvironmental characteristics (e.g. measures of area median income) or area physical characteristics (e.g. levels of air pollution, water hardness, or radiation).

Ecological studies are most appropriate when investigators are interested in explaining variation between groups (i.e. drawing inferences regarding the causes of inter-group variability in the outcome) and the constructs of interest can be conceptualised as group level properties. Because of the unavailability of information on the cross-classification of individual level independent and dependent variables within groups, ecological studies are limited in their ability to examine the role of individual level constructs. An ecological study cannot examine individual level variables as confounders[2] or mediators[3] of the observed ecological association. For example, an ecological study could not determine whether the relation between country industrialisation level and rates of heart disease is due to differences in the dietary habits of individuals. This could occur because living in an industrialised country causes individuals to have high fat diets (high fat diet as a mediator of the ecological relationship) or because something leads persons with high fat diets to live in industrialised countries (high fat diet as a confounder of the ecological association). Neither can an ecological study determine whether the ecological effect differs based on individual level characteristics (sometimes called effect modification[4]). For example, the ecological study described above could not determine whether the relation between country industrialisation level and heart disease differ in individuals of high and low occupational status. When the group level independent variables investigated are constructed by aggregating the characteristics of individuals within groups (sometimes called "derived" variables (Blalock, 1984; Diez Roux, 1998), ecological studies are unable to differentiate the true "contextual" effect of the variable from the effects of its individual level analogue. For example an ecological study documenting a relation between area unemployment and area mortality rates would be unable to determine whether the increased risk of death was associated with being unemployed or living in an area with high unemployment. Thus ecological studies are unable to differentiate "context" from "composition" (Duncan et al., 1998). Both the contextual and the individual level effect are mixed-up (or confounded) in the ecological association. (Of course, from a public health perspective, the ecological association may itself be of interest, regardless of whether it is confounded by individual level variables or whether it results from contextual or compositional effects.)

In contrast, individual level studies (the studies commonly referred to under headings of "Study Design" in epidemiological textbooks) are studies in which the units of analysis are individuals: both independent and dependent variables are measured for individuals and individual level factors associated with individual-to-individual variability in the dependent variable are investigated. For example, common individual level studies in epidemiology relate individual behaviours, such as smoking, to the probability of having cancer at a given point in time or developing cancer over a follow-up period. individual level studies are most appropriate when investigators are interested in explaining variation between individuals (i.e. drawing inferences regarding the causes of interindividual variability). individual level studies are also most easily (and commonly) used when the constructs of interest can be conceptualised as individual level properties. When studies with individuals as the units of analysis are limited to individuals from a single "group" they cannot examine the role of group level constructs in causing individual level outcomes because group level characteristics are obviously invariant within groups (Schwartz and Carpenter, 1999). For example, a study of the causes of hypertension in individuals drawn from a single society could not directly examine the role of society level factors (for example societal characteristics leading to increased stress levels in all members). Since all individuals are "exposed" to the society level factor, the factor will obviously not explain any interindividual variability in the outcome within the society. Although studies of individuals sometimes include individuals from several distinct "groups" they often lack information on characteristics of the groups to which individuals belong. For example, a study pooling individuals across countries but with no information on country level characteristics could not examine the role of country level constructs as antecedents of individual level variables (is country industrialisation a determinant of individual level diets?), as independent predictors of outcomes (is country industrialisation related to heart disease over and above the effects of individual level diet?) or as confounders of individual level associations (is the relation between high fat diet and heart disease partly due to the fact that persons with high fat diets tend to live in industrialised countries, which may place persons at higher risk of heart disease for reasons unrelated to diet?). In addition, studies of individuals with no information on group level constructs cannot determine whether the effect of a given individual level variable is only present in certain group contexts, or varies from group to group, as a function of group characteristics.

2.2. Fallacies related to the presence of multiple levels

The methodological problem inherent in drawing inferences regarding individual level associations based on group level data (the *ecological fallacy*) is well established and often discussed in epidemiology. The reasons for the ecological fallacy are developed in detail elsewhere (Piantadosi *et al.*, 1988; Greenland and Robins, 1994; Morgenstern, 1995; Diez Roux *et al.*, 2002) and can only be briefly summarised here. Fundamentally, the ecological fallacy has two sources. The first source is the absence of information on individual level confounders or effect modifiers (which may vary from group to group). Controlling for aggregate summaries of individual level confounders (for example, controlling for mean intake of fat in a study investigating the relationship between country industrialisation and heart disease rates, where individual dietary intake is conceptualised as a confounder) is often insufficient to control for their confounding effects (Greenland and Morgenstern, 1989; Morgenstern, 1995; Greenland and Robins, 1994). Most discussions of the ecological fallacy in epidemiology focus on the technical details of this problem. Another source (which is less often highlighted in discussions of the ecological fallacy because of the implicit assumption that all disease determinants are individual level constructs) is the presence of contextual effects of derived variables (an effect of the aggregate group level measure over and above the effects of its individual level namesake). Thus, even in the absence of individual level confounders or effect modifiers that differ from group to group, associations at the group and individual level may differ because the group variable (e.g. group mean income) and the individual level variable (e.g. individual level income) are tapping into different constructs. Both constructs may be differently related to the outcome. For example, even if within countries motor vehicle-related mortality decreases as individual level income increases (due for example to better automobiles in the higher classes, better road maintenance in high class neighbourhoods), across countries motor-vehicle related mortality may actually increase as mean country income increases (because of increased reliance on automobile transportation and increased traffic associated with industrialisation and higher mean country income). In this case, individual level income and mean country income are measuring different things. If an investigator assumes that both measures are tapping into the same construct and concludes that motor vehicle-related mortality increases as individual level income increases based on country-level associations, he or she would be committing the ecological fallacy.

The ecological fallacy is only one of a set of possible "fallacies" that derive from the existence of multiple levels of organisation (Diez Roux, 1998). Because at least recently, epidemiologists have been mostly concerned with drawing inferences regarding the causes of interindividual variability, the ecological fallacy has received much more attention than its counterpart, the atomistic fallacy. The *atomistic fallacy* is the fallacy of drawing inferences regarding variability across groups based on individual level data. As illustrated by the ecological fallacy example above, the effect of an individual level predictor on an outcome in a study of individuals is not necessarily the same as the effect of its group level namesake on group level outcomes. Thus the use of individual level associations to draw inferences regarding group level associations may also lead to incorrect inferences. Moreover, as we have noted, some individual level studies only include individuals from a single "group". Factors that explain variability across individuals within groups are not necessarily the same as those that explain variability across groups. For example, if stress levels are relatively invariant within groups (e.g. communities or countries), stress may not be important in explaining variability in coronary heart disease within groups, but may be strongly associated with differences in coronary heart disease rates across groups. This is another reason why the use of individual level data to infer group level effects may lead to incorrect inferences.

Both the ecological and atomistic fallacies can be thought of as methodological problems inherent in drawing inferences at one level when the data are collected at another level. These fallacies arise when the conceptual model being tested corresponds to one level, but the data are collected at another level, or in Riley's words when "the methods fail to fit the model" (Riley, 1963). As we have discussed, the sources of these problems lie in (1) the lack of information on constructs pertaining to another level of organisation; and (2) the failure to realise that a variable defined and measured at one level of organisation may tap into a different construct than its namesake at another level, and that constructs at both levels may be relevant to the outcome studied. Both of these issues point to a more general problem which is that even when making inferences about a given level, other levels of organisation may need to be taken into account. For example, the failure to consider group characteristics in drawing inferences regarding individuals, and the failure to consider individuals in drawing inferences regarding groups gives rise to another set of fallacies, which are closely related to the ecological and atomistic fallacies described above. In these fallacies (which have been termed the psychologistic and sociologistic fallacies), although the level at which data are collected may fit the conceptual model being investigated, important facts pertaining to other levels have been ignored, in Riley's words "the methods may fail to fit the facts" (Riley, 1963).

Ignoring relevant group level variables in a study of individual level associations may lead to what Riley has termed the *psychologistic fallacy*, i.e. assuming that individual level outcomes can be explained exclusively in terms of individual level characteristics. For example, a study based on individuals might find that immigrants are more likely to develop depression than natives. But suppose this is only true for immigrants living in communities where they are a small minority. A researcher ignoring the contextual effect of community composition might attribute the higher overall rate in immigrants to the psychological effects of immigration per se or even to genetic factors, ignoring the importance of community level factors and thus committing the psychologistic fallacy (Valkonen, 1969; Riley, 1963) (The term "psychologistic fallacy" is not the most appropriate because the individual level factors used to explain the outcome are not always exclusively psychological. Although the term "individualistic fallacy" may appear more appropriate, it has also been used as a synonym of the "atomistic fallacy" (Alker, 1969; Scheuch, 1969) it will be avoided here.)

Analogously, ignoring the role of individual level factors in a study of groups may lead to what has been termed the *sociologistic fallacy* (Riley, 1963). Suppose a researcher finds that communities with higher rates of transient population have higher rates of schizophrenia, and he/she concludes that higher rates of transient population lead to social disorganisation, breakdown of social networks, and increased risk of schizophrenia among all community inhabitants. But suppose that schizophrenia rates are only elevated for transient residents (because transient residents tend to have fewer social ties, and individuals with few social ties are at greater risk of developing schizophrenia).

That is, rates of schizophrenia are high for transient residents and low for non-transient residents, regardless of whether they live in communities with a high or a low proportion of transient residents. If this is the case, the researcher would be committing the sociologistic fallacy in attributing the higher schizophrenia rates to social disorganisation affecting all community members rather than to differences across communities in the percentage of transient residents.

Both the psychologistic and the sociologistic fallacies arise because relevant variables pertaining to other levels have been excluded from the model, which led to an inappropriate explanation for the association. Although it is didactically useful to distinguish both sets of fallacies (ecological and atomistic vs. psychologistic and sociologistic), they are closely interrelated and are essentially different manifestations of the same phenomenon: the failure to recognise that constructs defined at different levels may be important in understanding variability within a given level, and the failure to adequately distinguish constructs defined at different levels.

3. MULTILEVEL ANALYSIS

The recent interest in multilevel analysis in epidemiology and public health (Von Korff *et al.*, 1992; Rice and Leyland, 1996; Duncan *et al.*, 1998; Diez Roux, 2000; Blakely and Woodward, 2000) has been largely driven by the recognition that variables that refer to groups may be relevant to understanding the distribution of health outcomes (Duncan *et al.*, 1996; Schwartz, 1994; Susser, 1994a; Von Korff *et al.*, 1992; Diez Roux, 1998), and the need to be able to "control" for individual characteristics when drawing inferences regarding the effects of group properties on individual level outcomes. But more fundamentally, multilevel analysis allows the simultaneous investigation of between group and between individual variability and permits the examination of how group level and individual level constructs are related to variability at both levels, thus avoiding the fallacies outlined above. The method explicitly distinguishes "levels" and recognises that constructs defined at different levels may be important in understanding variability within a given level, i.e. things about groups may be important in understanding the causes of inter-individual variability and things about individuals may be important in understanding variability across groups.

In explaining the occurrence of a given phenomenon researchers can appeal to different types of theories, which may be more or less relevant depending on the particular question being investigated (Coleman, 1991; DiPrete and Forristal, 1994). In the simplest case, the outcome at one level is explained by independent variables that apply to the same level. This is the approach commonly taken in epidemiology when individual level outcomes are explained in terms of individual level variables (as in traditional cohort studies) or group level outcomes are explained in terms of group level variables (as in ecological studies aimed at drawing group level inferences). A second approach, is when the outcome at one level is explained in terms of variables defined at a lower level. This, for example, is the approach taken when differences in disease rates across groups are "explained" in terms of the characteristics of individuals comprising the groups. A third approach is to explain the outcome at one level as a function of variables defined at a higher level: for example, when an individual level outcome is explained exclusively as a function of the attributes of the group to which individuals belong. A fourth approach is to explain variation in the dependent variable at one level as a function of variables defined at various levels, plus interactions within and between levels. Multilevel analysis is one methodology that can be used to approximate the latter situation.

The statistical details of multilevel analysis can be found elsewhere (Bryk and Raudenbush, 1992; Goldstein, 1995; Kreft and de Leeuw, 1998; Snijders and Bosker, 1999). Only a brief and simplified summary is presented here for illustration. In the case of multilevel analysis involving two levels (e.g. individuals nested within groups), the model can be conceptualised as a two stage system of equations in which the individual variation within each group is explained by an individual level equation (first level equation), and the variation across groups in the group specific regression coefficients is explained by a group level equation (second-level).

In the first stage (level 1), a separate individual level regression is defined for each group or higher level unit.

$$Y_{ij} = b_{0j} + b_{1j}I_{ij} + \varepsilon_{ij} \qquad \varepsilon_{ij} \sim N(0, \sigma^2) \tag{1}$$

Y_{ij} = outcome variable for i^{th} individual in j^{th} group
I_{ij} = individual level variable for i^{th} individual in j^{th} group
b_{0j} is the group specific intercept
b_{1j} is the group specific effect of the individual level variable.

Individual level errors (ε_{ij}) are assumed to be independent and identically distributed with a mean of 0 and a variance of σ^2. The same regressors are generally used in all groups, but regression coefficients (b_{0j} and b_{1j}) allowed to vary from one group to another.

In a second stage (level 2), each of the group or context-specific regression coefficients defined in equation (1) (b_{0j} and b_{1j} in this example) are modelled as a function of group level (or higher level) variables.

$$b_{0j} = \gamma_{00} + \gamma_{01}G_j + U_{0j} \qquad U_{0j} \sim N(0, \tau_{00}) \tag{2}$$

$$\begin{aligned} b_{1j} &= \gamma_{10} + \gamma_{11}G_j + U_{1j} \qquad U_{1j} \sim N(0, \tau_{11}) \\ cov(U_{0j}, U_{1j}) &= \tau_{10} \end{aligned} \tag{3}$$

G_j = group level variable
γ_{00} is the common intercept across groups
γ_{01} is the effect of the group level predictor on the group specific intercepts
γ_{10} is the common slope associated with the individual level variable across groups
γ_{11} is the effect of the group level predictor on the group specific slopes.

Error terms (sometimes called macro errors) can be included in the second level equations (U_{0j} and U_{1j} in equations (2) and (3)) hence multilevel models are random effects or random coefficient models. By including error terms in the group level equations, these models allow for sampling variability in the group specific coefficients and also for the fact that that the group level equations are not deterministic (i.e. the possibility that not all relevant macro-level variables have been included in the model) (Wong and Mason, 1985). The underlying assumption, is that group specific intercepts and slopes are random samples from a normally distributed population of group specific intercepts and slopes (or equivalently, that the groups or macro errors are "exchangeable") (Diprete and Forristal, 1994). The inclusion of errors in the group level equations has several potential advantages. By quantifying the variability in macro errors (τ_{00} and τ_{11}) multilevel models allow estimation of group to group variability in the group specific regression coeffi-cients and examination of how it changes as individual and group level variables are added. In addition, the inclusion of these errors allows for the possibility that dependent variables for individuals within groups may be correlated even after accounting for the individual level variables and group level variables in the model. One reason for this correlation may have to do with the omission of important group level variables which individuals within groups share. By taking into account this residual correlation, multilevel models correctly estimate standard errors associated with the regression coefficients. In addition, the allowance for errors in the group level equations may be particularly appropriate if groups can be thought of as a sample of a larger population of groups (e.g. schools, neighbourhoods etc.) about which inferences want to be made. Multilevel models can of course be extended to more than two levels.

An alternative way to present the model fitted in multilevel analysis is to substitute equations (2) and (3) in (1) to obtain:

$$Y_{ij} = \gamma_{00} + \gamma_{01}C_j + \gamma_{10}I_{ij} + \gamma_{11}C_jI_{ij} + U_{0j} + U_{1j}I_{ij} + \varepsilon_{ij} \tag{4}$$

The model includes a common intercept (γ_{00}), as well as the effects of group level variables (γ_{01}), individual level variables (γ_{10}) and their interaction (γ_{11}) on the individual level outcome Y_{ij}. These coefficients (γ_{01}, γ_{10} and γ_{11}) which are common to all individuals regardless of the group which they belong are often called the fixed effects (or fixed coefficients). The model also includes a random intercept component (U_{0j}), and a random slope component (U_{1j}). The values of these components vary randomly across groups, and hence U_{0j} and U_{1j} referred to as the random effects (or random coefficients).

Multilevel analysis differs from traditional epidemiological approaches (i.e. ecological studies and studies of individuals) in that: 1) it allows the simultaneous examination of the effects of group level and individual level predictors on individual level outcomes (i.e. after adjustment for each other); 2) the effects of group level variables on group level outcomes (i.e. group specific intercepts or means and group specific slopes) can be investigated; 3) both inter-individual and inter-group variation are examined as well as the contributions of individual level and group level variables to variability at both levels (Snijders and Bosker, 1994); and 4) groups or contexts are not treated as unrelated, but are seen as coming from a larger population of groups about which inferences wish to be made. Thus, multilevel analysis allows researchers to deal with the micro-level of individuals and the macro-level of groups or contexts simultaneously (Duncan *et al.*, 1998). In a sense, both groups and individuals are the units of analysis and constructs at both levels can be investigated. Multilevel models thus provide a link between the traditionally distinct individual level and ecological studies in epidemiology.

Multilevel models allow investigation of a variety of interrelated research questions. They allow separation of the effects of context (i.e. group characteristics) and of composition (characteristics of the individuals in groups) (Duncan *et al.*, 1998): Do groups differ in average outcomes after controlling for the characteristics of individuals within them? Are group level variables related to outcomes after controlling for individual level variables? Multilevel models can also be used to examine the effects of individual level variables: Are individual level variables related to the outcome after controlling for group level variables? Do individual level associations vary from group to group, and is this partly a function of group level variables? Multilevel models also allow quantification of variation at different levels (e.g. within group and between group) and the degrees to which these sources of variation are "statistically explained" by individual level and group level variables. For example, is there significant variation in group specific intercepts or slopes? How does this variability change as individual level or group level variables are added? What percent of the variability in individual level outcomes in between and within groups?

Models in which individual level dependent variables are explained in terms of both group level and individual level independent variables are not new. These types of models have also been called *contextual models* (Blalock, 1984; Iversen, 1991). Although the terms contextual analysis and multilevel analysis have sometimes been used synonymously (Hermalin, 1986; Van Den Eeden and Huttner, 1982), today's multilevel models are more general than early contextual models. Early contextual models were simply models in which group level predictors were included in standard regressions with individuals as the units of analysis. This is equivalent to a multilevel model in which no errors are allowed for in the group level equations, hence, early contextual models were "fixed" effects models. (Special analytical methods may be required to account for non-independence of the outcomes within groups). Contextual analysis can be used to simultaneously investigate how group level and individual level constructs (and their interactions) are related to individual level outcomes but it does not allow examination of group-to-group variability per se or of the factors associated with it (as multilevel analysis does). In traditional contextual analysis, the unit of analysis remains the individual and only inter-individual variation is examined.

4. MULTILEVEL ANALYSIS IN PUBLIC HEALTH AND EPIDEMIOLOGY

A recent and innovative use of multilevel analysis in public health has been the investigation of the independent and interacting effects of group level and individual level factors on health outcomes. The groups or contexts investigated have included countries, states, regions, neighbourhoods or communities, schools, families, workplaces, and health care providers (see for example Duncan *et al.*, 1999; Duncan *et al.*, 1997; Entwisle *et al.*, 1986; Gatsonis *et al.*, 1993; Hedeker *et al.*, 1994; Sixma *et al.*, 1998; Soderfeldt *et al.*, 1997; Rountree and Clayton, 1999). In one of its first applications in the public health field, multilevel analysis was used to investigate how country and individual level characteristics are related to fertility and contraceptive use (e.g. Entwisle *et al.*, 1986; Hermalin, 1986). Health services researchers have used multilevel analysis to investigate geographic variations in use of health services as well as how hospital, provider, and individual characteristics are related to patient satisfaction and health-related outcomes (e.g. Gatsonis *et al.*, 1993; Jones and Moon, 1991; Leung *et al.*, 1998; Leyland and Boddy, 1998; Rice and Leyland, 1996; Sixma *et al.*, 1998). Multilevel analysis has also been used to evaluate the effects of community level and workplace interventions (Forster *et al.*, 1998; Hedeker *et al.*, 1991). In the study of alcohol and drug abuse, multilevel models have been used to examine the role of familial and peer group characteristics (Wang *et al.*, 1998; Rountree and Clayton, 1999). Multilevel models have also been used increasingly in the investigation of the social determinants of health. Both contextual and multilevel models have been used to investigate whether income inequality (by definition a group level property) is related to mortality and other health-related outcomes after accounting for individual characteristics (Daly *et al.*, 1998; Fiscella and Franks, 1997; Kennedy *et al.*, 1998; Le Clere and Soobader, 2000; Diez Roux *et al.*, 2000). One of the most common recent uses of these models in public health has been the investigation of the role of small areas, communities or neighbourhood environments in shaping health outcomes. A key issue in investigating neighbourhood effects on health is separating out the effects of neighbourhood characteristics (context) from the effects of individual level attributes which persons living in certain types of areas may share (composition). Because neighbourhoods can be thought of as groups or contexts with individuals nested within them, multilevel models have been used to investigate how neighbourhood factors, individual level factors, and their interactions, influence health (Pickett and Pearl, 2001). Researchers interested in area or neighbourhood effects have used multilevel models to investigate between and within area variability in health outcomes, and the extent to which between area differences persist after controlling for individual level variables (Boyle and Willms, 1999; Duncan *et al.*, 1993; Duncan *et al.*, 1999; Ecob, 1996; Gould and Jones, 1996; Hart *et al.*, 1997; Humphreys and Carr-Hill, 1991; Jones and Duncan, 1995; Shouls *et al.*, 1996). Multilevel models have also been used to investigate the extent to which area characteristics (such as measures of area deprivation) are related to health outcomes after accounting for individual level indicators of social class (Diez Roux *et al.*, 1997; Diez Roux *et al.*, 1999; Duncan *et al.*, 1999; Ecob, 1996; Humphreys and Carr-Hill, 1991; Jones and Duncan, 1995; Kleinschmidt *et al.*, 1995; Matteson *et al.*, 1998; O'Campo *et al.*, 1997; Shouls *et al.*, 1996; Yen and Kaplan, 1999; Sundquist *et al.*, 1999; Malmstrom *et al.*, 1999).

Although the above discussion has focused on the case of "individuals" nested within groups, multilevel models are applicable in many other situations involving nested sources of random variability. Other possible public health applications include multivariate responses (multiple outcomes nested within individuals) (Duncan *et al.*, 1996; Duncan *et al.*, 1998), the analysis of repeat cross-sectional surveys (multiple observations nested within time periods) (DiPrete and Grusky, 1990), the examination of geographic variations in rates (rates for smaller areas nested within regions or larger areas) (Congdon, 1995; Langford and Bentham, 1996; Langford *et al.*, 1998; Ware, 1985), and the examination of interviewer effects (respondents nested within interviewers) (Hox *et al.*, 1991). Multilevel analytical methods are also applicable in the analysis of repeat measures on individuals over time (for example a study examining factors associated with changes in blood pressure over time where blood pressure is measured every year on a sample of individuals) (Gibbons *et al.*, 1988; Manor and Kark, 1996; Rutter and Elashoff, 1994). In this case the higher level units are the individuals (rather than groups) and the measurement occasions are the lower level units nested within each individual. Multilevel models are also applicable when researchers are interested in pooling data from several different studies (meta analysis) (Bryk and Raudenbush, 1992; Hedeker *et al.*, 1991). In this case the higher level units (or groups) are the studies and the lower level units are the individuals participating in each of them. Another important application of multilevel models is their use to obtain improved estimates of parameters for a given group (for example, estimates of within group regression coefficients or rates for a particular group) by combining information from the group itself with information from all other groups investigated (i.e. Empirical Bayes estimates). This is particularly useful when estimating parameters for a group with few within group observations, for example when estimating death or disease rates for small areas with few observations (Clayton and Kaldor, 1987; Langford, 1994), or when estimating rates of different health outcomes for individual providers (hospitals, physicians etc.) (Thomas *et al.*, 1994). In other applications (which do not involve the structure of individuals within groups described here, although they are analogous to it), empirical Bayes estimates of regression coefficients have been used to obtain improved estimates of associations in studies investigating the role of multiple exposures (Witte *et al.*, 1994).

Multilevel models can easily be extended to data structures involving more than two levels (Bryk and Raudenbush, 1992; Goldstein, 1995). As noted above, time itself can be thought of as one of these levels. For example, multilevel analysis can be used to analyse repeat measures over time in individuals who are themselves nested within neighbourhoods. This allows the examination of the effects of both individual level and group level variables on changes over time in the outcome. In addition, both group level and individual level factors can be allowed to vary over time. One can thus examine how group level and individual level factors defined at multiple points over a person's lifecourse are related to outcomes measured at different times, as well to change over time in the outcome. Multilevel analysis thus opens up a broad range of possibilities related to the examination of how group level (or contextual) and individual level factors over a person's lifecourse affect his or her health.

5. CHALLENGES RAISED BY THE USE OF MULTILEVEL ANALYSIS IN EPIDEMIOLOGY

The advent of multilevel analysis in epidemiology has generated great expectation. The multilevel approach may help transcend the dichotomy of individuals/populations. It integrates the advantages of the traditionally distinct individual and ecological study designs while simultaneously avoiding several of the limitations that each has. In so doing, multilevel analysis holds promise for the development and empirical testing of more comprehensive explanations of the determinants of health and disease. However, the empirical uses of multilevel analysis in epidemiology and the insights that have been derived from its use are still limited in many ways. The reasons for this are both theoretical and practical. On one hand (as we will discuss below), there is still little theoretical development of models or hypotheses that involve factors defined at multiple levels in explaining health. On the other hand, limitations in the types of data available often hamper the adequate investigation of multilevel hypotheses. This section reviews some of the challenges raised by the use of multilevel analysis in public health. The discussion and illustrations will continue to focus on the case of individuals nested within groups, although the issues raised are often applicable to many other situations involving units at a lower levels nested within units at a higher level (for example, small groups nested within larger groups).

5.1. Theories of disease causation that incorporate constructs defined at different levels

In a 1984 review, Blalock (1984) described many of the theoretical and methodological challenges facing contextual analysis. Despite the methodological sophistication of multilevel models, many of these challenges are still valid today. Perhaps chief among these is the need to develop theories that specify how group level and individual level factors may jointly shape the distribution of health and disease, theories that can be operationalised and tested. Theory development and the testing of specific hypotheses will contribute to the development of substantive explanations. An important challenge to public health researchers is the need to develop such explanations and move beyond the use of multilevel analysis simply to document and "statistically explain" residual variability after accounting for individual level variables. These theoretical models will need to articulate the relation between group level factors and individual level processes, and move beyond simplistic models which treat individual level variables as potential "confounders" of any observed group level effect. The absence of theory development regarding the causes of disease (and the implicit acceptance of simple biomedical causality) has been noted as an important critique of epidemiology generally (Krieger and Zierler, 1997). The recent emphasis on method as opposed to theory and substantive explanations in epidemiology makes the field especially vulnerable to the adoption of the method for the method's sake, with little regard to the substantive questions that the method can (or cannot) help answer. In the absence of theories of how factors defined at multiple levels affect the causation of disease, multilevel analysis runs the risk of being reduced to a method which examines variation across meaningless groups or associations with meaningless group level variables, and of either not finding much or finding patterns that are difficult to understand.

5.2 Specifying relevant groups and group properties

A crucial component of multilevel analysis closely related to the theoretical model being tested, is the definition of the relevant group and of the relevant group level variables. The "groups" that are (or should be) investigated in multilevel analysis are not arbitrary or convenient groupings of individuals, but rather groups whose characteristics are hypothesised to be meaningful in explaining the outcome. The increasing sophistication of multilevel models now allows them to accommodate multiple or overlapping contexts (e.g. Goldstein, 1994), but the more substantial issues of defining relevant contexts, specifying the relevant group level variables, and collecting the necessary data remains a challenge.

A key component of the rationale for multilevel analysis is the notion of emergent group properties or the idea that group level variables may provide information which is not captured by individual level data. Several different types of group level variables (including both derived and integral variables, as reviewed elsewhere (Lazarsfeld and Menzel, 1971; Van Den Eeden and Huttner, 1982; Von Korff, 1992; Diez Roux, 1998) can be used in multilevel analysis. The key issue is that group level variables are used as measures of relevant group level constructs (rather than as proxies for unavailable individual level data). For example, the construct of neighbourhood unemployment is distinct from individual level unemployment, and both may be important to health. Similarly, inequality in the distribution of income within a group measures a different construct than individual level income. Defining what the relevant group level constructs are and how they should be measured is therefore key.

Sometimes the distinction between group level and individual level constructs (or variables) is clear-cut, but other times it may be complex. For example, individual level variables can be used to categorise people into groups, such as age groups; however age itself remains an individual level attribute. Of course, it is possible that age groups themselves may have emergent group level properties (related for example, to the types and patterns of interactions between individuals within a certain age group), which may be related to the outcome being studied. Another perhaps more subtle issue is that many variables measured at the individual level (such as individual social class or race-ethnicity) may only be meaningfully understood in the context of how individuals are related to each other in groups or societies. Their meaning and implications for health are tightly intertwined with (and dependent on), group level attributes. The fact that the appropriate unit for measuring a given characteristic is the individual, does not imply that it is individually-determined (as opposed to determined by characteristics of the social organisation of the group to which that individual belongs). In fact, many hypotheses regarding the social determinants of disease can and should be tested with individual level data. In some cases it may still be relevant to add another level to the analysis, for example, examine the effects of race/ethnicity (a socially defined construct measured at the individual level) across groups with different types of social organisations, social norms, or public policies related to race/ethnic discrimination (group level variables) (see e.g. Wong and Mason, 1991). Another example in which group level and individual level attributes are tightly intertwined is provided by patterns of interactions between individual within groups. Patterns of relationships or interactions between individuals may be important in understanding both group level and individual level health outcomes (Koopman *et al.*, 1991a, 1991b; Koopman and Lynch, 1999). In some cases these patterns of interactions can be summarised in the form of a group level attribute (for example, network size or structure), which may affect all individuals within a group, in which case they can be thought of as true group level properties (Lazarsfeld and Menzel, 1971; Van Den Eeden and Huttner, 1982). In other cases, they may pertain to smaller groups within a larger group, or may even vary from individual-to-individual depending on individual contact patterns (in which case they can be thought of as individual level variables that depend on how individuals are related to each other in groups). The specification of relevant constructs and the levels at which they are defined and measured (which is of course closely related to the underlying theoretical model) is a key challenge in multilevel analysis.

5.3. Avoiding excessive simplifications related to the artificial isolation of the effects of group level and individual level variables

As all models, multilevel models necessarily simplify complex processes. One limitation in this regard which multilevel analysis shares with other regression methods, is its focus on teasing apart "independent" effects of variables. Particularly relevant to multilevel analysis is the estimation of the "independent" effects of group level and individual level variables. The extent to which the group and individual level effects can be meaningfully separated or isolated depends on the model that hypothetically links them. It has often been argued that group level effects may simply reflect unaccounted for (or mismeasured) individual level predictors, or more generally, misspecification of the individual level model (equation (1)) (Diez Roux, 1998). However, the degree to which it makes sense to "control" for individual level attributes in examining group effects depends on whether the individual level variable is conceptualised as a true confounder or a mediator. If group attributes affect health they must "get into the body" and therefore are necessarily mediated through individual level processes. Strictly speaking therefore, group level attributes cannot affect individuals "independently" of *all* individual level attributes, but this does not imply that group level constructs are reducible to individual level ones. A related issue is that the measurement of group level constructs is often much more complex than the measurement of individual level attributes, of which there is already a long tradition in epidemiological research. As a result of these measurement problems together with difficulties in defining the relevant groups themselves (e.g. in specifying the boundaries of a neighbourhood or the members of a network of friends), "groups" or "contexts" are often underspecified. This makes estimation of their "independent" effects difficult (particularly after adjustment for better specified individual level variables) and may render comparisons of the relative strengths of group level and individual level variables problematic.

Multilevel models also do not allow examination of the full range complex and reciprocal interrelationships between variables (Blalock, 1984). They still posit a relatively simple regression structure in which a single variable depends on a number of other variables (Bryk and Raudenbush, 1992). For example, multilevel models do not model the possibility that individual level properties (or individual level relations between variables) may influence group characteristics (DiPrete and Forristal, 1994; Mason, 1991; Oppenheimer and Mason, 1991), and vice versa, that group characteristics may shape individual level independent variables. They do not contemplate reciprocal relationships between groups and between individuals within groups, both of which may be important in understanding health outcomes. Although modifications to multilevel models to account for some of these types of relations have been proposed (Entwisle, 1991; Mason, 1991), alternative and complementary methodological approaches may also be necessary.

5.4. The challenges of causal inference in multilevel observational studies

Although multilevel analysis is obviously applicable in randomized trials or experimental approaches, its use in epidemiology to date has been limited for the most part to observational studies.

The challenges of causal inference in observational studies, and especially in situations involving complex causal pathways, have recently received increasing attention in epidemiology. The limitations of using standard multivariate adjustment factors to estimate direct and indirect effects (Robins and Greenland, 1992) or to control for factors which are simultaneously mediators and confounders (Robins, 1989) have been noted and methods have been proposed to better account for these complex causal webs (Robins *et al,*. 1992; Robins *et al.*, 2000). These issues are of course relevant to multilevel analysis as well, where interest often centers around the estimation of "independent" or "direct" group level effects from observational data, after controlling for individual level variables which may be mediators, confounders, or simultaneously mediators and confounders of group effects. The presence of multiple levels also raises additional complexities for causal inference due to the possibility of omitted (and interrelated) variables at multiple levels. The development of more rigorous approaches to causal inference is an important challenge in the application of multilevel analysis to epidemiological questions.

6. LIMITATIONS AND COMPLEMENTARY APPROACHES

The implicit model of disease causation in a large part of current epidemiological research is the multicausal or "web of causation" model initially proposed by MacMahon *et al.* (1960). The multicausal model has been undeniably useful in epidemiology, allowing research to account for the possibility that several different factors may be involved in shaping patterns of health and disease. However the widespread application of this model has often resulted in the reduction of epidemiological research to the investigation of associations between a factor and a disease, after adjustment for multiple additional factors. Although the analytical strategies used (and the multicausal model itself) allow for joint and interacting effects, empirical applications are largely based the often artificial separation of the effects of multiple interrelated variables. Chains of causation and the different levels at which factors are defined are often ignored: hierarchies are collapsed and interest centres in the estimation of independent effects. In so doing, the model implicitly tends to favour more proximate (and therefore biological and individual level) deter-minants over more distal and society level ones (Krieger, 1994; Tesh, 1990).

The advent of multilevel analysis has stimulated thinking on how factors defined not only at the level of individuals but also at the level of groups may be important in understanding the causes of disease. By explicitly recognising the existence of emergent group properties and allowing the empirical examination of their effects, multilevel analysis challenges the dominant individual based and biological paradigm. Multilevel analysis also allows the examination of inter-group variability (which may itself be of interest) and the individual and group level factors associated with it. The risk, however, is that the adoption of multilevel analysis will imply merely the addition of yet another variable (now a group level variable) to the "web of causation", another variable whose "independent" causal effects need to be isolated. The limitations of estimating the effects of distal causes using multivariate adjustment strategies (of which regression methods including multilevel models are an example) have been recently emphasised (Kaufman and Kaufman, 2001). These limitations have to do with difficulties in partialling out causal effects when complex and interrelated sets of confounders and mediators are present. The estimation of the causal effects of group level variables on health may be especially vulnerable to these problems as group level attributes are likely to be related to health outcomes though complex sets of intervening variables and processes.

Although an advance over traditional individual level models, multilevel models may be limited in their ability to examine the full range of dynamic, reciprocal and nonlinear structural relationships within and between levels which are likely to be a feature of disease causation. Simplification is of course necessary and part of the process of scientific inquiry. The problem arises when the simplified model is reified into an ontological stance, a "true" and "complete" representation of reality (Levins and Lewontin, 1985) (i.e. "the world is like the model" rather than "the model helps us understand some aspects of the world"). Multilevel analysis, and the new research questions which it is likely to stimulate, will enhance our ability to investigate and understand the causes of disease. Nevertheless, new analytical strategies may be needed to complement existing approaches in order to allow the investigation of hypotheses based on more complex models of disease causation (Philippe and Mansi, 1998). The proposition and development of such strategies is beyond the scope of this chapter, and they can only be suggested here. A key issue is the theoretical and methodological development of strategies more suitable to the analysis of complex systems. Koopman, for example, has argued that "epidemiology is in transition from a science that identifies risk factors for disease to one that analyses the systems that generate patterns of disease in populations" (Koopman, 1996, p. 630), and Loomis and Wing have posited that "cause in epidemiology is not a property of agents but one of *complex systems* in which the population phenomena of health and disease occur."(Loomis and Wing, 1990, p 2). Recent critiques of the dominant epidemiological paradigm have emphasised the need to consider multiple systems at different levels of organisation in studying health outcomes (Schwartz *et al.*, 1999; Susser and Susser, 1996b). These nested systems span the range from molecules and cells to society. Each system can be thought of as nested within another level, and dynamically interrelated with the levels above and below it. Systems at a higher level influence systems at a lower level and vice-versa. Several authors have articulated the need for a multilevel and systemic approach in epidemiology (Susser and Susser, 1996b; Loomis and Wing, 1990; Koopman and Lynch, 1999). Such an approach may require moving beyond the use of linear models (in which outcomes are assumed to result from linear combinations of explanatory variables) to models that allow for the nonlinear dynamics which often characterise complex, multilevel systems (Phillipe and Mansi, 1998). However, the application of such an approach to the investigation of concrete problems remains in its infancy and the methods to be used in empirical analyses of have yet to be fully developed.

Another element may be the need to conceptualise "causation" (or more generally, "determination") in more complex ways than is usually done in epidemiological studies. For example, in his classical text on causation in modern science, Bunge (1979) defines "determination" (or "lawful production") as including more than traditional causation (or causal determination). He describes a spectrum of categories of determination applicable in science which are irreducible to one another but which are also interconnected. These include not only causal determination (determination of the effect by an external cause as in "in susceptible individuals, smoking causes lung cancer"), and statistical determination (as in "x % of persons with high cholesterol will develop a myocardial infarction") which are the types of determination commonly implicit in epidemiological research (Rothman and Greenland, 1998), but also other types of determination such as reciprocal causation (determination of the consequent by mutual action), structural or wholistic determination (of the parts by the whole), and dialectical determination (of the whole process by the inner "strife" and eventual subsequent synthesis of opposite components). As suggested by Almeida (Almeida Filho, 1992), different types of "determination" may be appropriate for different scientific questions and for different levels of analysis (i.e. along the continuum from molecules to society).

The advent of multilevel analysis has contributed to restoring the population dimension to epidemiology by explicitly recognising the fact that populations are more than collections of individuals. By allowing the rigorous empirical testing of hypotheses involving group level and individual level variables, it has stimulated researchers to develop and articulate such hypotheses. It also explicitly recognises that the examination of both between individual and between group variability may be important in understanding the causes of disease. More broadly, it has contributed methodologically to a growing movement in the field which recognises the need to consider multiple levels of organisation in studying the causes of disease. The challenge lies, however, in ensuring that the method does not become an end in itself, but rather an analytical tool, which together with other approaches, may help stimulate the development and empirical examination of more complex (and realistic) models of disease causation.

NOTES

1 Some of the ideas presented in this chapter were previously developed in Diez Roux, 1998; Diez Roux, 1999; Diez Roux, 2000; and Diez Roux *et al.*, 2002.

2 In epidemiology, confounding is said to occur when the relation between X and Y results from the presence of a third variable Z (the confounder) which is associated with X and causally related to Y (Szklo and Nieto, 2000).

3 A mediator is a variable in the causal pathway linking a factor to an outcome.

4 In epidemiology, a variable Z is said to be an effect modifier if it modifies the effect of another variable (X) on the outcome (Y). For example, if the relation between high fat diet (X) and risk of heart disease (Y) differs depending on an individuals stress levels (Z), stress is said to be an effect modifier (if modifies the relation between high fat diet and heart disease risk) (Szklo and Nieto 2000).

REFERENCES

Alker, H. R. (1969). A typology of ecological fallacies. In M. Dogan and S. Rokkam (Eds.), *Social Ecology* (pp. 69-86). Boston: The MIT Press.

Almeida Filho, N. (1992). *Epidemiología sin números*. Serie Paltex, 28. Washington DC: Panamerican Health Organization.

Blakely, T. A., & Woodward, A. J. (2000). Ecological effects in multi-level studies. *Journal of Epidemiology and Community Health, 54*, 367-374.

Blalock, H. M. (1984). Contextual-effects models: theoretical and methodological issues. *Annual Review of Sociology, 10*, 353-372.

Boyle, M. H., & Willms, J. D. (1999). Place effects for areas defined by administrative boundaries. *American Journal of Epidemiology, 149*, 577-85.

Bryk, A. S., & Raudenbush, S. W. (1992). *Hierarchical linear models: applications and data analysis methods*. Newbury Park, CA: Sage.

Bunge, M. (1979). Causation and determination, causalism and determinism. In *Causality in Modern Science* (pp. 3-30). New York: Dover Publications.

Catalano, R. (1979). Paradigm succession in the study of public health. In R. Catalano, & R. A. Catalano (Eds.), *Health, behavior, and the community. An ecological perspective* (pp. 87-137).Oxford: Pergamon Press.

Charlton, B. (1996). Should epidemiologists be pragmatists, biostatisticians or clinical scientists? *Epidemiology, 7*, 552-554.

Clayton, D., & Kaldor, J. (1987). Empirical Bayes estimates of age-standardized relative risks for use in disease mapping. *Biometrics, 43*, 671-681.

Coleman, J. (1991). Social theory, social research and a theory of action. *American Journal of Sociology, 91*, 1309-1335.

Congdon, P. (1995). The impact of area context on long term illness and premature mortality: An illustration of multi-level analysis. *Regional Studies, 29*, 327-344.

Daly, M., Duncan, G., Kaplan, G., & Lynch, J. (1998). Macro to micro links in the relation between income inequality and mortality. *Milbank Quarterly, 76*, 315-339.

Diez Roux, A. V. (1998). Bringing context back into epidemiology variables and fallacies in multilevel analysis. *American Journal of Public Health, 88*, 216-222.

Diez Roux, A. V. (1999). On genes, individuals, society, and epidemiology. *American Journal of Epidemiology, 11*, 1027-1032.

Diez Roux, A. V., Nieto, F., Muntaner, C., Tyroler, H. A., Comstock, G. W. *et al.* (1997). Neighborhood environments and coronary heart disease: a multilevel analysis. *American Journal of Epidemiology, 146*, 48-63.

Diez Roux, A. V., Nieto, F. J., Caulfield, L., Tyroler, H. A., Watson, R . A., & Szklo, M. (1999). Neighborhood differences in diet: the Atherosclerosis Risk in Communities (ARIC) Study. *Journal of Epidemiology and Community Health, 53*, 55-63.

Diez Roux, A. V. (2000). Multilevel analysis in public health research. *Annual Review of Public Health, 21*, 171-92.

Diez Roux, A. V., Link, B. G, & Northridge, M. E. (2000). A multilevel analysis of income inequality and cardiovascular disease risk factors. *Social Science in Medicine, 50*, 673-87.

Diez Roux, A. V., Schwartz, S., & Susser, E. (2002). Ecologic studies and ecologic variables in public health research. In *The Oxford Textbook of Public Health* (pp. 493-509). London: Oxford University Press.

DiPrete, T. A., & Forristal, J. D. (1994). Multilevel models: methods and substance. *Annual Review of Sociology, 20*, 331-357.

DiPrete, T. A., & Grusky, D. (1990). The multilevel analysis of trends with repeated cross-sectional data. *Sociological Methodology, 20*, 337-368.

Duncan, C., Jones, K, & Moon, G. (1993). Do places matter? A multi-level analysis of regional variation in health-related behavior in Britain. *Social Science & Medicine, 37*, 725-733.

Duncan, C., Jones, K., & Moon, G. (1996). Health-related behaviour in context: a multilevel modelling approach. *Social Science & Medicine, 42*, 817-830.

Duncan, T., Duncan, S., Hops, H., & Alpert, A. (1997). Multilevel covariance structure analysis of intrafamilial substance abuse. *Drug and Alcohol Dependence, 46*, 167-180.

Duncan, C., Jones, K., & Moon, G. (1998). Context, composition, and heterogeneity: using multilevel models in health research. *Social Science & Medicine, 46*, 97-117.

Duncan, C., Jones, K., & Moon, G. (1999). Smoking and deprivation: are there neighbourhood effects? *Social Science & Medicine, 48*, 497-505.

Ecob, R. (1996). A multilevel modelling approach to examining the effects of area of residence on health. *Journal of the Royal Statistical Society (A), 159*, 61-75.

Entwisle, B. (1991). Micro-macro theoretical linkages in social demography: a commentary. In J Huber (Ed.), *Macro-micro linkages in sociology* (pp. 280-286). Newbury Park, CA: Sage.

Entwisle, B., Mason, W., Hermalin, H. (1986). The multilevel dependence of contraceptive use on socioeconomic development and family planning program strength. *Demography, 23*, 199-216.

Fiscella, K., & Franks, P. (1997). Poverty or income inequality as predictor or mortality: a longitudinal cohort study. *British Medical Journal, 314*, 1724-1728.

Forster, J., Murray, D., Wolfson, M., Blaine, T., Wagenaar, A., & Hennrikus, D. (1998). The effects of community policies to reduce youth access to tobacco. *American Journal of Public Health. 88*, 1193-1198.

Gatsonis, C., Normand, S., Liu, C., & Morris, C. (1993). Geographic variation of procedure utilization: A hierarchical model approach. *Medical Care, 31*, YS54-YS59.

Gibbons, R., Hedeker, D., Waternaux, C., & Davis, J. (1988). Random regression models: a comprehensive approach to the analysis of longitudinal psychiatric data. *Psychopharmacology Bulletin, 24*, 438-443.

Goldstein, H. (1994). Multilevel cross-classified models. *Sociological Methods & Research, 22*, 364-375.

Goldstein, H. (1995). *Multilevel statistical models*. New York: Halsted Press.

Gould, M., & Jones, K. (1996). Analyzing perceived limiting long-term illness using U. K. Census microdata. *Social Science & Medicine, 42*, 857-869.

Greenland, S. (1992). Divergent biases in ecologic and individual-level studies. *Statistics in Medicine, 11*, 1209-1223.

Greenland, S., & Morgenstern, H. (1989). Ecological bias, confounding, and effect modification. *International Journal of Epidemiology, 18*, 269-274.

Greenland, S., & Robins, J. (1994). Ecologic studies- biases, misconceptions, and counter-examples. *American Journal of Epidemiology, 139*, 747-760.

Halloran, M. E. (1998). Concepts of infectious disease epidemiology. In K. Rothman and S. Greenland (eds.), *Modern Epidemiology* (pp.). Philadelphia: Lippincott-Raven.

Hart, C., Ecob, R., & Davey Smith G. (1997). People, places, and coronary heart disease risk factors: a multilevel analysis of the Scottish Heart Health Study archive. *Social Science & Medicine, 45*, 893-902.

Hedeker, D., Gibbons, R., Davis, J. (1991). Random regression models for multicenter clinical trials data. *Psychopharmacology Bulletin, 27*, 73-77.

Hedeker, D., McMahon, S., Jason, L., & Salina, D. (1994). Analysis of clustered data in community psychology: with an example from a worksite smoking cessation project. *American Journal of Community Psychology, 22*, 595-615.

Hermalin, A. (1986). The multilevel approach: theory and concepts. The methodology for measuring the impact of family planning programs on fertility. In *Population Studies* Addendum Manual IX. 66 (pp. 15-31). New York: United Nations.

Hox, J. P., de Leeuw, E. D., & Kreft, I. G. G. (1991). The effect of interviewer and respondent characteristics on the quality of survey data: a multilevel model. In P. P. Biemer, L. E. Lyberg, N. A. Mathiowetz, & S. Sudman (Eds.), *Measurement errors in surveys* (pp. 439-463). New York: John Wiley & Sons.

Humphreys, K., & Carr-Hill, R. (1991). Area variations in health outcomes: Artefact or ecology. *International Journal of Epidemiology, 20*, 251-258.

Iversen, G. (1991). *Contextual analysis*. Newbury Park, CA: Sage.

Jones, K., & Moon, G. (1991). Multilevel assessment of immunisation uptake as a performance measure in general practice. *British Medical Journal, 303*, 28-31.

Jones, K., & Duncan, C. (1995). Individuals and their ecologies: analysing the geography of chronic illness within a multilevel modelling framework. *Health Place, 1*, 27-40.

Jones, K., & Moon, G. (1991). Multilevel assessment of immunisation uptake as a performance measure in general practice. *British Medical Journal, 303*, 28-31.

Kaplan, G. A., Pamuk, E. R., Lynch, J. W., Cohen, R. D., & Balfour, J. L. (1996). Inequality in income and mortality in the United States: analysis of mortality and potential pathways. *British Medical Journal, 312*, 999-1003.

Kaufman, J., & Kaufman, S. (2001). Assessment of structured socioeconomic effects on health. *Epidemiology, 12*, 157-167.

Kawachi, I. (1999). Social capital and community effects on population and individual health. *Annual Report. New York Academy of Sciences, 896*, 120-130.

Kennedy, B. P., Kawachi, I., & Prothrow-Stith, D. (1996). Income distribution and mortality: cross-sectional ecological study of the Robin Hood index in the United States. *British Medical Journal, 312,* 1004-1007.

Kennedy, B. P., Kawachi, I., Glass, R., & Prothrow-Stith, D. (1998). Income distribution, socioeconomic status and self rated health in the United States: a multilevel analysis. *British Medical Journal, 31*, 917-921.

Kleinschmidt, I., Hills, M., & Elliott, P. (1995). Smoking behavior can be predicted by neighborhood deprivation measures. *Journal of Epidemiology and Community Health, 49*, S72-S77.

Koopman, J. S. (1996). Emerging objectives and methods in epidemiology. *American Journal of Public Health, 86*, 630-632.

Koopman, J. S., & Lynch, J. (1999). Individual causal models and population system models in epidemiology. *American Journal of Public Health, 89*, 1170-1174.

Koopman, J. S., Prevots, D. R., Vaca Marin, M. A., Dantes, H. G., Zarate Aquino, M. L., Longini, I. M., & Sepulveda J. (1991a). Determinants and predictors of dengue infection in Mexico. *American Journal of Epidemiology, 133*, 1168-1178.

Koopman, J. S., Longini, I. M., Jacquez, J. A., Simon, C. P., Ostrow, D. G., Martin, W. R., & Woodcock, D. M. (1991b). Assessing risk factors for transmisson of infection. *American Journal of Epidemiology, 133*, 1199-1209.

Koopman, J. S., & Lynch J. (1999). Individual causal models and population system models in epidemiology. *American Journal of Public Health, 1989,* 1170-1174.

Kreft, I., & deLeeuw J. (1998). *Introducing multilevel modeling*. London: Sage.

Krieger, N. (1994). Epidemiology and the web of causation. Has anyone seen the spider? *Social Science & Medicine, 39*, 887-903.

Krieger, N., Zierler, S. (1997). The need for epidemiologic theory. *Epidemiology, 8*, 212-214.

Langford, I. H. (1994). Using empirical Bayes estimates in the geographical analysis of disease risk. *Area*, 26, 142-149.

Langford, I. H., & Bentham, G. (1996). Regional variations in mortality rates in England and Wales: An analysis using multilevel modelling. *Social Science & Medicine, 42*, 897-908.

Langford, I. H., Bentham, G., & McDonald, A. (1998). Multi-level modelling of geographically aggregated health data: A case study of malignant melanoma mortality and UV exposure in the european community. *Statistics in Medicine, 17*, 41-57.

Lazarsfeld, P. F., & Menzel, H. (1971). On the relation between individual and collective properties. In A. Etzioni (ed.), *A sociological reader on complex organizations* (pp.499-516). New York: Holt, Rinehart, and Winston Inc.

LeClere, F. B., & Soobader, M. J. (2000). The effect of income inequality on the health of selected demographic groups. *American Journal of Public Health, 90*, 1892-1897.

Leung, K., Elashoff, R., Rees, K., Hasan, M., & Legorreta, A. (1998). Hospital- and patient-related characteristics determining maternity length of stay: A hierarchical linear model approach. *American Journal of Public Health, 88*, 377-81.

Levins, R, & Lewontin, R. (1985). *The Dialectical Biologist*. Boston: Harvard University Press.

Leyland, A., & Boddy, F. (1998). League tables and acute myocardial infarction. *Lancet, 351*, 555-558.

Lilienfeld, D., & Stolley, P. (1994). *Foundations of epidemiology*. Third Edition. New York: Oxford University Press.

Loomis, D., & Wing, S. (1990). Is molecular epidemiology a germ theory for the end of the twentieth century? *International Journal of Epidemiology, 19*, 1-3.

Mac Mahon, B., Pugh, T. F., & Ipsen, J. (1960). *Epidemiologic Methods*. Boston: Little Brown.

Malmstrom, M., Sundquist, J., & Johansson, S. (1999). Neighborhood environment and self-reported health status: a multilevel analysis. *American Journal of Public Health, 89*, 1181-1189.

Manor, O., & Kark, J. (1996). A comparative study of four methods for analyzing repeated measures data. *Statistics in Medicine, 15*, 1143-1159.

Mason, W. (1991). Problems in quantitative comparative analysis: ugly ducklings are to swans as ugly scatter plots are to. . .? In J. Huber (Ed.), *Macro-micro linkages in sociology* (pp. 231-243). Newbury Park, CA: Sage.

Matteson, D., Burr, J., & Marshall, J. (1998). Infant mortality: a multi-level analysis of individual and community risk factors. *Social Science in Medicine, 47*, 1841-1854.

McMichael, A. J. (1999). Prisoners of the proximate: Loosening the constraints on epidemiology in an age of change. *American Journal of Epidemiology, 149*, 887-97.

Morgenstern, H. (1982). Uses of ecologic analysis in epidemiologic research. *American Journal of Public Health, 72*, 1336-1344.

Morgenstern, H. (1995). Ecologic studies in epidemiology: concepts, principles, and methods. *Annual Review of Public Health, 16*, 61-81.

O'Campo, P., Xue, X., Wang, M., & Caughy M. (1997). Neighborhood risk factors for low birthweight in Baltimore: a multilevel analysis. *American Journal of Public Health, 87*, 1113-1118.

Oppenheimer, K., & Mason, K.O. (1991). Multilevel analysis in the study of social institutions and demographic change. In J. Huber (ed.), *Macro-micro linkages in sociology* (pp. 223-230). Newbury Park, CA: Sage

Pearce, N. (1996). Traditional epidemiology, modern epidemiology and public health. *American Journal of Public Health, 86*, 678-683.

Philippe, P., & Mansi, O. (1998). Nonlinearity in the epidemiology of complex health and disease processes. *Theoretical Medicine and Bioethics, 19*, 591-607.

Piantadosi, S., Byar, D. P., & Green, S. B. (1988). The ecological fallacy. *American Journal of Epidemiology, 127*, 893-903.

Pickett, K. E., & Pearl, M. (2001). Multilevel analyses of neighbourhood socioeconomic context and health outcomes: a critical review. *Journal of Epidemiology and Community Health, 55*, 111-122.

Poole, C., & Rothman, K. J. (1998). Our conscientious objection to the epidemiology wars. *Journal of Epidemiology and Community Health, 52*, 613-614.

Rice, N., & Leyland, A. (1996). Multilevel models: applications to health data. *Journal of Health Services Research & Policy, 1*, 154-64.

Riley, M. W. (1963). Special problems of sociological analysis. In R. K. Merton (Ed.), *Sociological Research I: A case approach* (pp.700- 725). New York: Harcourt, Brace, and World Inc.

Robert, S. (1999). Socioeconomic position and health: the independent contribution of community socioeconomic context. *Annual Review of Sociology, 25*, 489-516.

Robins, J. (1989). The control of confounding by intermediate variables. *Statistics in Medicine*, 8, 679-701.

Robins, J. M., Blevins, D., Ritter, G., & Wulfsohn, M. (1992). G-estimation of the effect of prophylaxis therapy for Pneumocystis carinii pneumonia on the survival of AIDS patients. *Epidemiology*, 3, 319-36.

Robins, J. M., Hernan, M. A., & Brumback, B. (2000). Marginal structural models and causal inference in epidemiology. *Epidemiology*, 11, 550-60.

Robins, J. M., & Greenland, S. (1992). Identifiability and exchangeability for direct and indirect effects. *Epidemiology*, 3, 143-55.

Rose, G. (1985). Sick individuals and sick populations. *International Journal of Epidemiology, 14*, 32-38.

Rothman, K. J., & Greenland, S. (1998). Causation and causal inference. In K. J. Rothman, & S. Greenland (Eds.), *Modern Epidemiology* (pp. 7-28). Second Edition. Philadelphia: Lippincott-Raven.

Rountree, P. W., & Clayton, R. (1999). A contextual model of adolescent alcohol use across the rural-urban continuum. *Substance Use and Misuse, 34*, 495-519.

Rutter, C., & Elashoff, R. (1994). Analysis of longitudinal data: random coefficient regression modelling. *Statistics in Medicine, 13*, 1211-1231.

Scheuch, E. K. (1969). Social context and individual behavior. In M. Dogan, & S. Rokkam (Eds.), *Social Ecology* (pp. 133-155). Boston: The MIT Press.

Schwartz, S. (1994). The fallacy of the ecological fallacy: the potential misuse of a concept and its consequences. *American Journal of Public Health, 84*, 819-824.

Schwartz, S., & Carpenter, K. (1999). The right answer for the wrong question: Consequences of type III error for public health research. *American Journal of Public Health, 89*, 1175-1180.

Schwartz, S., Susser, E., & Susser, M. (1999). A future for epidemiology? *Annual Review of Public Health, 20*, 15-33

Shouls, S., Congdon, P., & Curtis, S. (1996). Modelling inequality in reported long term illness in the UK: combining individual and area characteristics. *Journal of Epidemiology and Community Health, 50*, 366-376

Sixma, H. J., Spreeuwenberg, P. M., & Pasch, M. (1998). Patient satisfaction with the general practitioner: a two-level analysis. *Medical Care, 36*, 212-229.

Snijders, T. A., & Bosker, R. J. (1994). Modeled variance in two-level models. *Sociological Methods & Research, 22*, 342-363

Snijders, T. A., & Bosker, R. J. (1999). *Multilevel analysis: an introduction to basic and advanced multilevel modeling*. London: Sage.

Soderfeldt, B., Soderfeldt, M., Jones, K., *et al.* (1997). Does Organization Matter? A multilevel analysis of the demand-control model applied to human services. *Social Science & Medicine, 44*, 527-534.

Sundquist, J., Malmstrom, M., & Johansson, S. (1999). Cardiovascular risk factors and the neighborhood environment: A multilevel analysis. *International Journal of Epidemiology, 28*, 841-845.

Susser, M. (1994a). The logic in ecological: I. The logic of analysis. *American Journal of Public Health, 84*, 825-829.

Susser, M. (1994b). The logic in ecological: II. The logic of design. *American Journal of Public Health*, 84, 830-835.

Susser, M., & Susser, E. (1996a). Choosing a future for epidemiology I: Eras and paradigms. *American Journal of Public Health, 86*, 668-673.

Susser, M., & Susser, E. (1996b). Choosing a future for epidemiology: II. From black box to Chinese boxes and eco-epidemiology. *American Journal of Public Health, 86*, 674-677.

Susser, M. (1998). Does risk factor epidemiology put epidemiology at risk? Peering into the future. *Journal of Epidemiology and Community Health, 52*, 608-611.

Szklo, M., & Nieto, F. J. (2000). *Epidemiology: beyond the basics*. Gaithersburg, MD: Aspen Publishers.

Taubes, G. (1995). Epidemiology faces its limits. *Science, 269*, 164-169.

Tesh, S. N. (1990). *Hidden Arguments. Political ideology and disease prevention policy*. New York: Rutgers University Press.

Thomas, N., Lonford, N., & Rolph, J. (1994). Empirical Bayes methods for estimating hospital-specific morality rates. *Statistics in Medicine, 13*, 889-903

Valkonen, T. (1969). Individual and structural effects in ecological research. In M. Dogan, & S. Rokkam (Ed.), *Social Ecology* (pp. 53-68). Boston: The MIT Press.

Van Den Eeden, P., & Huttner, H. J. (1982). Multi-level research. *Current Sociology, 30*, 1-178.

Vandenbroucke, J. P. (1990). Epidemiology in transition: a historical hypothesis. *Epidemiology, 1*, 164-167.

Von Korff, M., Koepsell, T., Curry, S., & Diehr, P. (1992). Multi-level research in epidemiologic research on health behaviors and outcomes. *American Journal of Epidemiology, 135*, 1077-1082.

Wang, J., Siegal, H. A., Falck, R. S., & Carlson, R. G. (1998). Needle transfer among injection drug users: a multilevel analysis. *American Journal of Drug and Alcohol Abuse, 24*, 225-237.

Ware, J. (1985). Linear models for the analysis of longitudinal studies. *The American Statistician, 39*, 95-101

Witte, J. S., Greenland, S., Haile, R. W., & Bird, C. L. (1994). Hierarchical regression analysis applied to a study of multiple dietary exposures and breast cancer. *Epidemiology, 5*, 612-621.

Wong, G., & Mason, W. (1985). The hierarchical logistic regression model for multilevel analysis. *Journal of the American Statistical Association, 80*, 513-524.

Wong, G.,& Mason, W. (1991). Contextually specific effects and other generalizations of the hierarchical linear model for comparative analysis. *Journal of the American Statistical Association, 86*, 487-503.

Yen, I., & Kaplan, G. (1999). Neighborhood social environment and risk of death: multilevel evidence from the Alameda County study. *American Journal of Epidemiology, 149*, 898-907.

Mark TRANMER, David STEEL, Ed FIELDHOUSE

Chapter 4

EXPLORING SMALL AREA POPULATION STRUCTURE WITH CENSUS DATA

Opening. We have already indicated that census data were used since the early nineteenth century to determine the structure of the populations studied, at a given moment. Owing to their completeness, they could be used—in theory—to study not only regional or national populations but also local populations. The structures studied could also be very complex, as the census data documented a large number of characteristics of individuals. Unfortunately, however, the methods of statistical analysis used and certain confidentiality restrictions have prevented analysts from extracting all the information one might have hoped.

First, the structures identified from the census data are largely based on selections performed on the populations. As a result, the tables supplied by the selections seldom allow a cross-classification of more than three criteria at once. This is due to issues concerning the legibility of results, as the number of cells in the tables soon becomes too great. At the same time, because of the large number of cells, some population groups may be small (or even contain one or no individuals), preventing publication of the tables for confidentiality reasons. For example, a table classifying the labour force of a French département by age (56 groups), detailed socio-occupational category (42 groups, for example), and educational attainment (16 groups) already contains 37,632 cells: for many departements the number of individuals per cell would be very small, if not equal to unity or zero. It is therefore impossible to publish such a table, as it would allow the identification of many individuals.

The tabulations that are authorised and published must consequently avoid breaching the rules of statistical secrecy to which censuses are subjected. If we want a very detailed classification, we must make do with a fairly broad geographic level: we will then forfeit the possibility of comparing the results obtained on various sub-populations of the overall geographic level. If, instead, we want a table for a tiny geographic area, we must content ourselves with a very rough classification: we will then lose the possibility of comparing these results with those obtained using more detailed classifications. These examples show the double bind—geographic detail versus classification detail—to which census tabulations are subjected.

The more detailed correlation or regression analyses performed on such data are vulnerable to the ecological fallacy. If their purpose is merely to show the constraints that groups impose on their members, the analyses will effectively do so. But there is a great danger of inferring that the effects shown at the aggregate level also exist at the individual level. As a rule, that is not the case, and the results obtained at the two levels are often independent: sometimes, the relationship at the aggregate level may carry an opposite sign to the one observed at the individual level.

One way to avoid the ecological fallacy risk is to take a random sample of individuals from the census data in order to perform the same analyses at the individual level. In England, for example, a 2% sample was selected for the 1991 census, enabling analysts to work on a geographic definition far more detailed than the one used in many surveys covering smaller samples. But, even in this case, the risk of violating census confidentiality has led statistical offices to refrain from supplying over-detailed geographic information on individuals' places of residence. This prevents a comparison between the results obtained at the individual level with those obtainable at a more aggregated but nevertheless sufficiently detailed level.

Mark Tranmer, David Steel, and Ed Fieldhouse show us here the results we can obtain by using a multilevel approach: instead of concentrating on a given observation level—individual or aggregated according to various types of geographic segmentation (Districts, Wards, Enumeration Districts)—it tries to use all the information available at whatever level. The strength of these methods is that (1) they draw maximum information from these results—which are seemingly non-comparable as they are obtained from different samples—and (2) they summarise the information in a wholly satisfactory synthesis. The multilevel methods can therefore estimate and explain population structure at different aggregation levels, with matrices reflecting the link between several characteristics for two individuals situated in the same geographic area and according to the aggregation level examined. We may assume that two individuals living in the

D. Courgeau (ed.) Methodology and Epistemology of Multilevel Analysis, 121-156.

same "Enumeration District" will be more similar in regard to a set of demographic and socio-economic characteristics than two individuals living in two different "Enumeration Districts". This goes for any type of geographic segmentation.

The estimation of these degrees of resemblance, using multilevel analysis methods applied to both individual and aggregated data, makes it possible to grasp the complexity of groupings of similar individuals in the same areas and to assess the strength of the connection between characteristics measured at a given aggregation level, after eliminating the effects due to the other aggregation levels. This paves the way for innovative applications of multilevel analysis to geographical analysis and social statistics—applications whose far-reaching potential is described and discussed in the pages that follow.

D. C.

1. INTRODUCTION

The need to reflect the complex structure of populations in the statistical models used in the social sciences has been increasingly recognised in recent years. In this chapter we consider how multilevel models may be used with census data to reveal important aspects of the social structure of geographic areas. We will focus on two examples, which highlight issues associated with the analysis of census data and multilevel models. For each example we give theoretical details and also empirical results based on data available from the 1991 UK census. We consider how the forms in which census data are released affect the approach to multilevel analysis. The roles of aggregate area level and individual level sample data, or microdata, are identified. In particular, methods for combining aggregate and individual level data using the multilevel model framework are described. The issues considered here apply more widely than the field of census data analysis and are relevant to research methodology in the social sciences in general, and to human geography.

The two examples we will consider are:

- *Example 1: Methods for estimating and explaining population structure*

  Most populations of interest have a structure. For example, if we are interested in the population of a city, we know that people live in different areas within this city and that these areas differ in terms of a variety of factors, such as housing characteristics. This leads to a population structure with an individual and one or more area levels. We consider the way in which multilevel models allow us to analyse and explain population structure. We show how the parameters of these models may be estimated by combining the available aggregate and individual level data for the population of interest. We also consider how the model may be extended to include variables that characterise group structure.

- *Example 2: Investigating variations in unemployment using census microdata with area classifications*

  This example illustrates the way in which area classification information, added to census microdata, can be used in a multilevel modelling approach to allow the type of Enumeration District (ED) in which each person lives to be taken into account in the analysis of an outcome of interest, such as the risk of unemployment.

An ED is a small geographic area containing about 500 people. We consider issues relating to using a *classification* of ED type (e.g. prosperous, deprived), rather than the EDs themselves, as higher level units in the multilevel model.

A general issue, integral to these examples is *data availability*. Multilevel models can be specified in theoretical terms, but the parameters can only be estimated if data are available that include information on each level assumed in the model. A "standard" multilevel data set comprises a set of individual units with higher level group indicators. For example a data set may consist of a record for each person that includes an indicator of the ED in which the person lives. In the census, such data are not available for reasons of confidentiality. However, for a local population of interest, such as a city, town or a local administrative area, aggregate data are available for higher level geographically defined groups, such as EDs. For the same population, a sample of individual level microdata is often available but this does not include group or area indicators. However, by combining these two datasets, referring to the same population, we show how estimates of multilevel parameters may be obtained, even though the data are not of the standard form usually used for multilevel modelling. We briefly consider some further issues associated with the multilevel analysis of census data and multilevel modelling in general.

The remainder of this chapter is organised as follows. The next section discusses some issues affecting multilevel modelling using geographically based data. Section 3 describes census data availability, focusing on the situation for 1991 UK census data. Section 4 briefly describes some previous uses of multilevel modelling with census data. The two main examples are discussed in Sections 5 and 6, where technical and empirical results are included. In Section 7 we briefly consider some further issues associated with the multilevel analysis of census data and multilevel modelling in general, and general conclusions are given in Section 8.

2. THE CONCEPT OF MULTILEVEL MODELS FOR GEOGRAPHICALLY BASED DATA

It is common for geographically based populations to have a multilevel structure. The simplest case is a two level structure, for example where individuals are located in EDs. Each individual is a level 1 unit (the lowest level of the hierarchy) and each ED is a level 2 unit. Higher levels could also exist—for example, each level 3 unit could comprise several geographically contiguous EDs. In this case several level 2 units are nested into each level 3 unit. Although the units are often assumed to be nested into a hierarchy of levels, multilevel structures may also occur that are cross-classified, so that two or more sets of groupings of units overlap one another. This situation is illustrated in Example 2, discussed in Section 6.

As well as the geographic case, which we will focus on, multilevel structures occur in other situations. One important case is the institutional context where the higher level groups correspond to organisations or institutions. For example, a population of pupils may be of interest, each of whom attends a school. Indeed, much of the motivation for recent advances in multilevel modelling stemmed from research in the educational context (See, for example, Aitkin and Longford (1986), Goldstein (1995), Longford (1987)). The chapter by Goldstein in this book deals specifically with this topic. Multilevel structures may also be considered for cases that include a mixture of geographical and institutional contexts. For example, the ED level and the school level may both be of interest, and these levels may be cross-classified, so that two pupils from the same ED may each attend a different school, or two pupils from the same school may each live in a different ED.

We should recognise the fact that social populations have a multilevel structure when carrying out an analysis. If we do not, we are likely to obtain biased or misleading estimates of population parameters such as regression or correlation coefficients. Having recognised that the population structure exists, we can adopt one of two strategies for analysis. Firstly, the population structure may be regarded as a nuisance that is not of direct substantive interest. However, we should still allow for this population structure in our analysis, particularly because of the impact on second order quantities such as standard errors of estimates. Secondly, the population structure may be a phenomenon of substantive interest, which is the situation that we will focus on. In both cases, a statistical framework, that is, a multilevel model, should be specified that allows for the population structure.

Analysis based solely on aggregate data for geographic areas has raised a number of issues, in particular the ecological fallacy and scale and zoning. The ecological fallacy occurs when the results of an analysis of aggregate group level data are assumed to apply to individual level relationships. Steel *et al.* (1996) suggest that a multilevel modelling framework is needed to allow progress to be made in understanding the nature and extent of area effects, and hence the causes of phenomena such as the ecological fallacy. Issues associated with the analysis of aggregate data for geographical areas are of increasing interest as the development of Geographical Information Systems (GIS) allows data to be obtained at a variety of geographical levels, or scales, possibly from a number of different sources.

Openshaw (1984) used the term "Modifiable Areal Unit Problem", or MAUP, to describe two important phenomena that occur in the analysis of aggregated area level data. The first phenomenon is the scale issue: the fact that an analysis of area level data will, in general, give different results depending on the number of areal units into which the population is divided. In Example 1 discussed in Section 5, we will show how scale effects may be assessed through a three level model. The second phenomenon is the zoning issue: a population can be divided into a particular number of areas in many different ways and area level analyses from each of these will give different results. For example, a population could be divided into areal units with an average population of 500 people, as is the case for UK census. This could be done in many different ways. A correlation analysis of the means for one set of areal units will differ, in general, from that of another set using a different set of boundaries. The issue of aggregate data and scale and zoning effects has been discussed extensively in the literature (For example, Moellering and Tobler, 1972; Fotheringham and Wong, 1991; Holt *et al.*, 1996). More recently in the geographical literature, the use of multilevel models for geographical analysis has been discussed (for example, Jones and Duncan, 1996).

Both the scale and zoning phenomena occur because the population has structure. Two people that are located close to one another within the population of interest tend to be more alike than two people who are not located close to one another. That is, there is "within area homogeneity". Hence, a multilevel model of the population that allows for within area homogeneity is particularly valuable for investigating these effects.

Many countries release individual level data based on a sample of census records. In the UK this data set is referred to as the Sample of Anonymised Records (SAR). The samples of census data may contain some relatively high level geographic indicators, which enable some aspects of the hierarchical population structure to be taken into account at a fairly large geographical scale. Indeed, SAR data have been used to carry out substantive analyses in the multilevel framework (for example, Fieldhouse and Gould, 1998; Gould and Fieldhouse, 1997), but the higher levels units analysed in these studies are large because until 1998, the SAR data only included geographic indicators for areas of at least 120,000 people, called "SAR districts"; identifiers for the 278 such areas were available on the SAR for Great Britain (GB). However, much of the substantively interesting effects occur at lower geographic levels. There is likely to be a great deal of heterogeneity within an area of 120,000 people associated with smaller geographic areas in which people live. It is worth noting that for the 2001 UK census the population threshold for SAR districts is likely to be 75,000, but there will still be effects occurring at smaller geographic levels than this. Ideally we would have a hierarchical dataset with indicators of these smaller geographical levels and we would be able to fit a multilevel model. However, in practice, this is not the case for reasons of confidentiality. We have to adopt a different approach, where the available aggregate and individual data are combined in the multilevel modelling framework.

3. CENSUS DATA AVAILABILITY

3.1. Aggregate and individual level data

The standard approach to multilevel modelling assumes that data are available for a sample or census of individuals that includes indicators for each of the levels of the geographic groups of interest. This sort of data is not usually available from a population census. However, as we will show, a multilevel analysis can be carried out provided that some data sets are available that, between them, include information on each of the levels of the multilevel structure. Here we will review the types of data that are often available from a census that may be relevant to multilevel modelling. In the two examples we used 1991 UK census data in the multilevel modelling framework. Part of this section will therefore be a discussion of 1991 UK census data availability. Many of the attributes of the UK 1991 census data will also apply to data released from the recently conducted UK 2001 census, and censuses conducted in other countries.

The *census* represents a (near) complete count of the population, capturing information on place of residence, housing and social, demographic and economic characteristics at a single point in time. A large amount of aggregate data is made available, usually in tabular form, for small geographic areas, and these data do not have any sampling error. They are also available on a comparable basis across areas. This unique aspect of census data is of considerable importance in exploring small area population structure. It means that census data are widely used in policy analysis, for example, to determine the demographic profile of an area; to make comparisons about the relative needs of areas; to assess which areas have the greatest housing need or the poorest health. The value of this information operates at various levels. National governments need census data to assess the distribution of resources to the next tier of government, for example, states or local authorities; state, local government or health authorities may use these data to target resources within their area.

Information for some variables may be collected or processed on a sample basis but the sampling fraction used is usually quite high to provide estimates for geographic areas with reasonable standard errors. For example in the 1991 UK census information on "difficult to code" variables, such as occupation was available on a 10% sample.

In the UK, and in many other countries, samples of microdata are drawn from the census. The census provides an effective "sampling frame". The fact that the census is compulsory for the entire population means that all households should fall within the sampling frame, although there is always a small amount of census under enumeration, typically less than 2% (OPCS, 1994), sampling design of most social surveys includes an element of stratification and often a degree of geographical clustering—the latter in order to cut down costs. However, the method by which microdata samples are drawn from the census allows a high degree of stratification based on geographical location, with no requirement for any clustering. This is reflected in the size of design effects, which are the factors by which sampling errors are affected due to the use of a sample design more complex than simple random sampling (Kish, 1965). Therefore census microdata files should provide good coverage of the population and also have smaller design effects than most social survey data. The sample size, which is often equivalent to 1% or 2% of the population, is larger than most social sample surveys.

The size and unclustered sampling design of microdata files means that geographical areas can be identified at a more detailed level than is the case with most sample surveys. This opens up the possibility of including "place" in the analysis through multilevel modelling methods. Using the example of unemployment, area level effects could be modelled by assuming that overall levels of unemployment were greater for some areas than others given the values of other individual level characteristics. But the model can be developed further to allow different effects of the explanatory variables for different areas; and also cross-level effects which summarise the relationship between individual level characteristics and an area level—in this case, a SAR district level—characteristic (Jones and Duncan, 1996; Fieldhouse and Gould, 1998).

In most countries there is a legal requirement to complete a census form. This places a heavy responsibility on the national statistical office to guarantee the confidentiality of the data provided by the public. Whilst a census of population is usually conducted every ten years, or every five years, in response to a statutory requirement, the production of microdata files is discretionary. Their production is usually in response to demand from the user community. The structure and content of microdata files is therefore related to these user needs, the other data products available, and the legislation and policies governing data confidentiality.

The factors that influence the release of census data and microdata in particular vary between countries and also over time. Census offices may change their policy towards data release in response to public opinion or new research evidence on disclosure risk; changes in levels of public expenditure may impact upon the conduct of the census itself as well as the production of output products. For all of these reasons the detailed structure, content, cost and availability of census microdata—that is, the geographical detail, the amount of detail for each variable and the sampling fraction—is not static but is shaped over time by a range of different influences.

Generally census microdata is less readily available in Europe than in North America. However, France, Spain and Italy extract microdata files which are available for research purposes. In Australia, census microdata is released as 1% sample of households based on very large geographical areas. A more detailed account is given in Dale *et al.*, 2000.

3.2 1991 UK census data availability

The 1991 UK census data were used in both of the main examples. Hence, we will now focus on this situation. The availability of data from the 1991 census is summarised in Figure 1 (p. 128).

This figure summarizes the census data availability for the 1991 UK census for local populations, including the approximate date that each dataset was released. Once the census information had been collected and processed, aggregate data were released from the census in the form of Census Area Statistics (CAS) tables. These are a set of about 100 cross-tabulations based on user demand—mainly for local administrative policy use, and mainly based on 100% of persons enumerated. A further set of tables is available, based on a 10% sample. A similar set of data is likely to be available for the 2001 UK census, however these data will be based on a different census geography.

Tables are available at quite fine geographical levels, or scales, down to the ED level. The advantages of the CAS data are that they have quite small area detail, and most are based on all usual residents. Inferences concerning the association between two variables at the individual level can be made if the relevant cross-tabulation is included in the CAS tables. However, in general we cannot make inferences—concerning individual level relationships

AGGREGATE DATA:

Released 1993: CAS tables

A set of about 100 cross-tabulations of census variables based on census user demand.

Tables are available at the following local spatial scales:

- District: Administrative areas for Local Authorities. For example, the population of a city centre: "Manchester district".
- Ward: A small area containing about 5,000 to 10,000 people: between 10 and 20 Enumeration Districts (Eds).
- Enumeration District (ED): A small area, containing about 500 people in 200 households.

Advantages of CAS data:

- 100% Data
- Small area detail

Disadvantages of CAS data:

- Variables have limited detail and only certain cross-tabulations are available.
- This is aggregate data.

MICRODATA:

Released 1993: SAR data

A 2% sample of individual level micro data.

Units for which these data are available

- District: SAR data are available for most single districts, such as "Manchester". For districts with smaller populations (mainly rural districts) SAR data are available for populations of two or more contiguous districts.
- Individuals: SAR data are available for individuals but no details of the small areas (e.g. EDs) in which the live are given.

Advantages of SAR data:
- Individual level data
- Detailed varaibles, and ability to do own crosstabulations.

Disadvantage: no small area information.

1998: Addition of Area classifications to SAR
New units: ED *type* added to 2% SAR.

2000: Proposals for Small Area Microdata (SAM) from 2001 census.
Small area identifiers included for areas of 10,000-15,000, but limited variable detail. Preliminary work carried out using prototype dataset on contract from the Office for National Statistics (ONS). (Tranmer *et al.*, 2002).

Figure 1. Data availability from the 1991 UK census for a local population, with approximate dates of release for each dataset

from the results of analysis of these area level aggregate data—if we do, we risk committing the ecological fallacy (Robinson, 1950).

In 1993, census microdata files were released for the first time in the UK as Samples of Anonymised Records (SARs). Two SARs were released; the first was a 1% sample of households, with coarse geographical detail to maintain confidentially. Only the region of each household can be identified on the 1% SAR. GB comprises 12 regions. Hence the 1% SAR is not available for local populations. The second SAR is a 2% sample of individuals, and this includes geographical detail down to the SAR district level. A SAR district is equivalent to Local Authority District (LAD)—that is, a local administrative area—that contains at least 120,000 people, or a group of several contiguous

LADs with populations smaller than 120,000. There are 278 SAR districts in Great Britain. In urban areas SAR districts are equivalent to single LADs. For more rural parts of the UK, a SAR district is equivalent to two or three contiguous LADs. SAR data have a great deal of research potential in that they are individual data, with reasonably localised geographical detail and cross-tabulations may be specified by the user—these are not restricted to the set of cross-tabulations available on the CAS. A disadvantage of the individual SAR is that, for reasons of confidentiality, we cannot identify the area in which each person lives with any more geographical detail than the SAR district.

The example in Section 4 of his chapter looks at the possibilities for combining the aggregate CAS data with the individual SAR data for a local district of interest, when a multilevel modelling framework that includes small geographic areas such as EDs is assumed. This approach greatly increases the research potential of the census data.

Whilst census microdata can provide greater geographical definition than many surveys, geography is also seen as an important key to identification. Therefore the balance between the research value of greater geographical detail and the confidentiality risk is of great importance. In 2000, proposals were made for Small Area Microdata (SAM) to be released from the 2001 census. This data set would use a larger sampling fraction than used for the SAR and provide even greater geographical detail, including indicators of areas down to populations of about 10,000-15,000 people, but with limited details on the variables, to maintain confidentiality. To assess the feasibility of such a dataset some multilevel modelling has been carried out with a prototype data on contract to researchers at the University of Manchester. The results of this work are reported in Tranmer *et al.* (2002).

3.3 Area classifications

An innovative method of extending the value of geographical definition whilst retaining confidentiality has been adopted for the British SARs. This has involved the addition, in 1998, of an area level classification called "GB profiles" to each individual on the 2% individual level SAR (Dale and Openshaw, 1997). GB Profiles were developed by a team at Leeds University, led by Stan Openshaw. ED level data on approximately 80 census variables were used in a multivariate analysis to classify ED types into 49 categories (prosperous, deprived, etc. See les.man.ac.uk/ccsr/cmu/data/gblabels.html for a full list). Because the area classifications are groupings of similar EDs, the populations of each of the 49 categories are likely to be relatively homogeneous for a range of socio economic characteristics.

An alternative classification of areas, at the ward level, was developed by the Office for National Statistics (ONS) (Wallace *et al.*, 1995; Wallace and Denham, 1996). A ward is a group of typically between 10 and 20 contiguous EDs.

These area classifications provide additional geographical information without revealing the actual ED or ward in which each person or household included in the SAR is located.

These classifications have been added as follows:

- 2% Individual SAR—an "ED type" classification, as defined by GB Profiles has been added to each individual record. Thus we have some information about the type of ED in which individual lives, without knowing the actual ED.
- 1% Household SAR—now includes a definition of ward type as defined by ONS ward classifications. We now know the type of ward in which each household is located, without knowing the actual ward.

Before the addition of the area classification information to the SAR, the lowest level of geography that could be allowed for in an analysis was the district level on the 2% SAR. With the addition of area classification information to the SAR, we can also consider a ED or ward type level. For example, on the 2% SAR, we can now include levels for administrative areas, such as SAR district **and** also include a "ED type" level as defined by the 49 GB profiles.

For example, the individual level SAR for 1991 identifies the city of Manchester but does not allow areas within the city to be identified. However, each individual in the Manchester SAR has been allocated to one of 49 different categories of the ED-level classification, GB Profiles, (Openshaw *et al.*, 1994). Thus residents of Manchester may be analysed in terms of the characteristics of their ED. The value of this in a multilevel modelling framework is that it allows type of ED to be assigned within the identified geographical area. This allows multilevel models to be extended by fitting cross-classified hierarchical multilevel models where individuals (level 1) are cross-classified by SAR areas (geographical contexts) and area classification (residential contexts) both at level 2 (Jones and Duncan, 1996; Goldstein, 1995). These methods have been used to investigate the variation in unemployment between individuals, taking into account not just the local labour market in which they live, but also the type of ED, as identified by the area classification of ED type. This approach is outlined in Section 5. For a more detailed account, see Fieldhouse and Tranmer (2001).

4. SOME PREVIOUS EXAMPLES OF MULTILEVEL MODELLING WITH CENSUS DATA

Fieldhouse and Gould (1998) conducted an investigation into ethnic minority unemployment and local labour market conditions in Great Britain. These authors use SAR data to fit a multilevel model with two levels: the individual level and local labour market area (LLM). The LLMs were derived from the SAR district codes so that the original 278 SAR districts were grouped into 185 LLMs. Fieldhouse and Gould combine aggregate information for each LLM obtained from aggregate census data, with the SAR data in the multilevel analysis. The authors recognise that potentially important variations in ethnic minority unemployment at finer spatial scales, such as EDs cannot be considered because of the nature of the available data. Example 2 in Section 6 of this chapter extends the multilevel models assumed by Fieldhouse and Gould (1998) to include information on population structure at the sub-LLM level, so that ED type is also taken into account. In another multilevel analysis of SAR data, Gould and Fieldhouse (1997) investigated male unemployment by specifying a two level model with an individual level and a SAR area level.

The aggregate UK Census Area Statistics (CAS) have been used to create deprivation indices within local authorities, using linear combinations of various census variables. For example Jarman (1983) proposes an index with eight census variables. The purpose of these indexes is to identify underprivileged areas and to allocate resources within the local authority based on the values of the scores for this index. Several alternative indices have also been suggested (Morris and Carstairs, 1991). These indices, however, do not take into account the multilevel structure of the population. For example, an area may have a high proportion of rented accommodation, non-white ethnic groups and households without cars—all variables which tend to be associated with deprivation—but this does not imply that every person in this area rents their house, is from a non-white ethnic group and from a household without a car. A person experiencing deprivation may not live in an area that is classified as deprived and an area classified as deprived may contain many people who are not deprived. As this example illustrates, it is important to make the distinction between the area level and the individual (person) level. A multilevel approach allows the two levels to be considered simultaneously. Fieldhouse and Tye (1996) carried out a study of deprivation using the SAR. They constructed a person based deprivation index and compare the distribution of "deprived people" with the results of an area level index for the same population. They found some differences in the individual and area level results, suggesting evidence of the ecological fallacy.

Duncan and Moon (1993) considered the use of multilevel models with census data. They explain that when all of the variables are cross-tabulated, as is sometimes the case with the CAS data, it is possible to simply fit a multilevel logistic model to the tabular data. This is a relatively straightforward procedure in statistical packages such as MlwiN (Goldstein *et al.*, 2000). Such an approach is recommended when all of the variables of interest are cross-tabulated. However, cases where all the variables of interest in a study are cross-tabulated at a particular area level are rather limited. They argue that ecological inferences are being undertaken not because individual data are unavailable but because researchers may be interested primarily in the results at higher levels; the *ecologies* themselves are of interest. The results are different at each scale, but this does not mean that only individual correlations are meaningful. We believe that the value of multilevel models is that they enable the clear separation of individual and area effects or relationships.

5. ESTIMATING AND EXPLAINING POPULATION STRUCTURE WITH CENSUS DATA

5.1 A multilevel model for a census district

In this section, we discuss an example that makes use of the available aggregate data, and individual level data from the 2% individual SAR in the multilevel model framework.

Suppose we wish to investigate the structure of a population of interest with respect to a number of socio-economic variables. We can do this by specifying an appropriate multilevel model and then estimating the parameters of this model, by combining the available aggregate area level and individual level data. A statistical framework is needed to reflect the population structure. For a SAR district, a multilevel model with three nested levels is appropriate, where individuals are the level 1 units, EDs are the level 2 units and wards are the level 3 units, as shown in Figure 2.

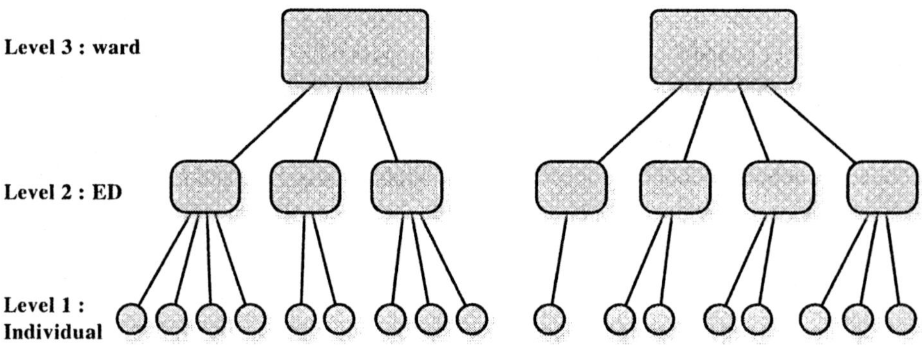

Figure 2. A three level nested population structure

The simplest model for this structure is a three level nested variance components model, which we will call "Model A". The technical details are given below. The model assumes that clustering or "within area homogeneity" may occur at the ED and ward levels, and that the level of homogeneity may differ for single variables and for pairs of variables. For example, two individuals who live in the same ED will tend to be a little more alike, for a range of socio-economic and demographic characteristics, than two individuals, each from a different ED. This phenomenon is called "within ED homogeneity". Because each ward contains several EDs, a similar phenomenon occurs at the ward level, leading to "within ward homogeneity". In this chapter the term "within area homogeneity" will be used to collectively refer to within ED homogeneity and/or within ward homogeneity. Estimation of the parameters in this model allows the extent of within area homogeneity to be assessed.

Although the available census data do not comprise the usual hierarchical data set used in multilevel modelling, it is still possible to fit a multilevel model for the population of a SAR area by combining the available CAS and SAR data for the same population (as shown in Figure 3). The CAS data provide information at the ward and ED levels, and the SAR data provides information at the individual level.

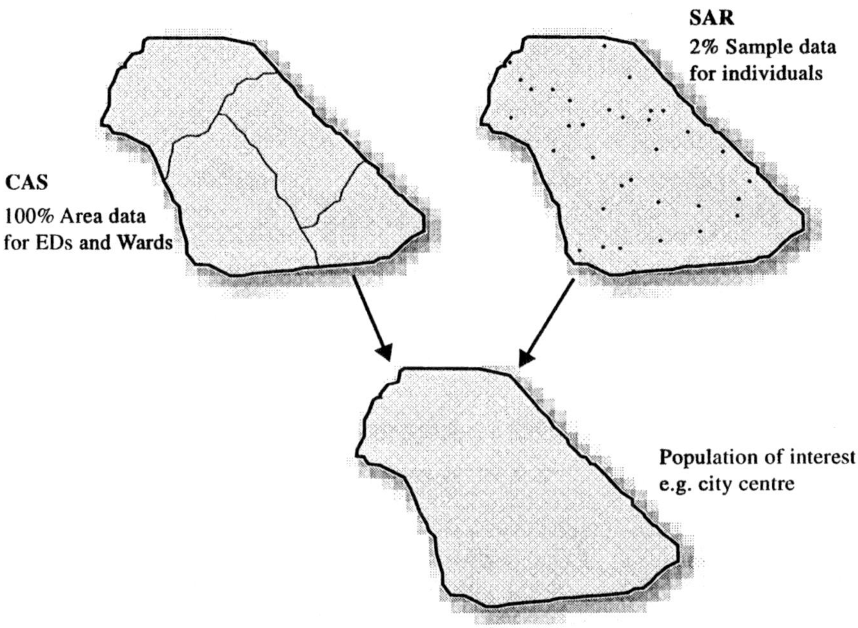

Figure 3. Combining the available data for a population of interest: a schematic map

5.2 The multilevel modelling framework: technical details

We will now give the technical details of the multilevel models used in this example.

Let Y_{ijk} be the vector of values of p census variables being analysed. The subscripts i, j and k indicate individuals (level 1), EDs (level 2) and wards (level 3) respectively. A superscript in brackets indicates the level that each variable, parameter or statistic relates to. The simplest model that may be specified is:

• *Model A*

$$Y_{ijk} = \mu + \varepsilon_k^{(3)} + \varepsilon_{jk}^{(2)} + \varepsilon_{ijk}^{(1)}$$

Where μ is a vector of p population means of the variables of interest and $\varepsilon_k^{(3)}$, $\varepsilon_{jk}^{(2)}$ and $\varepsilon_{ijk}^{(1)}$ are vectors of random variables representing ward, ED and individual effects respectively. It is assumed that the random variables have population means of zero, and covariance matrices $\Lambda^{(h)}$, where $h = 1,2,3$ indicates the level, and the random variables are assumed to be uncorrelated across levels. The model implies:

$$E[Y_{ijk}] = \mu \qquad V[Y_{ijk}] = \Lambda^{(3)} + \Lambda^{(2)} + \Lambda^{(1)} = \Sigma$$

Hence the expected value of the vector of variables of interest, $E[Y_{ijk}]$, is the population mean vector μ, and the overall population individual level covariance matrix of the variables of interest, Σ, comprises three components: $\Lambda^{(3)}$ for the ward level; $\Lambda^{(2)}$ for the ED level; $\Lambda^{(1)}$ for the individual level. The model also implies that:

$$Cov(Y_{ijk}, Y_{i'j'k'}) = \begin{cases} \Lambda^{(3)} + \Lambda^{(2)} \text{ if } k = k',\ j = j' \ \&\ i \neq i' \\ \Lambda^{(3)} \text{ if } k = k',\ j \neq j' \\ 0 \text{ if } k \neq k' \end{cases} \tag{1}$$

Thus, as Equation (1) shows, the covariance matrix reflecting the association between the variables for two individuals in the same ED ($k = k', j = j', i \neq i'$) is $\Lambda^{(3)} + \Lambda^{(2)}$, due to the common ward and ED effect. Two individuals from the same ward but different EDs ($k = k', j \neq j'$) have a covariance matrix, $\Lambda^{(3)}$, due to a common ward effect, and two individuals each from a different ward ($k \neq k'$) have uncorrelated values. This model accounts for the within area homogeneity or clustering that is often observed in social data.

The covariance matrix $\Lambda^{(1)}$ represents the association between variables at the individual level independent of the effects at the higher geographic levels, that is removing the effect of space or location. This can be called the "pure" individual level covariance matrix. Similarly $\Lambda^{(2)}$ represent effects at the ED level removing the individual and ward level effects and is the "pure" ED level covariance matrix, and $\Lambda^{(3)}$ is the "pure" ward level covariance matrix.

For this model, we can obtain expected values of the sample covariance matrices at each level. That is, the covariance matrix we calculate with the available census data at each level of the assumed three level hierarchy. Denote $S^{(h)}$ as the covariance matrix calculated from data at level h. Hence, $S^{(1)}$ is calculated from the individual level SAR and $S^{(2)}$ and $S^{(3)}$ are calculated from the CAS, at the ED and ward level respectively, using the population sizes as weights. The expected values of these covariance matrices are given as follows. Tranmer (1999) showed that a general expression for the expected value of the covariance matrix is:

$$E[S^{(h)}] = c_1^{(h)}\Lambda^{(1)} + c_2^{(h)}\Lambda^{(2)} + c_3^{(h)}\Lambda^{(3)} \qquad h = 1, 2, 3 \tag{2}$$

where $c_k^{(h)}$ are coefficients with approximate coefficients given in Table 1. Exact values are given in Tranmer and Steel (2001). $\bar{N}^{(2)}$ is the average ED-population size, and $\bar{N}^{(3)}$ is the average ward population size. For UK census data, EDs contain approximately $\bar{N}^{(2)} = 500$ people and wards contain an average of 10 EDs, hence is about 5000. Table 2 gives typical values of the coefficients for UK census data.

Table 1. Coefficients for components of variance-covariance matrices

		Approximate values		
Level	h	$c_1^{(h)}$	$c_2^{(h)}$	$c_3^{(h)}$
Individual	1	1	1	1
ED	2	1	$\bar{N}^{(2)}$	$\bar{N}^{(2)}$
Ward	3	1	$\bar{N}^{(2)}$	$\bar{N}^{(3)}$

Table 2. Coefficients for components of variance-covariance matrices (approximate values from UK census data)

		Approximate values		
Level	h	$c_1^{(h)}$	$c_2^{(h)}$	$c_3^{(h)}$
Individual	1	1	1	1
ED	2	1	500	500
Ward	3	1	500	5000

Equation (2) can be used to explain the scale effect. It shows that as we change scale the contribution of the pure covariance matrices change, see Tranmer and Steel (2002) for further discussion of scale effects. If $\Lambda^{(2)} = \Lambda^{(3)} = 0$ there is no population structure and all three covariance matrices have the same expectations.

5.3 Estimating population structure.

Assuming Model A, and given the available CAS and SAR data, we can estimate the parameters of the model using one of two possible approaches: a moments approach and an Iterative Generalised Least Squares (IGLS) approach. The former approach may be implemented in any computer package that handles matrices, such as SAS IML, the latter may be implemented in a multilevel statistical package such as MlwiN (Rasbash *et al.*, 2000). We outline the moments approach below. Full details of both approaches, including a comparative simulation study are given in Tranmer (1999). The two approaches are found to give very similar results.

Estimates of the individual, ED and ward level covariance matrices, $\Lambda^{(1)}$, $\Lambda^{(2)}$, $\Lambda^{(3)}$. may be obtained from Equation (2), using a moments approach. Let $\Lambda_{ab}^{(h)}$ and $S_{ab}^{(h)}$ be the ab^{th} elements of $\Lambda^{(h)}$ and $S^{(h)}$ respectively and set:

$$\Lambda_{ab} = \begin{bmatrix} \Lambda_{ab}^{(1)} \\ \Lambda_{ab}^{(2)} \\ \Lambda_{ab}^{(3)} \end{bmatrix} \qquad \boldsymbol{C} = \begin{bmatrix} c_1^{(1)} & c_2^{(1)} & c_3^{(1)} \\ c_1^{(2)} & c_2^{(2)} & c_3^{(2)} \\ c_1^{(3)} & c_2^{(3)} & c_3^{(3)} \end{bmatrix} \qquad S_{ab} = \begin{bmatrix} S_{ab}^{(1)} \\ S_{ab}^{(2)} \\ S_{ab}^{(3)} \end{bmatrix} \tag{3}$$

Then Equation (2) implies $E[S_{ab}] = \boldsymbol{C}\Lambda_{ab}$, and an unbiased estimate of Λ_{ab} may be obtained from $\hat{\Lambda}_{ab} = \boldsymbol{C}^{-1}S_{ab}$, provided $\boldsymbol{C}$ is non-singular, as is usually the case. Once estimates of $\Lambda^{(2)}$ and $\Lambda^{(3)}$ have been produced, the within area homogeneity can also be estimated, since these components determine the co-variance between individuals within the same ED, or in the same ward but different EDs. An alternative IGLS approach (Goldstein, 1995), making use of multilevel software packages such as MlwiN, is considered by Tranmer and Steel (2001), and this gives results that are similar to those obtained from the moments approach (Tranmer, 1999). An advantage of the IGLS approach is that it provides approximate standard errors for the estimates of variance components. Also, by implementing this approach in MlwiN, it is very easy to make changes to the specified model and to compare the results of several models. However, the moments approach is simple to implement and provides etimates very quickly as it is less computer intensive than the IGLS method.

5.4 Further explaining population structure through grouping variables

We have specified a multilevel model (Model A) which reflects the population structure and can be estimated using the available census data. We can now extend this model to include variables which characterise or "explain" the population structure to some extent.

Steel and Holt (1996) suggested two ways in which within area homogeneity may arise:

- Individuals who live in the same area are exposed to common influences. For example, administrative control, air quality.
- Individuals with similar characteristics tend to live in the same area. For example, people may move into certain areas of the city, or into certain types of housing, according to their income.

The authors refer to the set of variables that characterise these processes, and hence the group structure, as "grouping variables".

Suppose a set of q grouping variables exist which may at least partly characterise the within area homogeneity. Let Z_{ijk} denote the value of these grouping variables for individual i, in ED j, and ward k. Model A may be extended by making the model parameters conditional on these grouping variables. This model is referred to here as Model B, and may be written as follows:

• *Model B*

$$Y_{ijk} = \mu_{.Z} + \beta' Z_{ijk} + \varepsilon_k^{(3)} + \varepsilon_{jk}^{(2)} + \varepsilon_{ijk}^{(1)}$$

$$E[\varepsilon_k^{(3)} | Z] = 0 \qquad Var[\varepsilon_k^{(3)} | Z] = \Lambda_{.Z}^{(3)}$$

$$E[\varepsilon_{jk}^{(2)} | Z] = 0 \qquad Var[\varepsilon_{jk}^{(2)} | Z] = \Lambda_{.Z}^{(2)}$$

$$E[\varepsilon_{ijk}^{(1)} | Z] = 0 \qquad Var[\varepsilon_{ijk}^{(1)} | Z] = \Lambda_{.Z}^{(1)}$$

Now the model parameters are conditional on these grouping variables. The coefficients β relate the variables of interest to the grouping variables. If the grouping variables characterise the population structure well, the estimates of the variance components conditional on the grouping variables will be much smaller than the corresponding unconditional estimates from Model A. Steel and Holt (1996) provide details of a method for the identification of grouping variables, which they call a Canonical Grouping Variable (CGV) analysis. When considering the population structure for local populations, in a two level study with individuals at level 1 and EDs at level 2, Holt *et al.* (1996) found that older age groups and characteristics of housing were possible grouping variables.

Model B may be estimated using either the moments or the IGLS approach, as Tranmer (1999) showed. It enables us to examine how much of the ED or ward effect observed in the variables interest may be due to their association with these grouping variables. To estimate the parameters of the model the values of the grouping variables must be included on the individual and group level data sets, for example on the SAR and CAS.

5.5 Numerical results: estimating population structure using Model A

The population of interest was the SAR district "Reigate and Banstead with Tandridge LAD", which we will refer to as "Reigate" in this discussion. Reigate is a relatively prosperous commuter area, to the south of London. The results are based on five census variables:

— Non White (NONW);
— Employed (EMP);
— Unemployed (UNEM);
— Limiting Long-Term Illness (LLTI);
— Persons living in households without a car (CAR0).

We began by calculating the variances, $S^{(h)}$ at each of the three levels, and the aggregation effects between each pair of levels (see Table 3). The aggregation effects are the ratio of the higher level variance estimate to the lower level variance estimate. For example the ratio of the ward level variance to the individual level variance (Ward: Ind). If this figure is greater than one, it shows that there is some structure to the population, as it implies that there is some within area homogeneity. If the aggregation effects were all approximately one this indicates that there is no within area homogeneity at the different levels of the hierarchy. In these results the aggregation effects are all greater than one, indicating that there are effects in addition to the individual level effects for the five variables. The extent of these effects is different for each of the different variables, as the differences in the aggregation effects indicate.

Table 3. Variances and aggregation effects for five census variables of interest

	Variance at level			*Aggregation effect*		
	Ind.	ED	Ward	Ward: Ind	ED: Ind	Ward: ED
NONW	0.027	0.220	0.696	8.27	26.17	3.14
EMP	0.250	1.581	3.642	6.33	14.58	2.30
UNEM	0.027	0.062	0.148	2.27	5.40	2.39
LLTI	0.080	0.576	1.269	7.24	15.94	2.20
CAR0	0.097	3.186	11.032	32.98	114.20	3.45

Table 4. Estimates of variance components (x1000) for the variables of interest: moments approach

	Variance components		
	$\Lambda_{aa}^{(1)}$ Individual level	$\Lambda_{aa}^{(2)}$ ED level	$\Lambda_{aa}^{(3)}$ Ward level
NONW	26.233	0.275	0.109
EMP	247.338	2.168	0.468
UNEM	27.313	0.050	0.020
LLTI	78.649	0.826	0.157
CAR0	90.612	4.339	1.797

Using the moments approach we next estimated the variance components and these are given in Table 4. The variance component estimates are largest at the individual level, where they are similar to the values of $S^{(1)}$, for each of the five variables, and smallest at the ward level. Because we have considered a vector of variables of interest, we can also obtain covariance components at each of the three levels (these are not shown).

Using the variance component estimates, the associated intra area correlations, shown in Table 5 were calculated For example the

$$\text{intra area correlation for EDs} = \frac{\text{ED level variance component}}{\text{Total variance}}$$

Where: Total variance = individual component + ED level component + Ward level component. Similarly the intra-class correlation for the ward level effects may be calculated using the ward level variance component as the numerator in the above expression. These intra area correlations determine the similarity of

Table 5. Intra area correlations for the variables of interest: moments approach

Variables of interest, y:	*ED level*	*Ward level*
NONW	0.0103	0.0041
EMP	0.0087	0.0019
UNEM	0.0018	0.0007
LLTI	0.0104	0.0020
CAR0	0.0449	0.0186

the values of the variable of interest within areas. The intra-ward correlation is the correlation between values for people in the same ward but different EDs. The correlation between values for people in the same ED is the sum of the ED and ward level intra-area correlations. The higher the value of this measure, the more similarity in the values and hence the more within area homogeneity. We see from these results for all of these variables, the ED level component is greater than the ward level component and that CAR0 has the most within area homogeneity.

The approaches outlined here allow us to look at covariance components as well as variance components, so that the relationship between pairs of census variables may also be considered. Using the moments approach we calculated the "pure correlations" from the estimated covariance component matrices at the different levels, $\Lambda^{(h)}$. For example, the pure correlation between two variables, *a* and *b* at level *h*, is a function of the pure covariance and variance component and the variance components of the variables as follows:

$$\text{pure correlation at level } h = \frac{\Lambda_{ab}^{(h)}}{\sqrt{\Lambda_{aa}^{(h)}\Lambda_{bb}^{(h)}}}$$

The direct correlation at level *h* between the variables *a* and *b* is calculated directly from the sample covariance matrix at level *h*, $\boldsymbol{S}^{(h)}$, i.e.:

$$\text{direct correlation at level } h = \frac{S_{ab}^{(h)}}{\sqrt{S_{aa}^{(h)}S_{bb}^{(h)}}}$$

Pure correlations at the Ward and ED levels are shown below in Table 6, with the corresponding direct correlations in square brackets.

The results in Table 6 indicate that the ward level pure correlations are generally stronger than the corresponding direct correlations. The pure ward correlations estimate the effect at the ward level only, having taken into account

Table 6. Estimates of the pure correlation coefficients at the ED and ward levels, derived from $\Lambda^{(h)}$, with corresponding direct estimates calculated from $\boldsymbol{S}^{(h)}$ shown in square brackets

Ward level	*NONW*	*EMP*	*UNEM*	*LLTI*
EMP	.23 [.19]			
UNEM	.26 [.29]	.30 [.21]		
LLTI	.29 [.16]	−.52 [−.52]	.53 [.39]	
CAR0	.43 [.35]	−.18 [−.23]	.82 [.69]	.83 [.77]
ED Level	*NONW*	*EMP*	*UNEM*	*LLTI*
EMP	.13 [.13]			
UNEM	.14 [.13]	.30 [.21]		
LLTI	−.11 [−.03]	−.59 [−.52]	.27 [.22]	
CAR0	.10 [.18]	−.41 [−.33]	.57 [.47]	.74 [.71]

the effects at the ED and individual levels. As Equation 2 showed, the direct estimate, derived from $S^{(3)}$ is based on a composite of ward, ED and individual components, and even though the most weight is given to the ward level component, the other levels will have some influence on the estimates. Indeed, these effects lead to a reduction in the values of the direct estimates compared with the pure coefficients. Hence $S^{(3)}$ is a biased estimate of the correlations associated with the ward level effects At the ED level a similar pattern arises where the pure correlations are stronger than the corresponding direct values in most cases.

5.6. Explaining population structure: Model B

Having obtained results from the unconditional model (Model A) which allows the nature of the population structure to be investigated, it is of interest to see how we might explain this structure by including grouping variables in the model (Model B). We chose 5 grouping variables:

- — Person is aged 45-59;
- — Person is aged 60 +;
- — Person lives in an owner occupied household;
- — Person lives in a household rented from a Local Authority;
- — Type of house in which the person lives (detached, terraced, etc.).

These variables were chosen as previous analysis has shown the importance of age and housing structure in characterising the differences between areas (Steel *et al.*, 1996).

Table 7. Estimates of variance components from Model A and B

	Model A estimate	Conditional on 5 grouping variables (model B estimate)	$\frac{\text{Model A estimate}}{\text{Model B estimate}} \times 100$
Ward level variance components x 1000:			
NONW	0.1090	0.0620	57
EMP	0.4677	0.1175	25
UNEM	0.0196	0.0015	8
LLTI	0.1569	0.0394	25
CARO	1.7969	0.0687	4
ED Level variance components x 1000:			
NONW	0.2750	0.2554	93
EMP	2.1683	1.1141	51
UNEM	0.0496	0.0190	38
LLTI	0.8262	0.1405	17
CARO	4.3391	0.9050	21
Individual level variance components x 1000:			
NONW	26.2330	26.0045	99
EMP	247.3373	210.9013	85
UNEM	27.3081	27.1492	99
LLTI	78.6492	67.6950	87
CARO	90.6122	72.4700	80

Using the moments approach, we obtained variance components for the conditional model (Model B). These are given in Table 7. We can see that the estimates of components, conditional on the 5 grouping variables listed above are all smaller than the corresponding unconditional estimates obtained from Model A. This is because the grouping variables "explain" much of the within area homogeneity with respect to these variables. If the grouping variables explained all the within area homogeneity the conditional estimates of the variance components would be zero. We can see that while this is not the case, at the ward level, most of the variation is explained for the variable CAR0 (the most homogeneous of the five variables). There is slightly less of a reduction in the components conditional on 5 grouping variables at the ED level compared with the corresponding unconditional components but the grouping variables explain much of the variation at this level in all variables except NONW. At the individual level, there is little change in the conditional versus the unconditional estimates. This suggests that a variable can be effective in reducing area effects even though its explanatory power at the individual level is low.

The intra area correlations shown in Table 8 are conditional on the five grouping variables and are therefore much smaller than those obtained from the unconditional model (Model A—see Table 5). This is because some of the population structure (that is, the within area homogeneity) has been explained by the grouping variables.

Table 8. Intra area correlations conditional on 5 grouping variables

	ED level	*Ward level*
NONW	0.0093	0.0039
EMP	0.0051	0.0010
UNEM	0.0006	0.0003
LLTI	0.0028	0.0009
CAR0	0.0099	0.0129

5.7 Targets of inference

By specifying a statistical model that allows for within area homogeneity, as we have done for Models A and B above, it is possible to clearly state the population parameters to be estimated: that is, the targets of inference. In a population with a group structure (for example, individuals grouped into EDs, which are nested in wards), the targets may be across the groups or within the groups; in these examples the groups are geographical areas. For the across-group approach, interest focuses on the overall population once the group structure has been taken into account. For example, the overall population covariance matrix for individuals, Σ, may be of interest. In other words, for the across group approach the group structure is sometimes regarded as a nuisance. In a within-group approach interest focuses on the estimation of parameters within the groups in the population. For example the relationship of unemployment by sex within each ED or ward may be of interest, having taken the multilevel structure of the population into account. That is, it may be of interest to estimate the covariance for each ED, j, in each ward, k. Skinner, Holt and Smith (1989) provide an excellent discussion of these concepts, using the term "aggregated approach" to describe the across-group approach and "disaggregated approach" to describe the within-group approach.

Whether an across-group approach or within-group approach is taken may depend on the nature of the population. For a population with an institutional group structure, such as pupils in schools, the group structure is well defined and essentially unmodifiable. In these situations the within-group approach may seem more appropriate than an across-group approach. In populations with a geographical structure, the areas into which the population is divided are modifiable. For example, the boundaries of EDs could have been drawn up in many different ways to each contain 500 people 200 households, and hence their definition is essentially arbitrary and therefore modifiable.

For many aspects of social research, interest may focus on the overall individual population covariance matrix, Σ, or parameters that may be derived from this matrix. For example, the overall individual relationship of unemployment by sex may be of interest. In other applications the variance components $\Lambda^{(h)}$, (where h denotes the level) may be of interest as in Example 1. For example, the relationship between the unemployment and the proportion male at the "pure ED" level might be of interest, having taken into account ward and individual level effects. This reflects social processes operating at the ED level.

Functions of the elements of the estimate of $\Lambda^{(2)}$, such as the pure ED level correlation between two census variables may be compared with the corresponding pure ward level correlation derived from the estimate, $\Lambda^{(3)}$; this shows how the relationships between pairs of variables may change at different scales. Under Model (B) the role of grouping variables may be assessed by comparing $\Lambda^{(h)}_{.z}$ with $\Lambda^{(h)}$. This gives insight into variables that characterise population structure at a particular scale.

In multilevel modelling there is usually interest in each of the variance components: $\Lambda^{(1)}$, $\Lambda^{(2)}$ and $\Lambda^{(3)}$, as well as the fixed parameters of the model. In other words, the population structure is, itself, a phenomenon of interest, as opposed to being regarded as a nuisance. Multilevel analysis is usually carried out with a dataset that includes indicators for higher levels of the population. For example, individual level data with ED and ward level indicators would be required for "standard" multilevel modelling. Such data are not available from the census, but we have shown how the available CAS and SAR data can be combined to obtain the estimates of the variance components for multilevel models.

6. INVESTIGATING SMALL AREA VARIATIONS USING THE SAR WITH RECENTLY ADDED AREA CLASSIFICATIONS

There is increasing recognition of the importance of place in social statistics research. Developments in statistical methodology, such as multilevel modelling, have provided methods which allow us to investigate the nature and extent of variation in outcome variables of interest at one or more area levels. Multilevel models allow us to measure the degree of similarity within and between areas rather than treating the population structure as a nuisance factor (Goldstein, 1995). Because multilevel models can simultaneously model both the micro (individual) and the macro (area) level it is possible to assess whether area or place (contextual) differences are important having taken into account the characteristics of individuals or compositional differences (Jones and Duncan, 1995). Thus multilevel models allow the effect of "place" to be analysed net of the "confounding" effect of individual and household characteristics such as age, gender or ethnicity. Generally, if populations are geographically structured and/or contextual factors (such as neighbourhood effects or environmental effects) are influential, it will be possible to observe unexplained variation between higher level units. In turn this variation might be explained by (contextual) variables measured at the higher level (i.e. area characteristics).

However, such an analysis usually requires certain data to be available: in particular, information about the location of each individual unit . We have already explained, in Example 1, that on the SAR data, as originally released in 1993, no area indicator information relating to the EDs or wards in which the individuals live is available for reasons of confidentiality. In 1998, area classifications of ED type were added to the individual SAR. The following two examples draw on work using these data to explore individual and contextual influences on unemployment and deprivation.

6.1 Exploring labour market and neighbourhood variations in male unemployment risk using census microdata

Fieldhouse and Tranmer (2001) used the ED classifications, that were added to the 2% individual level SAR, to investigate variations in unemployment for 18-65 year old males in England and Wales. Previous research indicated that where a person lives can effect their propensity to unemployment (e.g Fieldhouse and Gould, 1997). However, the understanding of these relationships are confounded by the reciprocal nature of the relationship between unemployment, housing and geographical location. This research examined the relative importance of the individual, the type of neighbourhood of residence, and the local labour market in which one lives in explaining variations in unemployment risk. It also examined the role of housing tenure at an individual and contextual level in mediating this relationship. Two competing hypotheses were evaluated. The first was that local concentrations of unemployment are the result of the process of neighbourhood selection. The other suggests there are contextual effects on unemployment risk, which may include access to job opportunities and so-called "concentration effects" (Wilson, 1987). As well as offering insights into the relationship between unemployment and geographical location, this research demonstrates methodological innovations in the analysis of census microdata. In particular it shows how area classifications can be used in conjunction with microdata in a multilevel modelling framework, to get a better understanding of the role of individual and contextual factors in social processes.

In addition to individual or person level differences, two geographic levels (or scales) were considered. The first is an approximation of Travel to Work Areas (TTWAs), based on the SAR geography (see Fieldhouse, 1996), and these may also be regarded as the Local Labour Market (LLM) area. The second is the ED type classification. Since this is based on EDs, which are small areas with 500 people in 200 households, it may be regarded as a classification of small areas or neighbourhoods. Hence, the addition of the area classifications to the 2% SAR allows ED type variations to be investigated. Before the addition of this information, the smallest geographical scale that could be investigated was the SAR area level (there are around 250 SAR areas in England and Wales).

6.1.1 Model specification

Given the available data, Fieldhouse and Tranmer (2001) first considered two, separate, two level models for the data. These simple models allow the extent of within area homogeneity of different socio-economic variables to be assessed at two different geographic scales:

— Individuals in local labour markets;
— Individuals in ED type.

In the second model (B): area classification is used as a level in the multilevel model as opposed to including these classifications as a set of dummy variables. There are 49 area classifications and in theory these could be included in the model as 48 dummy "ED type" variables. However, this model would be difficult to interpret because it would include so many parameters. An alternative approach is to include classification as a level in the model, as long as it is understood that this level is the ED *type*, not the ED level itself. A number of other individual level explanatory variables were included which have shown in other research to influence the risk of unemployment (e.g. Pissarides and Wadsworth, 1992; Nickell, 1980; Fieldhouse, 1996).

6.1.2 The two level model

In this example the response, y_{ij} is a binary (or dichotomous) variable, such as whether or not a person is unemployed. This variable takes the value 1 if yes and 0 otherwise. For a binary response, a simple two level model can be expressed as:

$$y_{ij} = p_{ij} + e_{ij}$$

where

y_{ij} is the unemployment measure of individual i in area j. Where, for the two level model, the area is either the LLM or the ED type,

e_{ij} is the error term for individual i in area j (the level 1 residual),

p_{ij} is the probability of individual i in area j being unemployed.

The logit of p_{ij} can be expressed as a function of the individual level explanatory socio-economic and demographic variables as follows:

$$\text{logit}(p_{ij}) = \log\left(\frac{p_{ij}}{1-p_{ij}}\right) = \beta_0 + \sum_{m=1}^{r} \beta_m x_{mij} + u_j$$

The logit transformation is used to transform a probability, with range 0 to 1 to a variable with range plus to minus infinity, allowing a linear model to be fitted. A set of *r* explanatory variables, x_{mij}, is used to predict the probability of unemployment, p_{ij}, *m* is and index for the explanatory variables of interest $(m=1,2,...r)$.

Because the level one variance is related to the mean in these models, we are primarily interested in the estimates of variance components at higher levels. In the two level models σ_u^2 is a parameter which represents the area level variance component for unemployment. This is the variance of the u_j area level residual terms, i.e:

$$Var(u_j) = \sigma_u^2$$

In these two level models, this area level variance component represents **either**: 1. The extent of variation in unemployment at the LLM level, **or**: 2. The extent of variation in unemployment for ED types

When these models were fitted characteristics of housing were found to be the most homogeneous at each of the two geographic scales and generally, all socio-economic variables considered in this study were more homogeneous at the ED type level than at the LLM level. This is not surprising since the ED type level includes groups of small areas—EDs—with similar characteristics, whereas LLMs are relatively large. Full results from these two level models are given in Fieldhouse and Tranmer (2001).

6.1.3 Three level models

We have illustrated the two level models that may be assumed with the available data. Of course, it is better to consider a multilevel model that takes into account both the LLM level and the ED type level simultaneously. In terms of the way in which the area information is modelled, two different approaches can be taken: a nested approach and a cross-classified approach. There are important substantive differences in the approaches. In Figure 4 (p. 146), the two approaches are contrasted for a schematic map of three LLMs.

6.1.4 The nested approach

In the nested approach we assume that there is a hierarchy of ED types within each LLM. Or, in other words, that each ED type can be thought of as unique to each LLM. In Figure 4, the study population comprises three LLM, containing persons A-H. The smaller regions within the LLMs (with dotted boundaries) depict particular ED types. For example, these might be, in some sense, "prosperous" EDs. A, B and C are seen as having something in common as they are from the same type of ED in LLM 2, and these are regarded as being independent of F and J, as they are in LLM 3, a different LLM, even though A, B, C, F and J are all from the same, prosperous, type of ED. Despite some loss of information (i.e. that ED types are common across TTWAs) this approach is preferred because it has the advantage that neighbourhoods are treated as being at a lower level (reflecting the fact that this level, the neighbourhood type level is based on classifications of small areas—EDs). When this model is specified, the estimation procedure first estimates the variance at level three (Travel to Work Area) before estimating the variation between neighbourhoods. This model is therefore more suitable to represent the situation in which the characteristics of neighbourhoods are, to a large extent, a product of the type of local economy in which they are based. In other words these models acknowledge that each Travel to Work Area is not made up of a random selection of ED types.

6.1.5 The cross-classified approach

Referring again to Figure 4, we will now describe the cross-classified approach. In this approach, ED types are not assumed to be unique to each LLM as was assumed in the nested approach. Whereas, for the nested model we assume

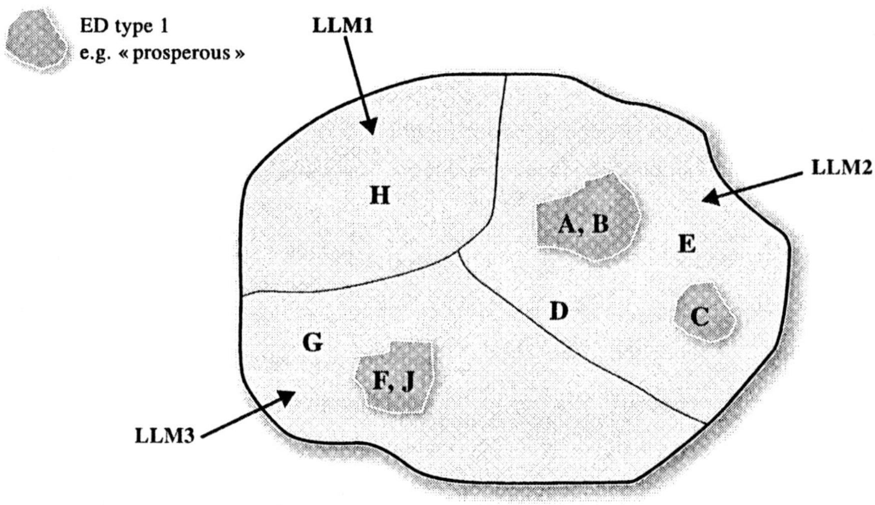

Nested Model:

ED type level A, B, C alike, but independent of F, J
LLM level: A, B, C, D, E alike
F, G, J alike.

cross-classified model:

ED type level A, B, C, F, J alike
LLM level: A, B, C, D, E alike
F, G, J alike.

But! A, B, C alike in 2 ways: LLM **and** ED type
F, J alike in 2 ways: LLM **and** ED type

Figure 4. A pictorial comparison of nested and cross-classified models

that prosperous EDs in LLM 2 are different from the prosperous EDs in LLM 3, in the cross-classified approach, A B and C are assumed to have something in common with F and J because they are all from the same ED type, despite being from different LLMs. The results of the cross-classified model of unemployment are not reported here as the nested model was preferred for reasons given above. Note also a technical difference: the cross-classified model is much more computer intensive than the nested approach. This approach is preferred where we do not have any *a priori* reason for prioritising the level, for example in the analysis of variation in deprivation, where we are interested simply in the nature of variation rather than a causal model (see below).

6.1.6 The three level nested model: technical details

Nested models can be specified where each ED type is treated as unique within each LLM. The three level nested model is specified as follows:

$$y_{ijk} = p_{ijk} + e_{ijk}$$

$$\mathrm{logit}(p_{ijk}) = \beta_0 + \sum_{m=1}^{r} \beta_m x_{mijk} + u_k + v_{jk}$$

The subscript: *i* represents person, *j* represents the ED type and *k* represents the LLM.

x_{mijk} is a set of *r* explanatory variables ($m = 1 \ldots r$), u_k is the LLM level error term, and v_{jk} is the ED type level within LLM term.

Because these models assume that the response is binomial, the level one variance is a function of the mean. The LLM level variance component is denoted by:

$$Var(u_k) = \sigma_u^2$$

and

$$Var(v_{jk}) = \sigma_v^2$$

is the level 2 variance component and represents the amount of variance at the level of the ED (ED type) within the LLM. However, because the models give precedent to the higher level, this represents the residual variance, not explained at the level of the LLM.

6.1.7 Empirical results

- *Fixed effects*

Individual level housing (whether an individual rents their house) and ED type level housing (the percentage of rented housing in each ED type), country of birth, ethnic group, family type, age and qualifications were all significantly associated with unemployment. In particular, higher qualifications, and being in a couple with dependent children were associated most strongly with lower probability of unemployment whereas most non-white ethnic groups, individual and ED level renting were associated most strongly with a higher probability of unemployment. This is consistent with other research.

• *Random effects*
Using a Taylor expansion method (Goldstein *et al.*, 2000) we were able to estimate the extent of variation at each of the three levels, including level 1, for each model we assumed the overall mean value of unemployment, p_{ij}, was around 12%. The results are shown in Table 9.

*Table 9. Estimated variance components and % share of variance for the nested model, assuming p_{ij} = 0.12 (12%)**

	LLM	*ED type*	*Indiv.*	*Total*	*% LLM*	*% ED tp*	*% Indiv.*
Model 1	0.001	0.006	0.105	0.111	0.9	5.0	94.1
Model 2	0.001	0.003	0.105	0.109	0.9	2.7	96.4
Model 3	0.001	0.001	0.105	0.107	0.9	0.9	98.2
Model 4	0.001	0.0005	0.105	0.106	0.9	0.5	98.6
* Results reproduced from Fieldhouse and Tranmer (2001).							

Looking at these results, it is clear that most of the variation in unemployment is at the individual level. However, at the higher levels the share of the variation is much greater at the ED type level than the LLM level for the null model (Model 1). For the model which includes all individual level explanatory variables except renting (Model 2) there is still a greater share of the variation at the ED type level. When tenure (renting) is added to the list of individual level variables (Model 3), the extent of variation at the ED type level reduces so that there is very little higher level variation and this is evenly split between the ED type and LLM levels. This demonstrates the role of housing characteristics in explaining the within area homogeneity at the ED type level; Tranmer and Steel (1998) also found housing to be an important grouping variable in three local census areas in England. When the housing profile (i.e. % rented housing at the ED type level) is added in to the model (Model 4), the higher level variation reduces still further, and two thirds of the residual variation is now at the LLM level as the combination of housing variables at level 1 (individual) and level 2 (ED type) has explained the within area homogeneity at the ED type level

The results of these analyses have provided some support for both hypotheses set out above, namely that spatial concentrations of unemployment are a result of both neighbourhood selection processes and neighbourhood contextual (or concentration) effects. However with respect to the latter hypothesis, there was little evidence of residual "spatial" effects at the level of the neighbourhood. The results suggests that neighbourhood effects are smaller than they first appear, and these are largely due to residualisation of the most vulnerable in particular housing types which are geographically clustered.

6.2 People, places, and deprivation: a multilevel approach to a multilevel problem.

Fieldhouse and Tye (1996) have pointed out that the "deprived" do not necessarily live in "deprived" areas (see also Sloggett and Joshi, 1998). Consequently, targeting resources on the basis of area need is unlikely to serve well those needy individuals who live in wealthier areas. Within the UK there has been very limited analysis of the relationship between area level and individual or household measures of deprivation. Fieldhouse and Tye used 1991 UK census data, in the form of the 2% Sample of Anonymised Records (SAR), to show that the rank ordering of local authority districts changes depending upon whether area or individual level measures are used. Furthermore, although many deprived people were shown to live outside of deprived areas, this finding was, in part, a product of the scale of analysis (the district). However, Fieldhouse and Tye (1996) concluded: "The geographical areas used in this analysis are large local authority areas and were always very unlikely to identify homogeneous pockets of deprivation". The addition of the area classification information allows us to overcome this problem.

A multilevel approach can be used to extend the work on deprivation of Fieldhouse and Tye (1996). Because the data are available to allow deprivation to be considered in a multilevel modelling framework, the ecological fallacy may be avoided since deprivation at both the area level and the individual level are considered in the same model. To some extent, such an analysis is possible using the SAR with the area classifications, using the approach as outlined above, with a measure of deprivation as the dependent variable, as opposed to unemployment. In this research we focus on the population of the North West, and adopt a similar strategy to Fieldhouse and Tye (1996) in defining deprivation based on eight key census variables. We concentrate on the North West of England as the models are complex and it is important to understand the local context in order to interpret the results. By using a cross-classified multilevel model, we can identify the relative importance of the 29 SAR areas (23 of which are single districts, the remainder amalgamations of smaller districts) in the North West and 46 types of ED in this dataset in identifying variations in deprivation, and determine how demographic characteristics such as sex, ethnic group and family structure are associated with deprivation.

6.2.1 The cross-classified model

It is argued that the cross-classified model was most appropriate for the deprivation research, as it assumes that people in a particular type of neighbourhood in one district have something in common with people who live in the same type of neighbourhood in another district. For example, a person living in Salford and a person living in Manchester may have something in common if they both live in an neighbourhood type as classified by GB profile 5, which is labelled as "Asian, high unemployment, overcrowded, terraced housing".

The individual part of the three level cross-classified model is written as follows:

$$y_{i(j,k)} = p_{i(j,k)} + e_{i(j,k)}$$

where

$$\text{logit}(p_{i(j,k)}) = \beta_0 + \sum_{m=1}^{r} \beta_m x_{mi(j,k)} + u_j + v_k$$

Define the indices as follows k = SAR area, j = ED type, and i = person. The brackets around the j and k subscripts indicate that these two levels are both regarded as "higher level units", without an assumed hierarchy. In other words, the units indexed by j and k may overlap.

In the cross-classified model variance attributable to ED type is given by:

$$cov(p_{i(j,k)}, p_{i(j,k')}) = \sigma_u^2$$

e.g. this would be the variance component for persons A and F in Figure 4.

The variance attributable to SAR areas is given by:

$$cov(p_{i(j,k)}, p_{i(j',k)}) = \sigma_v^2$$

e.g. this would be the variance component for persons A and D.

For two people from the same ED type **and** the same LLM the level 2 covariance is:

$$cov(p_{i(j,k)}, p_{i(j,k)}) = \sigma_v^2 + \sigma_u^2$$

e.g. this would be the variance component for persons A and C in Figure 4 (above).

6.2.2 Empirical Results

The results from the two models are presented in Table 10: a simple variance components model (Model 1), and a model that also includes demographic characteristics (age, born in UK, sex, family type, ethnic group) as fixed effects variables (Model 2). These two models allow us to assess to extent of variations in deprivation for districts and neighbourhoods in the north west, and to investigate the way in which demographic characteristics are associated with these variations. The results are based on an average deprivation level of 8% (i.e. $p = 0.08$) and these are calculated using the Taylor expansion method discussed in Goldstein *et al.* (2000).

This research suggests a high level of neighbourhood level variation in deprivation, compared with that at the district level. This is to be expected as small areas are much more homogenous than large districts. However even

Table 10. Variance components for Deprivation in the North West (cross-classified model, assuming a deprivation level of 8%)

%	District	ED type	Indiv.	Total	District %	ED type %	Indiv. %
Model 1	0.001	0.006	0.105	0.111	0.07	5.69	94.24
Model 2	0.001	0.003	0.105	0.109	0.09	4.31	95.60

having allowed for variations at the district and neighbourhood levels, by adding demographic information as explanatory variables, most variation still occurs at the individual level. In particular the fixed part of the model shows that ethnic minorities and young people are the most likely to be deprived. However, although the demographics explain some of the neighbourhood variation, there is still considerable neighbourhood level variation having allowed for these demographic variables. This suggest area based targeting policies do have some value. This approach may also have potential for identifying specific deprived areas at the sub district level, by looking at the ED type level residuals of the multilevel model.

7. FURTHER TOPICS

In the discussion of the two main examples, we have shown how multilevel models can be used with census data to conduct analyses that reveal important features of the social structure of geographical areas. Other issues also arise in the multilevel analysis of census data.

7.1 Missing out a level

In analysing census data we might omit one of the levels in the analysis —either by not having the data available at a particular level, or by mis-specifying the model. Tranmer and Steel (2001) consider the implications of using the general approach outlined in Section 5 when we incorrectly omit the ED, ward or individual level from the analysis. The results suggested that variations in the outcome of interest that occur at a level higher than those assumed in the model, will be reflected in the estimated components for the highest level that *is* included in the model. If the individual level is ignored it will affect the estimates for the lowest level included in the analysis. The effects of an ignored level that lies between two levels included in the model are redistributed between these two levels.

In practice not all the levels that may potentially be important in the population will be included in an analysis. These results derived by Tranmer and Steel (2001) show that the effects estimated at a particular level may include contributions from other levels. This result needs to be taken into account in carrying out and interpreting an analysis of the effects at different levels. For example, Tranmer and Steel (1998) assumed a two level model for a local census population, with an individual and an ED level. The estimates of these two components may be affected by the ignored household level, that exists between the individual and ED levels. Furthermore, any effects for the ignored ward level, that is the level *above* the ED, may influence the estimates of the ED level components.

7.2 Investigating the zoning issue using cross-classified multilevel models.

Openshaw (1984) Used the term "Modifiable Areal Unit Problem (MAUP)" to describe differences in results obtained from statistical analysis for different spatial units. He suggested that the MAUP has two components: Scale and Zoning. Scale effects occur when the results of the same statistical measure, such as a correlation or regression coefficient, give different results at different levels, or scales, of analysis. In practice, this is usually the case. For example, the correlation between two census variables calculated at the ED level will be different from the correlation at the ward level. In Section 5 we showed how we can investigate scale effects by assuming a three level nested multilevel model, and we described a method of estimating the parameters of this model by combining the available aggregate and individual level census data.

The other component of the MAUP is the zoning effect, where two different definitions of areas of the same target population give two different results in statistical analysis. For example if we were to take a population of interest and carry out an analysis at the ED level (areas of target population size 500) and compare this with results for an analysis based on an alternative definition of EDs (see Figure 5) also with target population size 500, the results would, in general, be different. Such a phenomenon raises important issues relating to the analysis of units with essentially arbitrary boundaries, as is almost always the case with geographical areas. Such issues can be explored by a cross-classified multilevel model as described Section 5 above. If two different area schemes, such as EDs (scheme A in Figure 5) and pseudo EDs (scheme B) were defined for a population of interest, it would be possible, with the appropriate data, to investigate zoning effects for particular variables of interest by modelling the two schemes as a cross-classification and comparing the values of the variance components at each level, for variables of interest.

7.3 Missing Identifier Models

In the second example, discussed in Section 6, we used area classification codes as an identifier of ED type, allowing the ED type level to be taken into account in a multilevel analysis. It is also of interest to consider how we might estimate the variation at ED level as opposed to the ED *type* level, given the available data. Goldstein (2001) suggested a method which may be applied to allow the estimation of the ED level variance from the available data even though these only give information on the ED type. This stems from work on missing identifier models (Hill and Goldstein 1998), and is based on specifying an appropriate weight structure to MlwiN. For the current example, we would need to know, or to estimate for our population of interest, how many EDs are in each of the 49 classifications. We then use this information to

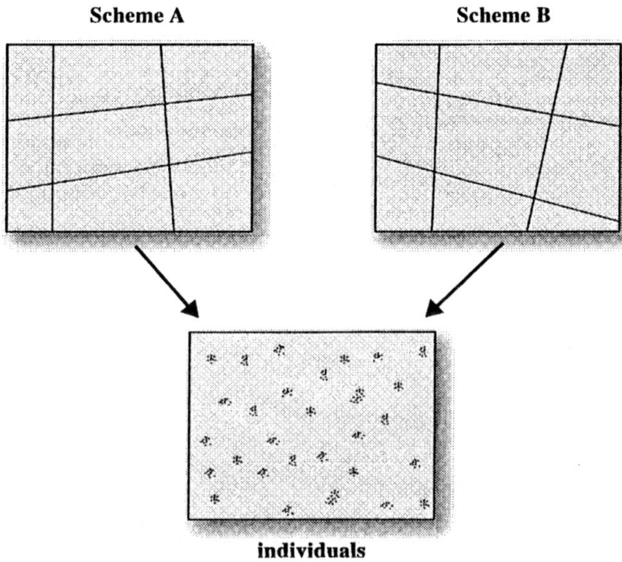

Figure 5. Two alternative ways of dividing a population of interest into nine small areas

specify the appropriate weight structure and hence to estimate the ED level variance component. Although on the SAR we do not know which EDs are in which area classification—these are the missing identifiers—we do know that EDs typically have a population of 500 and therefore on the 2% SAR we can assume that there will be 10 people per ED. Therefore if we divide each ED type classification by 10 we can estimate how many EDs are contained in each category and hence we know the approximate weights to use in the estimation procedure.

8. CONCLUSION

Through the two examples in Sections 5 and 6 , we have shown how the multilevel modelling framework may be used to estimate and explain population structure given the available census data. In Section 5 we have demonstrated the way in which area level aggregate data based on all persons enumerated may be combined with a sample of individual level data in order to fit a multilevel model. Such a model may be fitted even though the data are not of standard form for multilevel modelling. Since this model recognises that the population has structure we can make inferences about this structure for a range of socio economic variables through the parameter estimates. Furthermore, we can investigate the relationship between pairs of socio-economic variables at different levels of the population structure; measures such as the pure correlation allow us to assess the strength of the association between variables at a particular level of the population structure having removed the effects from other levels. The methods described in Section 5 can be easily implemented in standard statistical software such as SAS and multilevel modelling software such as MlwiN.

In Section 6 we considered the role of area classifications and the way in which this information may be used in a multilevel model. We compared the nested and cross-classified approaches, theoretically and substantively, for an example where the outcome of interest was male unemployment. We explained how the ED type information provided by the area classification could be used in the multilevel model. The fact that the area classification were added to the census data fairly recently demonstrates the desire amongst census data users for greater geographical detail, to allow population structure to be explored.

In general, we have explained the role of multilevel modelling in census data analysis, based on our work with UK census data, as an illustration of the way in which multilevel models may be used in the field of social statistics. It is clear that multilevel models are invaluable for the analysis of social data, but we must consider the way in which these may be estimated, given the available data. In many circumstances, it is necessary to combine data from several sources, and a different levels, in order to fit a model for a population of interest. However, in some cases data are not available at certain levels, and the implications for this are discussed in Tranmer and Steel (2001). When dealing with geographical areas as higher level units, it is important to bear in mind that these areas have modifiable boundaries. In the main examples, it was possible to assess the effects of scale through the multilevel model parameter estimates. The zoning issue, that is the modifiability of areas, must also be taken into account and this is the subject of on-going research by the authors.

ACKNOWLEDGEMENTS

The authors would like to thank Angela Dale and several other colleagues at CCSR for their useful comments on this research.

The 1991 SARs are provided through the Census Microdata Unit, at the Cathie Marsh Centre for Census and Survey Research (University of Manchester), with the support of the ESRC/JISC/DENI. All tables containing Census data, and the results of analysis, are reproduced with the permission of the Controller of Her Majesty's Stationery Office (Crown Copyright).

REFERENCES

Aitkin, M., & Longford, N. (1986). Statistical modelling issues in school effectiveness studies (with discussion). *Journal of the Royal Statistical Society (A), 149*, 1-43.

Dale, A., Fieldhouse, E. A., & Holdsworth, C. (2000). *Analysing census microdata*. London: Edward Arnold.

Dale, A., & Openshaw, S. (1997). *Adding area-based classifications to the samples of anonymised records (SAR)*. From http://les.man.ac.uk/ccsr/ccsrnew/areaclas.htm and SARs newsletter No 12. Manchester: CCSR: Manchester University.

Duncan, J., & Moon, G. (1993). *People and places: the multilevel model as a general framework for analysing census data*. Working paper. Portsmouth: Department of Geography.

Fieldhouse, E. A. (1996). Putting unemployment in its place: using Samples of Anonymised Records to explore the risk of unemployment in Great Britain in 1991. *Regional Studies, 30*, 119-134.

Fieldhouse, E. A.; Gould, M. I. (1998). Ethnic Minority Unemployment and Local Labour Market Conditions in Great Britain. *Environment and Planning (A), 30*, 833-853.

Fieldhouse, E. A., & Tranmer, M. (2001). Concentration Effects, Spatial Mismatch, or Neighbourhood Selection? Exploring Labour Market and Neighbourhood Variations in Male Unemployment Risk Using Census Microdata from Great Britain. *Geographical Analysis, 33*, 353-359.

Fieldhouse, E. A.., & Tye R. (1996). Deprived people or deprived places? Exploring the ecological fallacy in studies of deprivation with the samples of anonymised records. *Environment and Planning (A), 28*, 237-259.

Fotheringham, S., & Wong, D. W. S. (1991). The Modifiable Areal Unit Problem in Multivariate Statistical Analysis. *Environment and Planning (A), 23*, 1025-1044.

Goldstein, H. (1995*). Multilevel Statistical Models.* London: Edward Arnold.

Goldstein, H. (2001). *Modelling multilevel census data with aggregation of unit identifiers*. Personal Communication.

Goldstein, H., Browne, W. J., & Rasbash, J. (2000). *Extensions of the Intra-unit correlation coefficient to complex generalised linear multilevel models*. London: Multilevel models project.

Gould, M. I., & Fieldhouse, E. A. (1997). Using the 1991 Census SAR in a multilevel model of male unemployment. *Environment and Planning (A), 23*, 1025-1044.

Hill, P. W., & Goldstein, H. (1998). Multilevel modelling of educational data with cross-classification and missing identification of units. *Journal of Educational and Behavioural statistics, 23,* 117-128.

Holt, D., Steel, D., Tranmer, M. & Wrigley, N. (1996). Aggregation and ecological effects in geographically based data. *Geographical Analysis, 28*, 244-262.

Holt, D., Steel, D., and Tranmer, M. (1996). Area Homogeneity and the Modifiable Areal Unit Problem. *Geographical Systems, 3*, 181-200.

Jarman, B. (1983). Identification of underprivileged areas. *British Medical Journal, 286*, 1705-1709.

Jones, K., & Duncan, C. (1996). People and places: the multilevel model as a general framework for the quantitative analysis of geographical data. In P. Longley and M. Batty (Eds.), *Spatial analysis: modelling in a GIS environment* (pp. 79-104). Cambridge: GeoInformation International.

Kish, L. (1965). *Survey Sampling*. New York: John Wiley and Sons.

Longford, N. (1987). A fast scoring algorithm for maximum likelihood estimation in unbalanced mixed models with nested random effects. *Biometrika, 74*, 817-27.

Moellering, H., & Tobler, W. (1972). Geographical variances. *Geographical Analysis, 4*, 34-50.

Morris, R., & Carstairs, V. (1991). Which deprivation? A comparison of selected deprivation indexes. *Journal of Public Health and Medicine*, 13, 318-326.

Nickell, S (1980). A Picture of Male Unemployment. *Economic Journal, 90*, 776-794

Office for National Statistics (2001). *A guide to the one number census: final version*. Titchfield: Office for National Statistics.

OPCS (1994). Undercoverage in Great Britain. *1991 Census User Guide 58*. London: HMSO.

Openshaw, S. (1984). Ecological Fallacies and the analysis of areal census data. *Environment and Planning, (A) 16*, 17-31.

Openshaw, S., Blake, M., & Wymer, C. (1994). *Using neocomputing methods to classify Britain's residential areas*. Working paper 94/17. Leeds: School of Geography.

Pissarides, C., & Wadsworth, J. (1992). Unemployment Risks. In McLaughlin (Ed.), *Understanding Unemployment. New Perspectives on Active LabourMarket Policies.*

Rasbash, J., Browne, W., Goldstein, H., Yang, M., Plewis, I., Healy M., Woodhouse, G., Draper, D., Langford, I., & Lewis, T. (2000). *A user's guide to MlwiN.* Multilevel models project. London: Institute of Education.

Robinson, W.-S. (1950). Ecological Correlations and the behaviour of individuals. *American Sociological Review, 15*, 351-357.

Skinner, C., Holt, D., & Smith T. (1989). *Analysis of Complex Surveys.* Chichester: Wiley.

Sloggett, A., & Joshi, H. (1998). Indicators of deprivation in people and places: longitudinal perspectives. *Environment and planning (A), 30*, 1055-1076

Steel, D.G., & Holt, D. (1996). Analysing and Adjusting Aggregation effects: the ecological fallacy revisited. *International Statistical Review, 64*, 39-60.

Steel, D. G., Holt, D., & Tranmer, M. (1996). Making Unit Level Inferences from Aggregated Data. *Survey Methodology, 22*, 3-15.

Tranmer, M. (1999). *Using census data to investigate the multilevel structure of local populations.* Unpublished PhD thesis. Department of Social Statistics, University of Southampton.

Tranmer, M., & Steel, D. G. (1998). Using census data to investigate the causes of the ecological fallacy. *Environment and Planning (A), 30*, 817-831.

Tranmer, M., & Steel, D. G. (2001). Ignoring a level in a multilevel model: evidence from UK census data. *Environment and Planning (A), 33*, 941-948.

Tranmer, M., & Steel, D. G. (2001). Using local census data to investigate scale effects. In N.J Tate and P.M. Atkinson (Eds.), *Modelling Scale in Geographical Information Science* (pp. 105-122). Chichester: John Wiley.

Tranmer, M., Steel, D. G., Martin, D., Gardner, C., Fieldhouse, E., Eliot, M., Dale, A., & Brown, M. (2003). Microdata for Small Areas. To appear in the *Journal of the Royal Statistical Society (A).*

Wallace, M., Charlton, J., & Denham, C. (1995). The new OPCS area classification. *Population Trends 79*, 15-30.

Wallace, M., & Denham C. (1996). *The ONS classification of wards.* SMPS 60. London HMSO.

Wilson, W. J. (1987). *The Truly Disadvantaged.* Chicago: University of Chicago Press.

Bernard WALLISER

Chapter 5

ORGANIZATIONAL LEVELS AND TIME SCALES IN ECONOMICS

Opening. Since its inception—traditionally identified with Adam Smith's The Wealth of Nations (1776)—economics has gradually detached itself from the other social sciences and rapidly gained autonomy. Its field has been defined by the quantitative relationships between the individuals in a society arising from the production, exchange, and consumption of goods and services. Today, it is one of the disciplines closest to the physical or biological sciences, having developed highly sophisticated objective methods to describe, explain, and analyse the phenomena it studies. Of course, it is out of the question here to attempt even a concise summary of the history of economics; rather, this chapter aims to show the originality of its approach, relative to the other social sciences, and to identify the concepts of temporality and socio-economic space that it applies to different levels. It is important, therefore, to outline the theoretical foundations of the arguments developed in the following chapter.

One of the original features of economics, as Bernard Walliser shows us, lies in the theoretical models that it uses as its starting points. The models rely not only on variables that can be observed from sources such as the National Accounting System, but also on non-observable variables, such as the beliefs and preferences of economic players, or the satisfaction of the needs of merchandise traders. Economists can thus validate the models by empirical means. That is not the approach customarily adopted by other social sciences such as epidemiology, demography or education: they begin with observable, measurable variables (percentages of patients, number of births, or individual grades in a classroom test), which they integrate into a broader theoretical framework. Only the models combining economics with these sciences can incorporate non-observable variables from the outset: in demography, for example, we saw how fertility-transition models were reworked by economists and could incorporate non-observable variables such as individual preferences—for example, the choice between child-raising and other forms of consumption (Becker, 1960). The perspective adopted in economics paves the way for formal models, which enable us to "identify the sufficient if not necessary conditions for the emergence of a phenomenon, and to gradually define its field of logical validity" (Walliser, 2001, p. 129). Empirical facts can then confirm or invalidate the models' robustness.

The second important point is to define the aggregation levels at which economic objectivation will operate. Again, we are not dealing with levels located in a geographic space, as in other social sciences, but with subtler levels whose analysis came to be seen as essential in the course of the development of economics. For the founders of "abstract" economics—Jevons, Menger, Walras, Pareto, ...—the dynamics of an elementary economic situation are located at the level of the individual subject. By assuming that individuals seek maximum satisfaction for a minimum effort or inconvenience, these economists founded their science on a postulate of agent rationality. But this theory, which is essentially a theory of the consumer, was to prove incomplete when examining larger institutions or communities, such as a market where firms compete. When we move to the level of these macrostructures, we need to formulate the issues in different terms, as aggregation generates a new structure that differs altogether from the sum of its parts because it incorporates entirely new interactions between them. Bernard Walliser takes a detailed look here at how the problems due to different types of aggregation are generated, the information lost in this aggregation, the new properties it creates, and, lastly, how microstructures can be inserted into macrostructures.

Third, we must have an accurate view of the way in which time or, more precisely, different time scales are taken into account in economic analysis. Time has long been absent from economic theory, whose practitioners focused exclusively on the final state of equilibrium without concerning themselves with the path followed or the time taken to reach the end-point. Bernard Walliser describes the new temporal approaches in economics, both in the ambitious form of a search for an explanation of long-term movements, and in the more modest form of a description of short-term changes. This dynamic approach enables economists to make allowance for different

D. Courgeau (ed.) Methodology and Epistemology of Multilevel Analysis, 157-173.

response speeds that characterise economic mechanisms, and to achieve coexistence between linked sub-systems possessing distinct dynamics.

The analysis is performed here using two contrasting theories. First, the classical theory of trade rests on the notion of equilibrium realised by prices between producers'offers and consumers' demand in markets that can be competitive. It can, in some cases, lead to multiple equilibria, with no possibility of choosing between them. The second theory is game theory, which is situated at a more general level. It holds that a player's behaviour will be the best response to the behaviour of the other players, players being producers and consumers who fix quantities or prices. The outcome is an equilibrium between players, known as a Nash equilibrium: it does not introduce any overall property of the socio-economic system, but depends solely on the players' behaviour; as in the previous case, it can be a multiple equilibrium. To offset the intrinsic limitations in this type of equilibrium, we can introduce dynamic processes involving successive interactions between players. This makes it possible, for example, to solve the problem of multiple equilibria (Walliser, 2001).

Lastly, the article examines the attitude of economics toward methodological holism and individualism. It shows that, despite the modest role of holism in economic research, we cannot regard economics as wholly informed by methodological individualism: economics uses collective characteristics, such as prices, and economic equilibria are seldom reached by purely individual means. The author therefore outlines a more nuanced scenario, where weaker forms of holism and individualism meet, and where interactions between the two approaches can play a role.

D. C.

1. INTRODUCTION

In economic theory, two main **organizational levels** are abstractly defined by specific entities (and the outputs they produce):

— at individual level, several basic agents take some actions in a rational way, under the influence of the states taken by a physical environment called "nature" and of the signals taken by a social environment symbolised by "institutions" of several kinds;

— at collective level, agents' actions, nature's states and institutions' signals interfere to give rise to global phenomena of several types: distributional (distribution of agents' actions), relational (network between basic agents) and emergental (original collective entities).

Agents are individuals like consumers or already social groups like firms; institutions (assumed to co-ordinate the agents) are physical like markets or conceptual like money.

In economic theory, two main **time scales** are defined as concern the links between variables (each variable being attributed to some entity):

— at short-term (within a period), some present conjonctural variables (for instance present prices) adjust to each other, given the past conjonctural variables (past prices) as well as past structural variables (past equipments) considered provisionally as fixed;

— at long-term (between two periods), the present structural variables (for instance present equipments) adjust themselves to the preceedingly adjusted conjonctural variables (present prices) as well as to the past structural variables (past equipments).

Moreover, the former objective time scales may be simulated by two corresponding subjective time scales when agents are able to expect the future path of the system.

The organizational levels and the time scales are independent in principle, since the individual variables can be classified in short-term and long-term ones and the same is true for the collective variables. However, in practice, one observes a fuzzy relationship between the two taxonomies of variables, since the individual variables adjust rather at short-term while the collective variables react rather at long-term. The paper aims at making such a relationship more precise through the various equilibrium notions usually considered in two main economic fields. *Exchange theory* is devoted to the confrontation on (competitive) markets of purely reactive and specialised agents, i.e. producers and consumers; *game theory* is devoted, at a higher level of generality, to strategic interactions between undifferentiated players without mediation of institutions.

In a first part, the paper describes four steps in the history of economic thought as concerns the interweaving of levels and the treatment of time. In a second section, time is frozen and agents' actions adjust instantaneously in order to define a one period equilibrium. In a third section, objective time stays fixed while subjective time spreads out and defines an intertemporal equilibrium. In a fourth section, while subjective time vanishes, objective time becomes sequential and leads to discriminate short and long-term equilibria. In a fifth section, objective and subjective time are mixed, and agents' adaptive actions may converge towards an asymptotic equilibrium.

In a second part, the paper considers the epistemological positions held in economics about methodological individualism in relation with time. In a sixth section, the distinction between methodological individualism and methodological holism is re-examined in the light of the foregoing framework. In a seventh section, two related problems are considered, emergence of institutions and social conditioning of agents. In an eighth section, the distinction between microeconomics and macroeconomics is involved with the so called aggregation problem. In a ninth section, the transition from theoretical models to empirical models leads to modulate the number of organizational levels and time scales.

2. FROZEN TIME

In economic theory, three entities are usually considered in order to explain social phenomena, each endowed with specific behaviour rules:

— agents, eventually of several types, choose their actions in a rational way after observing their environment, in accordance with three choice characteristics: opportunities (which delimit their action sets), beliefs (which allow to expect the effects of their actions), preferences (which evaluate the consequences of their actions);

— nature, gathering all physical and technological factors, takes states in an autonomous and mechanical way, according to a deterministic or stochastic rule;

— institutions, symbolising various social mediating devices, emit signals in a more complex way, according to institutional rules relating them to individual actions.

Any agent follows a deliberation process from observations to actions ruled by two complementary forms of **rationality** which concern specific characteristics (Walliser, 1989):

— instrumental rationality deals with the adequation realised between the alternative means available to him and the goals pursued by him;

— cognitive rationality deals with the adequation realised between the information gathered by him and the beliefs formed by him.

If cognitive rationality allows the agent to expect accurately the consequences of his actions on his environment by using his information and prior beliefs, instrumental rationality allows him accordingly to choose the best actions to implement by confronting his opportunities and his preferences.

The interrelation between agents, nature and institutions is given by the following scheme where, in a single period, physical states act on individual actions without feedback while institutional signals and individual actions are mutually determined:

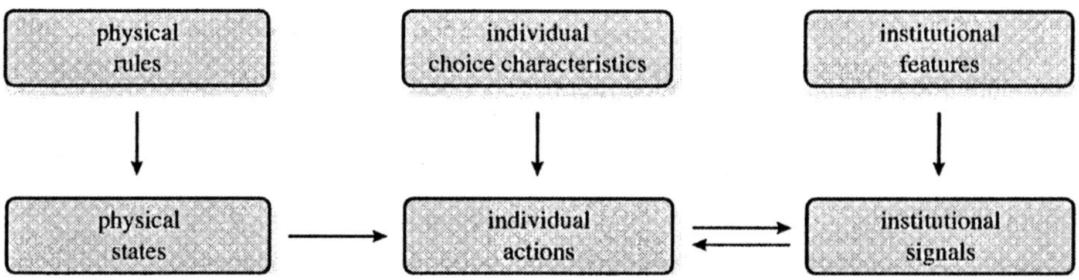

With such a configuration, an **equilibrium state** is defined as a fixed point (conditional to the state of nature) of the loop linking individual actions and institutional signals, hence as a rest point in the absence of outside perturbations. A first question asks how equilibrium variables can be simultaneously defined, a sort of paradox since agents choose individually their actions by observing the signals in the same time that they contribute collectively to fix the signals. A second question asks if there exists some equilibrium state compatible with agents' behaviour and institution's functioning, and in case of multiple equilibria, how one specific equilibrium is selected. The two former problems of simultaneity and multiplicity can only be solved by exhibiting (as seen later) a concrete process followed conjointly by the agents and the institution and able to converge towards some equilibrium.

In *exchange theory*, the standard example is given by the "Walrasian equilibrium" between producers, consumers and the "market", considered as an institution symbolised by the Walrasian auctioneer (Arrow and Debreu, 1954). Each producer, allowed with a production function (linking technically his factors and products) and a profit function (defining the generated profit), chooses his demanded inputs and offered inputs by optimising his profit, after observing their prices. Each consumer, allowed with a budget constraint (restricting their consumption basket by his or her revenue) and a utility function (defining the satisfaction given by some basket), choose the demanded goods by optimising his utility, after observing all prices. The Walrasian auctioneer fixes the prices of the goods by equalising their offers and their demands, hence the prices appear as institutional signals simultaneously observed and determined by the agents.

In *game theory*, the standard example is given by the "Nash equilibrium" between players, determined by an implicit and fictitious institution symbolised by the Nashian regulator (Nash, 1951). Each player, endowed with a utility function depending directly and strategically on all players' actions, defines a best response to others' actions by optimising his utility function under his constraints. The Nashian regulator searches for an equilibrium which is a fixed point of the loop defined by mutual best responses, hence a configuration from which no player has interest to deviate unilaterally when already achieved. Here, there is no specific institutional variable common to all players, since players have bilateral relations without a mediating entity, but the profile of players' actions fulfils formally a similar function of (multi-dimensional) public signal.

3. SPREAD OUT TIME

Agents, nature and institutions are now involved in a sequence of similar interactive situations, the agents' characteristics being adapted in consequence (sequentially interdependent opportunities, intertemporal preferences). Each agent exploits his cognitive rationality in order to expect the future path of the system, i.e. the future states adopted by nature, the future signals emitted by institutions and even the future actions taken by the other agents. He exploits his instrumental rationality in order to choose an optimal strategy, a strategy being defined as the action he will use in all possible circumstances according to nature's observed states and others' past actions. Once chosen before the first occurrence of the successive situations, the actions are implemented by the agent as they result from chosen strategy, without needing to be reevaluated as new information is coming in.

However, the agent is not omniscient and faces two forms of **uncertainty**, "factual uncertainty" concerning past actions, states and signals, "structural uncertainty" concerning others' choice characteristics or nature's law. For tractability reasons, structural uncertainty is domesticated in three steps: structural uncertainty is reduced formally to a factual one, factual uncertainty is summarised in a subjective probability distribution, probability distribution is assumed to be common knowledge among agents. To reduce his uncertainty, each agent revises his prior belief each time he receives some new message, either some external information about the true state of nature or some observation of another's implemented action. But here again, he is assumed to expect before the beginning of the play the future revisions he will make for all possible messages, and to choose his strategies accordingly before implementing the corresponding actions.

The interrelation between agents, nature and institutions can now be summarised by the following scheme where everything is instantaneously expected for all future periods, the implementation of actions and signals which faithfully follows being not represented :

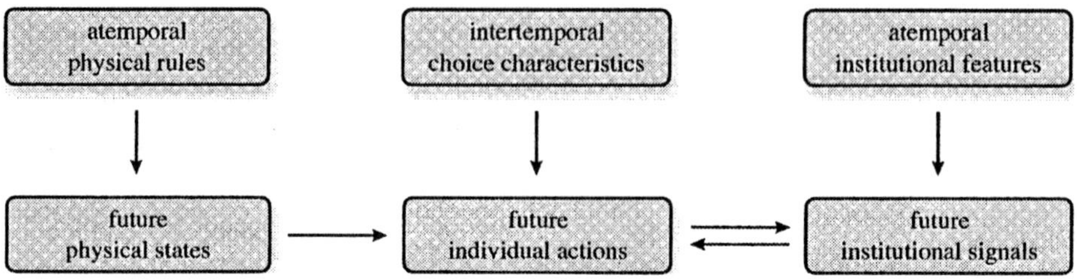

An equilibrium is again stated as a fixed point of the loop between the future actions and future signals on all future periods, with either each period defining an autonomous loop or all periods being interrelated and treated together. In case of uncertainty, an equilibrium is moreover a fixed point for each player between his actions and his beliefs, present beliefs being revised according to past actions while future actions are adapted to present beliefs. Such an equilibrium happens to be "dynamically consistent", in the sense that it has not to be reevaluated as time is unfolding, since all contingencies have already been correctly envisaged at the very beginning of the game. It reduces the long-term objective (realised) future to a short-term subjective (simulated) future, but such a "belief equilibrium" among agents turns into an "action equilibrium" as time unfolds and actions are implemented.

In *exchange theory*, when only probabilistic uncertainty about nature is involved, a « rational expectations equilibrium » can be defined not constructively but formally by three rather demanding conditions about price signals (Muth, 1960). First, the agent has a perfect specification of the system in which he is going to act with other agents, especially about the way the market fixes real prices by gathering offers and demands (depending on expected prices). Second, the agent observes without bias all past relevant variables of his environment, especially the past values of the prices of all goods as well as the past states of nature influencing them. Third, the agent is a perfect statistician who computes from the former sources of information the best estimation of the future value of the price signal (for instance by minimising the square value of error).

In *game theory*, for extensive-form games (defined by a game tree), several equilibrium notions were defined by the modeller and may be computed by the players themselves (Selten, 1975). Without uncertainty, the "subgame perfect equilibrium" is obtained by a "backward induction" procedure : the last player plays his best response to all past moves, the preceding one plays his best response expecting the opponent's future one and so on. With uncertainty, concerned with the other's probabilized type (summarising his choice characteristics), the "Bayesian perfect equilibrium" includes moreover the revision of the other's type when other's action is observed. These abstractly defined equilibrium notions receive epistemic justifications, when considering sophisticated players endowed with even more demanding beliefs such as common belief about game structure, player's rationality or player's independence.

4. SEQUENTIAL TIME

In sequential time, the structure of the system is no more fixed but adjusts from period to period, and the agents act myopically by making their choice by reference only to the expected effects of actions on the ongoing period. Several time scales lexicographically ordered may be considered, but practically only two time scales are explicitly introduced, which are symbolised by three types of variables endowed with different speeds of evolution. At short-term (within each period), variables of a first group adjust simultaneously to each other under the influence of all others, considered as temporarily or definitively time invariant. At long-term (between two periods), variables of a second group adjust under the effect of the past (first and second group) ones and in the general frame determined by variables of a third group, which are fixed for all periods.

More precisely, the agents' actions, the nature's states and the institutional signals form together the conjectural level and act on some more fundamental features, previously fixed. The agents' opportunities and preferences are decomposed into fixed variables (analytical form of the utility function or of the action set) which frame structural ones (parameters of the utility function or of the action set) also influenced both by actions and signals; the agents' beliefs evolve even more naturally through observations, but the belief revision rules are again considered as fixed. In the same way, the institutional features are decomposed into fixed ones (generic frame) and structural ones (specific rules) influenced by actions and signals. The nature's states are themselves determined by environmental rules influenced in a retroactive way by individual actions.

The interrelation between agents, nature and institutions involves now short-term influences (plain arrow) and long-term ones (thick arrow):

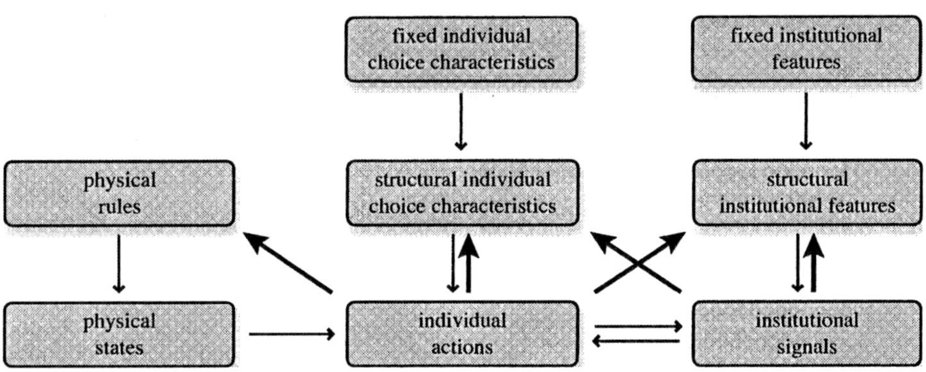

With such a configuration, two nested equilibrium notions can be defined, ordered in a lexicographic way, since the (unique) long-term equilibrium results from a whole sequence of (one period) short-term equilibria. A short-term equilibrium takes place within each period by mutual adjustment of actions and signals, given the present choice characteristics and institutional features, which are provisionally, unchanged. The long-term equilibrium happens asymptotically, when the structural individual characteristics and institutional features have converged, under the constraint of the corresponding fixed properties and the influence of the successive actions and signals. Hence, the long-term equilibrium is defined constructively by the process followed by the short-term ones, while the short-term equilibrium remains defined formally without concrete process leading to it.

In *exchange theory*, one considers for instance an "endogenous" evolution of the consumer's preferences, which are no more exogenously given to him but vary through time (Peleg-Yaari, 1973). At short-term, each consumer chooses his consumption basket according to his ongoing preferences, assumed to be dependent only on the presently consumed goods, hence he expresses a short-term demand. At long-term, the consumer's preferences evolve due to exogenous factors (age), to his past actions (addiction) and eventually to past signals (advertising), hence his behaviour evolves too and may converge towards a long-term demand. Other endogenous evolutions of characteristics can be considered, especially as concerns the action set of a producer, the implementation to-day of a more flexible equipment allowing to-morrow a larger set of possible equipments.

In *game theory*, one considers for instance an "endogenous" evolution of the players' interaction network, which is no more exogenously given but is changing through time (Schelling, 1971). At short-term, each player meets the opponents situated in his private interaction context, eventually by a sampling procedure, and chooses his best action in response to the sorted out opponents' actions. At long-term, each player sees his interaction context modified, due to exogenous factors (emergence of new players) or past actions (selection of players having provided to him performant previous interactions), leading progressively to a long-term interaction network. Other endogenous evolutions arise, especially for players' beliefs revised between two periods according to new messages, as was considered in a previous section, but assumed to be expected rather than experienced by the agents.

5. ADAPTIVE TIME

The actor's rationality becomes now severely bounded, due to his limited computational and informational capabilities, and leads to several alternative formulations of an adaptive behaviour to the context (Simon, 1959). Cognitive rationality is bounded, since the agent has only partial information about his environment and contents with rather myopic expectations about the surrounding system or even no expectations at all. Instrumental rationality is bounded, since the agent no longer looks for an "optimising" action, but contents with some "satisfying" one nevertheless seeking the good with regard to his objectives and past observations. The whole process, taking place in objective time with some remaining subjective expectations, can be summarised in four principles, knowing that agents stay endowed with given opportunities and preferences (Lesourne *et al.*, 2002).

The interaction principle makes explicit, in some interaction neighbourhood where each agent meets the others, if they meet randomly or not, in an anonymous or personalised way, two by two or in groups. The information principle makes precise, in some information neighbourhood where each agent gathers observations, if the data are sampled or not, with random or prior criteria, in individualized or already aggregated form. The evaluation principle makes precise how each agent gathers and synthesises the preceding information in specific indexes : other's past frequency of actions, own's past mean or summed utility of actions. The decision principle shows how each agent chooses an action in response to the preceding indexes : strict or perturbed best response to other's past actions, probabilistic response enforcing own's actions with best performances.

The interrelation between agents, nature and institutions implies again short-term effects (choice of actions) and long-term ones (adjustment of indexes):

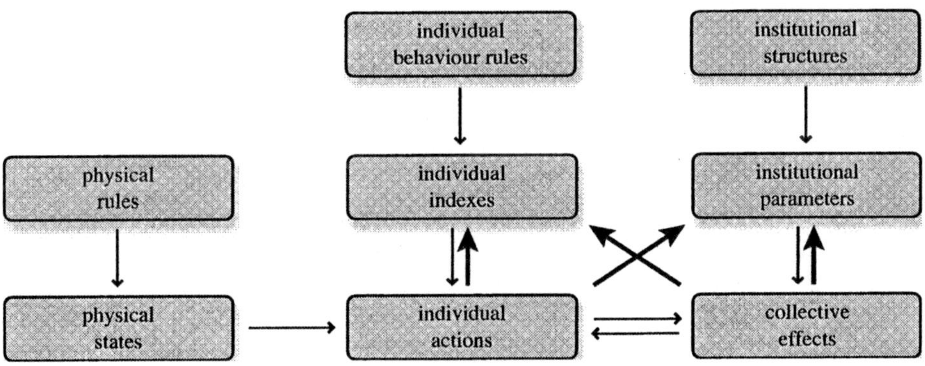

At short-term, the system adopts some social state no more interpreted as an equilibrium, since each agent chooses his ongoing action independently of the others' present actions or present global phenomena. But at long-term, the dynamical path of the system may be seen as a concrete process converging eventually towards an asymptotic state interpreted as an equilibrium since all agents appear duly co-ordinated in that state. The simultaneity problem (previously considered) is solved : agents' actions follow agents' observations at next period, hence the present social state is perfectly (even if sometimes randomly) determined by the past. The multiplicity problem is solved too : even if the process may not converge (cyclical or chaotic attractor), if it converges (punctual attractor), it converges towards a social state selected by initial state, context and history.

In *exchange theory*, one considers for instance a labour market where employers and employees are matched two by two randomly after search processes and negotiate a short-term contract under bounded rationality (Lesourne, 1991). At any period, each employer (employee) proposes (accepts) a task at a given reservation wage and a contract is mutually accepted at some intermediate wage as soon as the respective wages are compatible. At next period, if the employer (employee) was unable just before to find an employee (employer), he increases (decreases) his reservation wage, and is matched again to an employee (employer). If that self-organizational process is without friction, the wages converge towards the unique competitive equilibrium wage, but otherwise (with research or negotiation costs), multiple wages or even cyclical paths may appear.

In *game theory*, two main learning processes are generally considered, according to decreasing cognitive capabilities ascribed to the agents, more and more compensated by the constructive work of time (Fudenberg and Levine, 1998). In epistemic learning, each player observes the other's past frequency of actions, transforms it in a probabilistic belief about other's future action, and chooses a best response to such a belief at each period. In behavioural learning, each player observes the past utility obtained by each implemented action, computes an index of the past performance of each action and chooses an action with a probability increasing with its index. Some classical equilibrium notions may then receive dynamic justifications as asymptotic states of such a process, especially the pure Nash equilibrium for a large class of games or the subgame perfect equilibrium for a restricted class.

6. INDIVIDUALISM VS HOLISM

When considering two organizational levels and two time scales, the relations between individual and collective levels can be exhaustively enumerated in the following scheme:

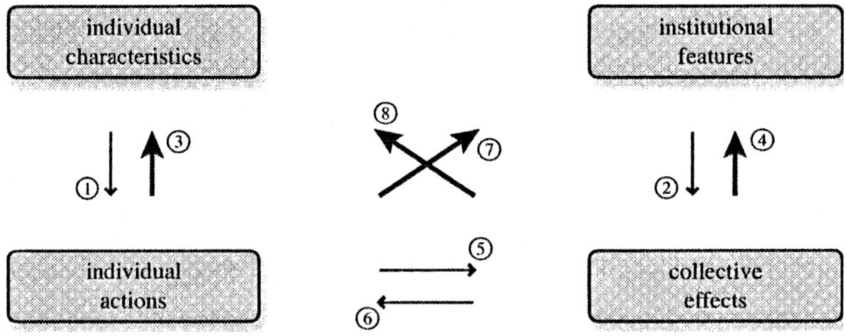

In that scheme, nature has been omitted since it acts always in the same way: it influences the agents' behaviour and institution functioning at short-term and may be influenced back mainly at long-term. Moreover, there is no direct influence of individual characteristics on institutional features (or the other way around) since institutions are assumed not to act structurally on agent's behaviour, but only through operational variables they emit. Two extreme epistemological positions (Agassi, 1960) deny the existence of links between the individual and the collective levels, each being respectively self-contained (influences ⑤, ⑥, ⑦ and ⑧ are void). Strong holism asserts that the social level is the only one to be meaningful (influences ② and ④ only) while strong individualism asserts that the individual level is the only one that makes sense (influences ① and ③ only).

Strong methodological holism considers that there are no relevant individual entities, hence that the social phenomena can only be explained by some other social facts while looking for an internal consistency. Adopted in sociology by Durkheim or in anthropology by the structuralists, such a position has no great influence in economics where the agents are always singularised, except perhaps in the physiocrats' work. *Strong methodological individualism* considers that there are no relevant collective entities, hence that the so called social phenomena can always be analysed as a superposition of individual entities or actions. Unknown in sociology except for some microsociologists, such a position is followed neither in exchange economics where prices are already collective variables nor in classical game theory where equilibria are not achieved by purely individual means.

When the entities are accepted at the individual as well as at the collective level, these not only internally connected (influences ① and ③, ②and ④) but mutually linked at lower scale (influences ⑤ and ⑥). Four more elaborated methodological positions are defined according to the acceptance or not of relations involving the upper level, either from individual to social (influence ⑦) or from social to individual (influence ⑧):

⑧ / ⑦	yes	no
yes	crossed interactionism	weak individualism
no	weak holism	autonomous interactionism

Weak methodological holism asserts the social level to be prominent, i.e. collective effects are able to modify the individual features while individual actions have no influence on the institutional features. For instance, it assumes that the agent's characteristics are socially conditioned, a usual position in sociology which was seldom shared in economics where such a potential influence is at best treated as exogenous. *Weak methodological individualism* asserts the individual level to be prominent, i.e. individual actions are able to determine institutional features while social phenomena have no bite on the individual characteristics. For instance, it assumes that the institutions are designed (consciously or not) by the agents, a position generally denied by sociology, but sometimes considered by economics for some specific institutions.

Autonomous methodological interactionism considers that both levels are on an equal foot, symbolised by autonomous individuals and institutions which interfere only at lower time scale through their actions or signals. Unusual in sociology, it is reflected in economics by the market mechanism where the agents and the market coexist from the beginning of time and are related through the equilibration of offers and demands by prices. *Crossed methodological interactionism* considers that individuals and institutions are able to influence indirectly the others' features, without real existence anteriority or influence anteriority of one over the other. In economics, it is symbolised by evolutionist game theory, where the players' characteristics are influenced by some social effects, while institutions are long-term consequences of individual actions.

7. ECONOMIC EPISTEMOLOGICAL POSITIONS

Starting from autonomous interactionism, a first evolution in economics was to achieve weak methodological individualism, hence to explain all social phenomena from individual actions, especially the co-ordinating institutions and the interrelating networks. However, these social entities or links can be obtained by agents endowed with more or less sophisticated rationality principles, giving rise to corresponding forms of methodological individualism. "Perfect individualism" states that the agents have strong cognitive and instrumental rationality, hence are able to fully expect the social effects they produce at short and long-term by their deliberate and voluntary actions. "Bounded individualism" states that the agents have limited instrumental and overall cognitive rationality, hence may face ex ante unforeseen social effects and may even not attribute ex post these effects to their ongoing actions.

The endogenous emergence of economic institutions has been studied essentially for two main global institutions, markets and money, both in charge of co-ordinating the agents' exchanges. With perfect individualism, markets are voluntarily designed by some specialised agents (new financial markets) while money is explicitly created by specific institutions (king's money, credit cards). With bounded individualism, markets are unexpected devices (Smith's invisible hand) emerging through unintended actions (Hayek's selection process) while money results from spontaneous actions selecting convenient means of exchange (shells, silver). However, more local institutions can likely be considered such as firms or syndicates, both creating coalitions of agents for more efficiency, initiated by an initial germ and growing by association of interested agents.

It is possible to combine sequentially the two approaches, by considering that an institution emerges in two phases, eventually under the influence of already mature institutions at higher level. In the "formation phase", the institution emerges from the actions of boundedly rational agents learning through time or imitating one another and materialises an asymptotic equilibrium showing some regular pattern. In the "naturalisation phase", the institution is recognised as such by the agents and becomes an explicit entity, hence influences the agents' actions which reinforce it since it precisely corresponds to an equilibrium. The process may be completed by a "legalisation phase" where the institution receives from some representative authority a legal recognition and is protected if necessary by material constraints or financial incentives and sanctions.

Starting now from weak individualism, a second evolution of economics is to accept crossed interactionism, hence to take into account some influences of society on actors' behaviour, especially through social and ethical channels. Here again, global phenomena and especially institutions act on agents endowed with more or less sophisticated rationality principles, giving rise to corresponding forms of interactionism. "Perfect interactionism" states that the agents have strong rationality, hence they are socially conditioned precisely through their choice characteristics, essentially their preferences and their beliefs. "Bounded interactionism" states that the agents have plain behaviour rules linking some context to some action, hence they are conditioned by internalisation of a newly experimental rule or by modulation of parameters of an already implemented rule.

The influence of institutions on agents' behaviour can be examined for two usual conceptual institutions, social norms and collective representations, which aim at co-ordinating agents without being of an economic nature. With perfect interactionism, social norms act on preferences through moral sanctions or ethical incentives while collective representations act on beliefs by educational training or media diffusion. With bounded interactionism, social norms act on behaviour rules by reinforcement mechanisms or mimetic contagion while collective representations act by imposing a dominant interpretation of the application domain of the behaviour rule. Some other social institutions can likely be considered, for instance churches or clubs, but their influence on participants' behaviours is even less precise since they mix various elements, which need to be isolated.

It is again possible to combine the two approaches by considering that an institution modifies the agents' behaviour in two phases, eventually with the support of other institutions having complementary roles. In the "enforcement phase", some types of behaviour are imitated from other agents since they seem performing or are simply imposed by external sources having sufficient physical or moral authority. In the "internalisation phase", these behaviours are consciously rationalised by the agents' (eventually adapted) preferences or are unconsciously considered as acceptable under constraints. But the conditioning process suggested by sociology stays difficult to translate in economic terms since the channels by which institutions act on behaviour are restricted to beliefs and preferences on one side, to actions and signals on the other side.

8. MICRO AND MACRO-ANALYSIS

Economics makes a traditional distinction between microeconomics and macroeconomics, but these two approaches cannot be plainly associated with the two former studied organizational levels, i.e. basic agents and collectivity. Both approaches consider the economic system as a whole, but differ by the fact that goods and agents are maximally decomposed in the first while they are **aggregated** in « compound goods » and « representative agents » in the second. The reason for the distinction is that it is quite impossible to deal practically with a lot entities or variables and it is much easier to construct empirical relations with aggregated variables. Hence, if microeconomics is essentially devoted to theoretical analysis (except for partial analysis of exchanges among a few agents), macroeconomics is essentially fitted for empirical analysis (except for already global phenomena like money).

The first aggregation problem concerns the quantities and prices of goods which are produced, exchanged or consumed by an agent or a set of agents, especially when these goods are qualitatively different. For an homogeneous good, the quantities can be simply added if they are used in a similar way (total consumption), but need to be more subtly combined if not (total production obtained algebraically by eliminating what is produced by some firms and consumed by others). For heterogeneous goods, the quantities are aggregated in value and not in volume, the total quantity being the weighted sum of the singular quantities obtained with relative prices as weights. Always for heterogeneous goods, the prices are aggregated in a dual way (prices weighted by quantities), giving rise to various price indexes, which are in fact only defined in variation from one period to the other.

The second aggregation problem concerns the gathering of a set of basic agents under a representative agent of same type, who deals with aggregated variables in an aggregated environment (Kirman, 1992). An aggregation procedure defines the representative agent's behaviour which is equivalent to the conjunction of the individuals' ones in some specific context, for given aggregation rules for goods and revenues. On one hand, "rationalistic aggregation" implies, for strongly rational agents, an aggregation procedure directly defined on their choice characteristics which are duly formalised, not only their opportunities, but also their beliefs and preferences. On the other hand, "behavioural aggregation" implies, for agents with limited rationality, an aggregation procedure directly defined on their behaviour rules, expressing in a short-cut how their actions are linked to signals and states.

The aggregation procedure concerns mainly the definition of aggregated consumers and producers in a competitive equilibrium framework, and is rigorously defined only under drastic and even unrealistic conditions. The consumers' utility functions and the producers' production functions can be perfectly aggregated only when agents have sufficiently similar characteristics and well dispersed resources. The consumers' demand functions and producers' offer functions can be rigorously aggregated, for a given price system of goods, only if agents' reactions to prices are identical and revenue distribution among agents smooth enough. The aggregation procedure is still harder to achieve when considering an imperfect competition context or taking into accounts more heterogeneous goods, even if it is sometimes replaced by approximate aggregation.

It must be noticed that the two agents' aggregation procedures may become close, since the aggregation of behaviour rules stemming from rational agents leads to an aggregate behaviour which no longer appears as rationally grounded. More precisely, the individual demand function of a rational agent, linking the demanded quantities of goods to prices and revenue, obeys to some specific constraints known as Slutzky conditions. However, the total demand function obtained by additive aggregation of goods no longer obeys to corresponding constraints and appears similar for agents endowed with more or less strong rationality (Debreu, 1974 ; Sonnenschein, 1973). Hence, at a macroeconomic level where aggregate agents are represented by behaviour rules, a lot of precise information concerning the individual agents' types of behaviour is lost in the averaging procedure.

A related problem is to examine how some randomness can be taken into account and interpreted at each organizational level and how such randomness may be transmitted from one level to the other. In microeconomics, randomness is usually explained by some intrinsic indetermism in agents' behaviour, even if it is sometimes attributed to hidden psychological factors formally not taken into account. In macroeconomics, randomness results more convincingly from external shocks related either to technological change (random innovations) or to foreign trade influences (unexpected international crisis). But it is possible to state neither that the micro randomness is compensated by aggregation to give rise to a macro deterministic order nor that the macro randomness is absorbed by the agents who act more deterministically.

9. FROM THEORETICAL TO EMPIRICAL ANALYSIS

Only two organizational levels were previously considered, but it is possible to consider more for practical applications, the successive levels being always considered as dealing with nested entities. Between micro and macro level, one sometimes considers a meso level of groupings of basic agents, grounded on qualitative as well as spatial criteria, such as syndicates, holdings or otherwise regions. A supra-macro level may be concerned by the exchanges taking place between several national economic systems and an infra-micro level by the multiple "selves" which are assumed to compete inside any individual agent. The considerations made so far continue to apply separately between each couple of contiguous levels, an original problem appearing only when some shortcuts exist between two non contiguous levels.

Only two time scales were previously considered, but it is possible to consider more in empirical cases, the embedded scales dealing again with variables evolving at different speeds with asymmetric influences between them. For a firm, quantities adapt at short-term, prices may adjust at middle term, quality of goods and technologies are revised at long-term and the firm structure is even modified at ultra long-term. Incidentally, rather than to specific variables, time scales may be defined as more and more extended periods showing different types of evolution for each variable. For macroeconomic policy, short-term corresponds to one year (budget periodicity), middle term to three to five years (planning periodicity) and long-term to about ten years; in financial markets, the corresponding intervals are rather of one hour, one day (opening period) and one week.

On the empirical side, the observations collected by agents, statistical institutes or academic researchers are either basic data expressed in a quantitative form or already empirical regularities extracted qualitatively from them ("stylised facts"). Historical observations stem from the spontaneous functioning of the economic system, and are further aggregated by the National Accounting System at different scales (for instance, from hundred goods to only three ones). Experimental observations stem from laboratory experiments which develop more and more as concerns exchange theory (market mechanisms, auction procedures) as well as game theory (negotiation processes, coalition formation). In fact, more and more individual data become available (with regard to aggregated ones) and data are available on longer and longer periods even if some are reconstituted (19th century corn prices).

On the theoretical side, theoretical models are transformed by deduction and specification into empirical models, which are composed of testable relations and are associated with precise fields of application. All theoretical variables (utilities, expectations) are eliminated in order to keep only observable ones (quantities, prices), even if more and more variables become observable (series of expectations become available). Simultaneously, all non-standard formalisations (for instance agent's optimisation programs) are resolved to give rise to usual stochastic equations between variables, which remain too often linear. However, these relations allow to treat simultaneously variables at different organizational levels, but it is harder to introduce more than three time scales since variables are just indexed by the unidimensional physical time.

An empirical model is then confronted (globally or relation by relation) to (more or less pre-treated) observations along two main procedures which appear as complementary and lead to modify or adjust it. In a projective way, a model is formally tested against the data and is confirmed or refuted in accordance with some statistical criteria, generally of a conventional kind (five per cent admissibility level). In an inductive way, a model is given in its analytical form (which is preserved in the process) and its parameters are simply estimated against the data by various statistical methods (statistical induction). However, it does not follow that a model refuted by observations is automatically revised since empirical violations need to be repeated many times to do so and since empirical arguments are completed by pragmatic ones (simplicity, operationality) when validating a model.

Besides the preceding interpretation of randomness as intrinsic uncertainty, two more interpretations of stochastic terms are introduced in order to ensure a better fit between theoretical models and empirical relations. Stochastic factors are assumed to represent specification errors, concerning either the analytical form of a relation (such as linear approximation) or omitted variables in the relation (such as non-economic factors). Stochastic factors are also assumed to incorporate measurement errors concerning the data, even if no error intervals are generally evaluated and published for basic data as well as aggregated data (except for sampling errors). In any case, all forms of randomness are mixed in an empirical model and it is possible in principle to compute the confidence interval of its results, but this is rarely done in practice and would lead to despairing values.

REFERENCES

Agassi, J. (1960). Methodological individualism. *British Journal of Sociology, 11*, 244-70.

Arrow, K., & Debreu, G. (1954). Existence of an equilibrium for a competitive economy. *Econometrica, 22*, 265-290.

Becker, G.S. (1960). An economic analysis of fertility. In *Demographic and economic change in developped countries*. Princeton: Princeton University Press.

Debreu, G. (1974). Excess demand functions. *Journal of Mathematical Economics, 1*, 15-23.

Fudenberg, D., & Levine, D. (1998). *Theory of learning in games*. Cambridge, Massachussetts: MIT Press.

Kirman, A. (1992). What or whom does the representative individual represent ? *Journal of Economic Perspectives, 6*, 117-136.

Lesourne, J. (1991). *The economics of order and disorder*. Oxford: Clarendon Press.

Lesourne, J., Orléans, A., & Walliser, B. (2003). *Leçons de microéconomie évolutioniste*. Paris: Editions Odile Jacob.

Muth, J. (1960). Rational expectations and the theory of price movements. *Econometrica, 29*, 315-35.

Nash, J. (1951). Non cooperative games. *Annals of Mathematics, 54*, 286-95.

Peleg, B., & Yaari, M. (1973). On the existence of a consistent course of action when tastes are changing. *Review of Economic Studies, 24*, 56-68.

Schelling, T. (1971). Dynamic model of segregation. *Journal of Mathematical Sociology, 1*, 143-86.

Selten, R. (1975). Reexamination of the perfectness concept for equilibria points in extensive games. *International Journal of Game Theory, 4*, 25-55.

Simon, H.A. (1959). Theories of decision-making in economics and behavioral sciences. *American Economic Review,49*, 249-83.

Smith, A. (1776). *The Wealth of Nations*, in four volumes. Edinburgh

Sonnenschein, H. (1973). Do Walras identity and continuity characterize the class of community excess demand functions. *Journal of Economic Theory, 6*, 345-54.

Walliser, B. (1989). Instrumental rationality and cognitive rationality. *Theory and decision, 27*, 7-36.

Walliser, B. (2001). La science économique. In Berthelot J.-M. (ed.), *Epistémologie des sciences sociales* (pp. 117-147). Paris: Presses Universitaires de France.

Robert FRANCK

Chapter 6

CAUSAL ANALYSIS, SYSTEMS ANALYSIS, AND MULTILEVEL ANALYSIS: PHILOSOPHY AND EPISTEMOLOGY

Opening. The previous chapters, written by specialists in different social sciences, have examined multilevel analysis as a new methodology that can encompass multiple levels of aggregation, with a view to answering novel questions raised in their respective fields. In education, for example, the multilevel approach can analyse an individual's responses to tests as a function not only of individual characteristics, but at the same time of the characteristics of the student's class, school, neighbourhood, etc. The joint analysis of these aggregation levels provides a far more accurate view of the effects of the characteristics than a study conducted at a single level. The contributors to this volume have therefore adopted an essentially methodological approach to show how multilevel analysis can overcome the difficulties encountered when working at a single aggregation level, whether individual or aggregated. By observing some of the gaps and inconsistencies between the results obtained using other analytical methods, the authors have shown the value of the multilevel approach, which solves most of these problems and offers an overall view of the characteristics operating at each aggregation level.

But, while the examination of new methods is essential to understanding the improvements they bring to the social sciences, it should not make us forget that methodology is not a branch independent from epistemology. Epistemology is the equivalent of Philosophy of Science. The last term suggests that the sciences are the focus of the investigation, while epistemology is concerned with the nature of knowledge in general. In fact, philosophy of science is, more often than not, concerned—as is epistemology—with scientific knowledge in general, discussing for instance the nature of scientific theories, the ways of their validation, the role of experience in scientific investigation, the meaning of probability, etc. Many works in the philosophy of science refer to the sciences only in order to illustrate by examples the ideas put forward. Other philosophers of science try to give a new insight by a thorough examination of the scientific practices. Following this course, Robert Franck emphasises the importance of methodology. According to him, a close examination of the methods in use allows us to bring nearer to each other the research practices and the philosophical concepts. The advantage for philosophy is obvious. But as long as the social sciences are feeling their way, a deeper assessment of the significance and of the limitations of the methods in use might also help to improve the research practices. And the philosophical concepts are of great help for this assessment. Robert Franck invites us to take that step, with an in depth examination of the concepts of "cause" and of "system". The goal is to show the advances that the multilevel analysis allows in the social sciences, and to find stronger underpinnings for it.

First, the introduction of multilevel models gives a totally new twist to the still lively debate over the relations between society and the individual, or between holism and methodological individualism in the social sciences. This dualist approach, which sets the whole against the parts, effectively raises the more fundamental issue of the priority of one over the other. Holism—defended, for example, by Durkheim (1895/1937)—gives precedence to society's action on human behaviour, and treats social facts as external to individual conscience. By contrast, methodological individualism—defended by Boudon (1988), among others—aims to explain the same facts by reconstructing the motives of the individuals concerned and presenting the facts as the result of the aggregation of individual behaviours dictated by those motives. But once we adopt the hierarchical or multilevel approach—where the opposition between the whole and the part is abolished, but where an entity we regard as a whole can become a part of a more aggregated level and vice versa—it no longer makes sense to choose between holism and individualism, and the opposition vanishes (Franck, 1995). On the other hand, we now need to explore the connections between levels and study the mechanisms that will enable us to integrate the levels. This takes us into a far more theoretical study.

D. Courgeau (ed.) Methodology and Epistemology of Multilevel Analysis, 175-198.

The reason is that we are confronted with the theoretical issue of the organisation of the levels and the existence of an underlying functional structure, which would help us better understand how human societies live and evolve. For example, the functional structure of a migratory system is not found in the linkage between (1) individuals' probability of migrating and (2) their own characteristics and those of the regions they inhabit; rather, the structure is to be found in the economic functions, family functions, spatial-distribution functions, and other functions implied by migration. The approach suggested by Robert Franck will thus use multilevel analysis differently from earlier contributions, with the aim of going further and identifying the functional structure underlying behaviours. Instead of seeking only to identify the individual and aggregated characteristics that can influence a given behaviour, multilevel analysis seeks to identify and understand the functions that the aggregation levels will perform in the multilevel system considered.

In order to explore the nature of the connections between levels, Robert Franck carries out an examination of several types of causal determination and of their impact on multilevel analysis. Then, he clarifies the nature of levels, by the aid of the philosophical concept of hylemorphism. This concept allows us to understand the emergence of systems, at a higher level, from factors acting reciprocally at the lower level. Under these conditions multilevel analysis may be enlarged to deal with the influences of factors over the emerging system, and to the influence of the emerging system over the same factors, leading to new procedures for the analysis of system functions.

An advance of this kind in the social sciences is, for the moment, a theoretical possibility more than a reality. We have no choice but to recognise that the identification of a functional structure that objectivates lived human experience, and the transition from that structure to an active recapture of lived experience, are still far from totally effective. The social sciences have not yet "managed to define the categories that allow, even in a temporarily satisfactory manner, the objectivation of human experience" (Granger, 1988). But we shall see that Robert Franck raises new possibilities here for moving closer to that functional structure, by making creative use of the paths opened up by multilevel analysis. These possibilities attest to the social sciences' ever greater proficiency in their approach to human reality, and augur well for objectivation in the future.

D. C.

1. INTRODUCTION. OBJECT OF THIS CHAPTER

Many efforts are made in the social sciences to establish causal relationships between social phenomena, and statistical analysis is the privileged means of establishing such relationships. Multilevel analysis comes under this general heading for social science research. It offers the advantage of being able to take collective as well as individual variables into account, and of being able to hierarchize these variables with respect to two or more levels. In this way multilevel analysis refines the statistical study of causal relations which generate observed phenomena, and improves our understanding of social life.

Are the determinative relationships which we manage to establish in social science between two or more phenomena always of a causal nature? This is a widely held opinion. To be more precise, researchers hesitate to speak of *causes*, preferring to refer to *factors,* a term which seems less burdened with philosophical connotations. They also know that a relationship of functional dependence is far from always indicating a determinative relationship. But in general they think that when there is a relation of determination between social phenomena, that determination can only be causal. However, Mario Bunge (1979) showed as early as 1959 in his famous work on causality that physical and biological sciences resort to various kinds of non-causal determination in order to explain natural phenomena. In the field of social phenomena, determinations are not limited to causal relationships either. Would greater attention to the nature of non-causal determinations at work between social phenomena augment the potential of multilevel analysis? That's what I will attempt to show in the second part of this chapter. The examination of non-causal determinative relationships should also allow us to understand the nature of relationships between levels.

Aside from the fact that there are different kinds of non-causal determination, there are also different kinds of causal determinations. For example, alongside the type expressed by the phrase "same cause, same effect" there are *interactions* in the sense given this term by Raymond Boudon (1967), which Paul Lazarsfeld previously described by multivariate analysis. I will examine a number of forms of causal determination from which multilevel analysis can benefit, and I will point out some of their theoretical implications. The examination of these different kinds of causal determination will be the object of the first part of this chapter.

The world is varied and changeable. This is as true of nature as of society. How then can we arrive at lasting and generalisable knowledge? This question gave rise to European philosophy (see Parmenides, Heraclitus, Plato, Aristotle, etc.). It concerns the natural sciences as much as the social. However, our awareness of socio-cultural differences has given the question a particular shape in social science. We see that social life is diverse and variable, differing from one place to another and from one period in history to another—and within a single time and place, social groups differ. Must we resign ourselves to admitting, as we see our analyses made more and more sensitive through multilevel analysis, that in the social realm there is no knowledge which is not particular? The examination of different possible forms of causal determination, in the first part of this chapter, will permit us to find out how necessary and relatively durable relationships can be established between social phenomena.

Ana Diez Roux describes, in this book, the challenges and limitations of multilevel analysis, and some possible alternative and complementary approaches to it. I will return presently to the methodological difficulties she has identified, and attempt to make a contribution to solving them. This chapter thus takes up where her chapter leaves off. I will begin by responding to her invitation to doubt the notion that effects are always separable ("dissection of risk"): I will present a kind of inventory (as mentioned above) of some other forms of causal determination which should be useful in epidemiology, and indeed in other disciplines. Among the points of difficulty raised by Diez Roux, one seems to me crucial for the future of multilevel analysis. Koopman (1996, p. 630, cited by Diez Roux) sums it up this way: "(...) epidemiology is in transition from a science that identifies risk factors for disease to one that analyses the systems that generate patterns of disease in populations." What must we do, to go from identification of factors to analysis of systems? Or better, how can we combine, in analysis, factors and the systems they belong to? Can multilevel analysis be open to the analysis of social systems? In other words, can multilevel analysis accommodate the structure of groups, of contexts, and of levels in its operation? The problem of combining factors and systems is not specific to epidemiology, but is shared by all social sciences

(M. Loriaux, 1994). I will try to show how a system of factors determines, in a non-causal way, the effects these factors can have, and how, inversely, factors generate and determine non-causally the structure of the system they belong to. That will help us to grasp the specific nature of relationships between levels (must we, following Susser and Susser (1994), think of these as being like Chinese boxes?), and allow us to consider the extension of multilevel analysis as applying to determinations of a new kind.

2. THE CAUSAL PRINCIPLE

2.1. The advantages of the principle "same cause, same effect"

Tradition connects the relation of cause and effect to the principle: "the same cause produces the same effect". According to this principle, one cause can have only one effect, and an effect can have only one cause. For example, Emile Durkheim noted that if there were different causes of suicide, there must also be different kinds of suicide, and that every kind of suicide had to have a different cause. But in the last fifty years the principle, "the same cause produces the same effect", has been fighting in retreat, while notions of multiple causation have gained ground. I will speak about multiple causation in a moment, but first I would like to draw attention to the advantages of the principle of "same cause, same effect" at the methodological level. These advantages are quite large. We forego them if we abandon the principle, if we for example admit (as is done in multilevel analysis) that a phenomenon is the result of a combination of the influence of several causes operating at different levels.

First advantage: if it is true that an effect can have only one cause, then when the cause is known it is unnecessary to ask whether in other places or at other times the same effect can have a different cause. Thus a causal explanation can be generalised. Every time the effect is observed, we can identify the cause without having to search for it all over again. The cause is known once and for all. Cavils about socio-cultural differences which otherwise would forbid generalisations of causal explanations which may be put forward are overcome if we stick to the principle of "same cause, same effect". But if we give up the principle, how can we guarantee that our analysis is valid outside the time and place of our investigation?

Second advantage: if it is true that a cause can have only a single effect, we know that the cause will never, here or elsewhere, produce any effects but those it is known to produce, whatever the context. Knowledge of the effect can be generalised. That is no longer possible when we have given up the principle, "same cause, same effect".

Third advantage: we can be equally certain that the effect will not be produced if its cause is not present.

Fourth advantage: if the effect is present, we can be sure the cause also is, even if it has not been observed. The effect implies its cause, not by a logical implication, but because the existence of the effect supposes that it has been produced by its cause.

2.2. According to this principle, causes are necessary, but their effect is contingent

Does the principle also mean that the existence of a cause implies the existence of its effect? In other words, when the cause is present, are we sure that its effect will follow? No. Contrary to a widely held opinion the principle "same cause, same effect" does not tell us whether a cause is always followed or accompanied by its effect. And that obviously limits the predictive power granted by the principle. The principle does let us predict that a cause will have no other effect than the one already known, and also to predict that the effect will not occur if the cause is absent. That is quite a lot. And I underline once more that as soon as we give up the principle, "same cause, same effect", we lose any means of making that kind of prediction or forecast. But having noted that, we should recognise also that the kinds of prediction the principle allows us to make still do not tell us what is going to happen. The principle tells us that the effect cannot occur if its cause is absent, but since we don't know if that cause will be present in the future or not, we don't know if the effect expected will be produced or not in the future. Neither does the principle permit us to say what is not going to happen. It guarantees that if the cause in question occurs, it will produce no other effect than the one it is known to produce—but a thousand other effects may occur as a result of the action of a thousand other causes. In short, the power of prediction gained through "same cause, same effect" is not a power of predicting the future. It is the power to expect an effect, though only as a *possibility*, and only if the presence of the known cause has been observed.

Why does the principle stipulate the necessity of the cause but not that of the effect? Where does the asymmetry in the principle of causality come from? It is the result, quite simply, of the traditional ontology which is the inspiration of the principle. One assumes that a cause is capable of producing its effect by its very nature (it is not a question here of accidental effects, but of one or another effect which is specifically linked to the given cause). The cause, obviously, cannot produce any specific effects other than those which its nature permits. And these specific effects, just as obviously, cannot be produced if the nature (of the cause) which can produce them is absent. On the other hand, why should the cause imply the production of its effect? Nothing forces us to think that a cause must necessarily produce its specific effects; it can produce them or not, according to circumstances. Thomas Aquinas, for example, writes (c.1272, part I, Q. CXV, a.6):

> It is not true that, given any cause whatever, the effect must follow of necessity. For some causes are so ordered to their effects, as to produce them, not of necessity, but in the majority of cases, and in the minority to fail in producing them. But that such causes fail in the minority of cases is due to some hindering cause.

I repeat this citation from Bunge (1979, pp. 103-104), who adds :

> Leibniz had an idea of this when he said that it is necessary that everything have a *cause,* but it is contingent that every cause should produce its *effects* (...)

If the production, by a cause, of its effect is not necessary but rather contingent, the question of determinism must be examined anew. One is not obliged to give up determinism (which states that "everything has a cause" or that "everything is determined") in order to avoid believing that the world is pre-determined, or that human beings are pre-determined to act as they do. Bunge demonstrated this convincingly (*op. cit.* p. 101-107). He writes:

> an essential mark of causality and, indeed, of every other type of lawful determinacy, is conditionality (...) statements of causal laws assert that *if*, and only if, certain conditions are met, certain results will follow. A change in the conditions will therefore ensure a change in the results (...).

Bunge observes that many researchers have opposed causality and determinism, pleading in favour of the possibility of indeterminacy, in order to protect themselves against falling into pre-determinism. The distinction Bunge emphasises, between determinism and pre-determinism should be taken as placing causality and determinism beyond the reach of these opposing pleas, if their purpose was to guard us against pre-determinism. Causal determinations are conditional; further along we shall present another argument in favour of a separation of the question of determinism ("everything that happens has a cause") from that of pre-determinism ("a cause necessarily produces its effect").

3. MULTI CAUSAL MODELS

For half a century now social science has taken an interest in the plurality of the causes of a single event. Econometrics played a pioneer role in the modelling of a variety of factors which may contribute to the determination of a phenomenon. Diez Roux drew our attention to the limited usage of multicausal models in epidemiology. Epidemiologists often assume that various risk factors act separately, and they attempt to differentiate their several effects. This leads them to neglect the presence of causal chains, and the effect of interference between certain factors in the etiology of diseases which occur in individuals or in populations. Diez Roux fears that calling in multilevel analysis will add only another different kind of variable, a group-level variable. She wants to see multilevel analysis in epidemiology become aware of causal interferences and non-causal determinations (in speaking of the latter she of course refers to Bunge).

I will examine possible kinds of interferences, and I will underline some of their theoretical implications, as I did above regarding the principle, "same cause, same effect".

3.1. Disjunctive multiple causation

The emphasis on "dissecting risk" in epidemiology corresponds to that which Bunge has called *disjunctive multiple causation* (*op. cit.* pp. 122-125). This occurs in situations in which several causes can produce a single effect, that is, any one of them is a sufficient cause of the effect, although the effect of one cause cannot be added to the effect of another cause. Each cause might produce the effect independently of each other, and thus we can believe that there is no interference between them. Still, there is one sort of interference whose consequences can be decisive in demographic forecasting, as Guillaume Wunsch has pointed out (1988, p. 45). What happens when two causes which can produce the same effect separately or disjunctively do not act simultaneously? For example, heart attacks and cancer are two causes of death; if one dies of a heart attack, one can no longer die of cancer, and vice-versa. Each cause only produces the effect if the other has not acted beforehand. Disjunctive multiple causality is of course not limited to two causes. For example, there is a large number of causes of death which act separately. We see in this way that the effect of time on causal determinations is sometimes decisive.

3.2. Conjunctive multiple causation

A second type of multiple causation occurs when two or more causes together produce an effect, though each alone does not produce it. Here the interference is evident. One supposes that each of the causes which act together is a *necessary* but not a *sufficient* condition of the production of the effect (Nowak, 1975). In other words, each of the causes is unable by itself to produce the effect, but none of them can be lacking in the causal combination, or the effect will not be produced. If none of the causes are lacking, the causal combination is a *sufficient* cause of the production of the effect. *Sufficient*, but not *necessary*, however. Other causes or other causal combinations might also produce the effect. When we give up the principle, "same cause, same effect" in favour of multiple causation, no cause continues to appear *necessary* for the production of the effect. The number of possible causes of an effect appears thus unlimited in principle. This allows us—and condemns us!—to continue putting forward new causal hypotheses : however convincing the results obtained in the course of verifying or corroborating a causal hypothesis, a thousand other causes could just as well produce the same effect, at other times or under other circumstances.

Still, conjunctive multiple causation introduces us to a new kind of causal necessity. What meaning is to be given for this kind of necessity? Each cause necessary for the production of the effect is necessary *relative to* the required combination of causes. In reality, this kind of necessity is not well known in empirical social science. Any choice of hypothetical factors is hardly based on the necessity of their complementarity. Is this type of causal necessity an illusion? An examination of the "INUS condition" (Mackie 1965 and 1974) will help us answer.

3.3. INUS condition

INUS is an abbreviation for : "an Insufficient but Necessary part of a condition which is itself Unnecessary but Sufficient for the result." John L. Mackie illustrates the INUS condition in this example: a short-circuit is the cause of the fire in the house, a *non-sufficient* cause because flammable materials must also be present, yet still necessary in order for the flammable material to catch fire. The short-circuit and the flammable material together form a *sufficient* condition for a fire occurring—but while sufficient, the combination is not *necessary* because a fire could be caused in other ways. Mackie's example has the merit of throwing into relief that odd mixture of contingence and necessity which is found in all causal processes in which the effect results from the conjunction of multiple causes. But it is precisely this mixture which begs the question. Isn't the necessity referred to illusory?

Mackie has also had the merit of showing how "a unique sequence can be immediately recognised as causal". If the police chief can establish, first, that there was a short-circuit, and secondly that all other possible causes of the fire were absent, he might legitimately conclude that the short-circuit caused the fire. He does not have to support his conclusion by means of repeated observations or statistical regularities. On this point, one can understand the interest which has been shown in the INUS condition, since it appears to elude a requirement of the empiricist philosophy in the Humean tradition which was thought unavoidable, namely that causality requires regularity in the relation between cause and effect, and that the establishment of a causal relation requires us to have observed a regular connection between two events.[1] The INUS condition is, according to Marc-Wogau (Marc-Wogau K., 1962, pp. 226-227), "a necessary condition *post-factum*" which corresponds to causal explanation in history.

A match or a cigarette falling from an ashtray, or the pilot light of a gas stove might cause a fire as the short-circuit did. Thus the short-circuit is in no way a necessary condition for a fire. So why did Mackie insist that the short-circuit is a necessary part of the conditions for the fire? He explains that the police chief was able to eliminate all other possible causes of a fire, and that he had verified that a short-circuit had occurred. That was sufficient to establish that the short-circuit was the cause of the fire breaking out. Is that sufficient for calling this cause a necessary one? The short-circuit is a necessary cause *post-factum*, as Marc-Wogau put it. That means that without the short-circuit, the fire could not have occurred, since all other possible causes were not present. The short-circuit was therefore necessary, but in a quite particular manner : it was necessary since any other cause capable of carrying out the function of setting fire to flammable material was lacking. We might say that such a necessity is... contingent! The necessity of the cause—for the production of the effect—is contingent because it depends on the presence or absence of other causes which could have fulfilled the same function (the function of setting fire to flammable material) as part of a particular combination of causes. But is it not then true that behind the necessity of the short-circuit, there is another sort of necessity hidden, the necessity of its function?

Flammable materials do not set themselves on fire. Something has to set them on fire. The necessity of the short-circuit (that which I called a contingent necessity) is based on another kind of necessity, the necessity attached to its function within the singular combination which caused the fire. The INUS condition is deduced from the necessity of its function within a particular combination of causes and from the absence of other factors which might have fulfilled that function. Mackie did not pay much attention to that kind of necessity, which is not causal but functional. And yet it is this latter sort which is—it seems to me—the basis of the INUS condition.

3.4. Two new kinds of necessity

The causal necessity brought to light by Mackie under the name of the INUS condition is not an illusion. This type of necessity is quite different from the one which went along with the principle, "same cause, same effect", which stipulated that a single effect can have only a single cause. For Mackie's necessity is *relative to* a given combination of causes. One cause can cease to be necessary, or on the contrary become necessary to the production of an effect, according to the context, that is, according to the presence or absence of individual or social characteristics of different levels. It is apparent that this type of necessity must be of interest to multilevel analysis since it shows the decisive role of a context in relation to the pertinence of a proposed causal explanation.

Underlying the Mackie's INUS condition, we found another kind of necessity : the necessity of the functions which have to be carried out in order for the effects to occur. These functions guided the police chief's investigation into the causes of the fire. What flammable materials were present in the house, and what possible sources of a spark were there? His knowledge of combinations of functions necessary for the production of the observed effect allows him to reduce drastically at the outset of the investigation the number of *possible* causes. Similarly, someone using multilevel analysis does not have to explore all the factors and levels which are imaginable. If the researcher knows which functions have to be carried out in order for the phenomenon (which he or she is trying to explain) to occur, then the combinations of factors at various levels chosen for testing will be those which *can* fulfil those functions. This second type of necessity should also interest multilevel analysis since it can guide the researcher in the choice of pertinent factors at various levels.

I am convinced that researchers in social sciences raise questions spontaneously concerning functions which must be carried out in order for a given observed effect to be produced, in the course of their proposing a causal hypothesis to explain it. But what we have just learned leads us to conduct this questioning, about functions necessary for the production of an effect, in a methodical fashion. We will reach this same conclusion at the end of the second part of this chapter, at which time we will have established the usefulness of opening up multilevel analysis to systems analysis.

In the introduction to this chapter I stated that we would seek to know whether there existed determinations which can lead to generalisations, even though all evidence indicates that social life is unstable. We will no longer seek help from the principle, "same cause, same effect". Help must come from the methodical study of combinations of functions which are necessary for the production of the observed effects. That which can be generalised over several different social contexts as concerns observations of a single effect, is the combination of functions which are necessary for the production of the effect. It is because this combination is *necessary* (and on condition that it is really necessary) for the production of the effect, that it can give rise to generalisations applicable to any situation or social context in which the effect is actually observed.[2] That is not how things stand with the combination of factors which produces the observed effect within a given context, because the same combination of functions can be carried out, in different contexts, by different combinations of factors.

In the second part of this chapter, I will show how the study of combinations of functions fits into the framework of systems analysis. We will then find out that a combination of functions has a real power to determine phenomena. But this determination by combinations of functions is not causal in nature. The importance of studying combinations of functions in relation to causal analysis will then become apparent.

3.5. Interactions

Up to this point we have noted how multiple causes can produce a single effect, disjunctively and conjunctively. Now we move to situations in which a single cause produces different effects. A cause can produce different effects by being associated with some other causes. The principle, "same cause, same effect", is once again set aside.

We say that two or more causes *interact* if the effect of one cause is modified by the action of one or more other causes. This is the type of causal determination which Paul Lazarsfeld described by multivariate analysis. Interaction was the topic of an in-depth analysis by Raymond Boudon (1967). Multilevel analysis provides many illustrations of this type of causal conjunction, and Boudon's book provides a powerful critical and theoretical framework for an examination of multilevel analysis.

Beyond the causal interaction analysed by Lazarsfeld and Boudon, there is another kind of interference which explains how a single cause can produce different effects. That is what we shall now examine.

4. THE STOIC PRINCIPLE OF CAUSALITY

4.1. The thing which undergoes the effect cooperates in the production of the effect

There is a type of interference which reverses current conceptions of causality, even more than the interferences between several causes which we have spoken of above. This type was central to the Stoic conception. Michael Frede wrote a fascinating study about the Stoic conception of causality (1980). The type of interference is this: the thing which undergoes the effect cooperates in the production of the effect.

A cylinder, a cone, or a top cannot begin to move without being pushed. The person who provides this push is thus the antecedent cause. But once the initial motion has been imparted, Chrysippus thinks that the rest of the action comes from the thing itself, and that is what makes the cylinder roll or the top turn. The actual movement is the result of joint action by the external antecedent cause and the thing which undergoes the effect. According to Chrysippus this kind of causal interference exists in all causal relations.

A given effect is not simply the result of the action of external factors, but also the result of the action of the thing which undergoes the effect. Chrysippus also observes that the nature of a cylinder, a cone, or a top (that is, their matter and form) determines their movement : a cone does not roll like a cylinder, or turn like a top. The explanation of a phenomenon cannot therefore be found entirely on the side of the action and of the nature of the external factors which gave rise to the phenomenon. We must also look for part of the explanation on the side of the action and the nature of the thing which has undergone the effect.

Frede adds that for Chrysippus the thing which undergoes the effect is through its own action most often the principal cause of the effect undergone. I offer this example : the water I put on my tomato plants is a cause of their growth, but the causal auto-determination of the plants, acting jointly with the water, seems more important. In fact, if I watered stones, that would not cause them to grow. The water is only a *synergon* (something which cooperates in some work) for the growth of my tomato plants, but the plants themselves are *autotele* (they determine their own growth).

The mundane example of the tomato plants shows that the kind of causal interference which conditions, according to the Stoics, all causal relations, is easily observed and even belongs to common sense. But it is often left out of the debate over causality in philosophy of science[3] and has hardly been utilised in social sciences. By contrast it is quite familiar in psychology, at least since differential psychology drew attention to the fact that the same stimulus applied to different subjects can produce different responses.

The causal interference noted by the Stoics has a major theoretical implication. A single cause can produce different effects according to whether its action is applied to one thing or another. The variety of effects is the result of a type of causal interference different from that identified by Lazarsfeld. The principle "same cause, same effect" is disqualified once again. Another principle of causality emerges which Frede states in this way : each time something does something there are at least two active causes in play, an *external* cause and an *internal* cause (belonging to the thing which undergoes the effect). External and internal causes both have something to contribute to the production of the effect.

The relation between external cause(s) and the effect produced, and between internal cause(s) and the effect produced, are both not pre-determined, because they determine each other. But this does not lead us to conclude that the effect is indeterminate. It is determined by the nature and the joint action of external causes and the thing which undergoes the effect. The effect cannot be determined by antecedent causes or by their actions alone, nor by the thing which undergoes the effect or by its action alone.

Here we encounter again the distinction between pre-determinism and determinism drawn by Bunge, mentioned above. But the argument now is different. This time, it is not merely a question of conditions which must be fulfilled in order for a cause to produce its effect. It is a question of the auto-determination of the thing which undergoes the action of external causes. The causal principle of the Stoics was admittedly inspired by their desire to safeguard moral responsibility without giving up the principle that everything is determinate.

4.2. Two ways of explaining why a cause is followed by its effect

Let's stay with the Stoics a little longer. For the Stoics there are two ways of explaining *why* a cause is followed by its effect. In order for a thing to be the cause of an effect, it is not enough that it be merely present, but in addition it must do something, be active. The cylinder will not move if I stand in front of it, but only if I push it. The knife does not kill unless it pierces the heart. And in order for a cause to come into effect, the thing which undergoes the effect must also be active. This is what Chrysippus illustrates by showing the movements of the cone, the cylinder, and the top. The conjunction of the actions of the cause and of the thing which undergoes the effect is the first of two explanations of the causal relation.

The second kind is as follows : Why do some things and not others produce the actions and reactions observed? The effect would not be produced if the thing which acts and that which reacts did not have the matter and the form that they do (Chrysippus refers to the *aitiai* of Aristotle; the reference is to what we would call today, loosely, the nature of things). The knife would not kill if it were not of iron (its matter) and if it were not pointed (its form). Thus there is a second way of explaining why a cause is followed by its effect. But this is more a matter of necessary conditions, Seneca explains; and it is fruitless to study them, in the opinion of many Stoics, because necessary conditions are often hidden or obscure, uncertain or too difficult even to imagine (what, for example, are the matter and form of tomato plants?). Posidonius is the exception. Though he belongs to the Stoic school, he carries out significant investigations of etiology in physiology, psychology, and meteorology.

The reluctance of most Stoics to study the nature of things should not be confused with the skepticism of Hume and empiricist philosophy. The Stoics judged explanation by the nature of things (their matter or form) to be pertinent but arduous and uncertain. The empiricist position, in contrast, is that the explanation of causal relations by the nature of things is an illusion, because the nature of things is not accessible through our senses. We will never know, said Hume, why heat is a constant concomitant of flame. If perchance the day should arrive, when we discover to Hume's stupefaction the reason why a flame is regularly accompanied by heat, the Stoic would rejoice, and cease to maintain that it was useless to seek to know the nature of heat. Why should we then continue, following empiricist philosophers, to hold that scientific investigation must limit itself to the establishment of absolute or statistical regularities between two or more events?

In medicine, in order to explain a disease, we look both at the physiological or biochemical structures of an organism (forms and matters of the organism) and at the actions which may have caused the sickness : what did he eat last night? Have there been other such cases at his school? Has he been smoking long? etc. This is a familiar example of a scientific investigation which tries to explain certain effects not only by seeking the action of causes which might have called forth the effects, but also by searching on the side of the nature of the things which undergo the effects.

5. NON-CAUSAL DETERMINATIONS

At the end of a long and meticulous work of elucidation of the traditional notion of causality, Mario Bunge (1979) identified three major characteristics of causal determination: linearity, unidirectionality, and externality. These three characteristics which are attributed by the tradition to causality are mostly borne out by experience. To question the linearity of causal determination is to assume the obligation of taking into account, all at once, all the factors which might contribute immediately or distantly to the production of an effect. This makes analysis impossible, and fails to recognise that chains of events exist which can be distinguished from the circumstances which accompany them. Similarly, we must retain the unidirectionality of the causal relation because it accounts for the preponderance of action which one variable quite often exerts over another. Finally it goes without saying that many causes are external to the thing which undergoes an effect. There can then be no question of giving up these three characteristics of causality. But must we then ignore determinations which are not linear, not unidirectional, or which are internal to the thing which undergoes an effect? Quite the contrary—when we specify the nature of causal determinations as Bunge has done, we see more distinctly the existence, in nature as in social life, of forms of determination which are not linear (the case with multiple causation), not unidirectional (the case with reciprocal actions), and whose determining factors are not exclusively external to the thing which undergoes the effect (as in the case noted by the Stoics, and this is also the case with phenomena of emergence, which we will discuss below). Such determinations are not causal, in the sense that they lack one or another of the three characteristics of causal determination.

The forms of multiple causation I have examined are not strictly causal because they do not satisfy the criterion of linearity. One may nonetheless speak of them as causal determinations for this reason : these forms of multiple causation restrict significantly the number of factors considered as causes of the effect, and try to differentiate these factors from all the circumstances which contribute to the production of the effect. This is not absolute linearity, but it is sufficient for us to isolate, from out of the welter of all kinds of factors which may contribute immediately or distantly to the observed effect, a core or chain of causes which generate the effect.

Besides causal determinations, Bunge lists seven other kinds of determination : quantitative self-determination, reciprocal action, qualitative self-determination (dialectical determination), statistical determination, structural determination, teleological determination, and mechanical determination which combines quantitative self-determination, reciprocal action, and causal determination. Bunge adds that this inventory is not complete and underlines the fact that in scientific practice, causal and non-causal determinations are combined in different ways.

The way in which Bunge differentiates non-causal determinations is open to debate. One might propose other classifications or lists (see Franck, 1994) since, as Bunge says, the types of determinations can combine in different ways in the practice of research and explanation. But this is not the place to discuss that. My aim is rather to draw attention to the gain which multilevel analysis can realise from considering non-causal determinations. I will begin by reviewing the manner in which the 18th century discovery of reciprocal action, in physiology and even earlier in mechanics, allowed people to account in rational terms for phenomena of emergence. I will base myself upon the concept of emergence in order to propose a theoretical definition of the notion of a social "level". Then, I will associate the concept of level with that of system, and try to show how causal analysis and systems analysis can be combined, in order to do justice to relations of determination between social levels.

6. THE NOTION OF RECIPROCAL ACTION

The various causal interferences which we have examined up to this point are unidirectional : they do not take into consideration the action which the very thing which undergoes an effect can exercise in its turn upon the thing or things which exert the first causal action. We will now look into the implications of reciprocal action.

The need to call on a notion of reciprocity of actions between the thing which determines and the thing which undergoes that effect became evident in the new science of physiology born in the 18th century, and reciprocal determination was commented on in philosophy quite early. The different parts of a living organism, Kant says (1790), form a whole by being reciprocally cause and effect of each other. Drawing attention to reciprocal causality as it had been observed in the physiology of living organisms, Kant inspired Hegel's dialectical logic, and he started the philosophy of nature which flourished during the period from Schelling to Bergson. Still later, the notion of reciprocal action reappeared in currents of systems analysis : a system gets defined as a complex of elements which determine each other. Reciprocal action also inspired the notion of *feedback*, and determinations of this type have become quite familiar to us as involved with the automatic control systems which operate household appliances.

Still, the concept of reciprocal action was already central in classical mechanics before it was established in physiology, as Mario Bunge emphasises. By affirming the principle that for every action there is an equal and opposite reaction (Newton's Third Law), Newton broke with the unidirectional character attributed to determination by Scholastic thinkers. Before Newton, Galileo and Descartes had introduced the principle of inertia, abandoning the scholastic principle which stated "everything that moves is moved by something else, opening thus the way for the idea of self-determination". Bunge (1979, II.4.4 and *passim*) combats over many pages the long-standing confusion between mechanics and causal explanation. The same confusion, in the 19th century and still in the 20th, fed arguments made by those who demanded a specific methodology for the study of living things, different from the one which ruled physics[4]. The same confusion between mechanics and causal explanation still nourishes the demand in some schools of social science for a specific methodology for the study of Humankind, one different from the supposedly causal methodology employed in physical and biological sciences.

This brief historical review must suffice to suggest that the concept of reciprocal action, far from being marginal with regard to the concepts of linear and unidirectional causality, is on the contrary a prize possession of both physics and biology. That is why the concept has had so much importance in the history of ideas since the 19th century, up to the present. The attention which social science has given it in certain periods, for example in Marxist economy, or in the systemic current of thought, was quite well founded.

Still, it would be imprudent to present reciprocal action as an alternative to unidirectional causality, as has often been done. There are at least two reasons for not reopening that area of controversy. These were clearly set forth by Bunge (*op. cit.*, ch. 6) and I will review them here.

First, the ontological point of view must be distinguished from the methodological. Bunge was not afraid to write that the unidirectionality of causation is ontologically inadequate since all known actions are accompanied or followed by reactions, that is, since the effect always reacts back on the input unless the latter has ceased to exist. But unidirectionality of causation is often a hypothesis leading to adequate approximations and, more often than not, it is the sole practical course that can be taken in many cases; hence, it is methodologically justified.

Second, if unidirectionality of causation does often lead to adequate approximations, it is because in reality most reciprocal actions are not symmetrical, that is, there is a strong dependence of the effect upon the cause, with a negligible reaction of the output back on the input. Bunge underlines the necessity of being able to isolate predominant aspects, and definitely genetic, hence irreversible, connections. To view society as a muddle of reciprocal actions standing all on the same level would make all explanation impossible. We are thus led to recommend, on the methodological level, a complementarity between unidirectional causal determinations and reciprocal determinations.

This valuable review encourages us, on one hand, to look cautiously into ways of introducing reciprocal determination into multilevel analysis, but also to seek means of identifying, among the numerous interconnections which may exist between factors of various levels, those interconnections which predominate. Multilevel analysis will always be doing less than it should in the eyes of those who wish science to be the representation of the totality of the universe—or the social universe—as a system of reciprocal action. But it is more important not to disappoint those who, less ambitiously, will ask why these interconnections have been chosen, and not others which are in their view as important or more so. But as I showed above, the way to identify the most important of the many interconnections which may exist between factors at different levels is to take as guide the combination of functions which is necessary for the production of the phenomenon one wishes to explain.

7. THE NATURE OF LEVELS

7.1. Emergence

Reciprocal determination can lead in the direction of two different kinds of effects. In the first kind, it is observed that the factor which exerts a primary action on some other thing also in turn undergoes, in reaction, a quantitative or qualitative variation. A classic example is that of the predator and its prey : the predator progressively decimates the prey species until that species becomes too few to feed it, and then its own numbers decrease, which permits the prey species to multiply, allowing the predator species to expand once again. We have here an example of a *causal cycle*, analogous to those which operate in automatized machines. But factors acting reciprocally can also integrate into a new unity. This second kind of effect due to reciprocal determination is the one which has so influenced the history of ideas since the 19th century. The emergence of new unified wholes due to the reciprocal action of certain components is a spectacular effect among living creatures. How can we explain the fact that the various components of an organism, by being reciprocally cause and effect of each other, form a whole? This question has always been an intriguing one. Still, the emergence of new wholes as a result of reciprocal action among their parts is not particular to living organisms. Hegel at an early date raised this type of reciprocal determination to the level of a universal principle, and sought to conceive the logic underlying it.

One part of the mysterious character one has often seen attributed to phenomena of emergence comes, I think, from the fact that many are tempted to picture to themselves the emerging entity as something different from the elements from which it emerges. Is the organism other than its cells? Is water something other than the hydrogen and oxygen which it is made up of? The whole does not subsist beside, or above, or around its parts. The organism is not an envelope which contains the organs or cells, the container of a content. The emergent entity is nothing but a combination of reciprocal actions between component parts of that entity, in conformity with a determinate structure.

We must nonetheless recognise that the emergent entity has properties which its component parts do not have. Water has properties that neither oxygen nor hydrogen have. Organisms have properties that cells don't have. This means the combination of reciprocal actions between the component parts in conformity with a determinate structure is not less real than the parts themselves. Think of a clock. It is the combination of reciprocal actions between the parts which makes them a clock. The clock is not less real than the parts of which it is made.

Can the concepts of reciprocal action and emergence help us attack the question of the nature of social levels, and the question of the nature of determinations between social levels? That is what we shall now see.

7.2. Matter and form

In his book La logique du vivant (1970, p. 323), Nobel laureate François Jacob wrote:

> Living beings construct themselves (...) through a series of packages. They are arranged according to a hierarchy of discontinuous groupings. At each level, unities of fairly well-defined size and more or less identical structure, unite to form a whole at the next level. Each of these unities constituted by the integration of sub-unities can be designated by the general term integron. An integron is formed by the assembly of integrons of a lower level; it participates in the construction of an integron at a higher level.

Molecules form cells, cells form "populations" of cells, and those populations form organisms. But Jacob added that organisms themselves unite to form "integrons" of a higher level, as populations of individuals. Individuals are linked together by "systems of communication which no longer function within the organism, but between organisms" (*op. cit.*, p. 339). In humans,

> this brings about new systems of communication, regulation, memory, which function at a higher level than the organism. (...) Thus is constituted a new hierarchy of integrons. From the organisation of families to the modern State, from ethnic groups to coalitions of nations, an entire series of integrations is founded on a variety of cultural, moral, social, political, economic, military, or religious codes, etc. (...) with their codes, their regulations, their interactions, the objects which are constituted by cultural and social integrons go beyond the explanatory schemas of biology. Once again we have to do with the integration of elements which are themselves integrated (*ibid.*, p. 341-342).

Jacob's approach is hierarchical, and this approach is customary in biology, though the determination of hierarchical levels may vary according to one's program of research. But Jacob had the audacity to extend the hierarchy beyond biology, while admitting that the explanatory schemas of biology could not explain any modes of integration which might be at work at higher levels.

How can we conceive this hierarchy? Can we represent such a hierarchy to ourselves as a "series of packages" or as a "box made of boxes" or "Russian dolls", as Jacob writes? Susser and Susser (1996) have more recently employed the image of Chinese boxes. But such metaphors are misleading. They risk making us forget what Hegel commented on often, which I recalled above : the emergent entity is nothing but the combination of the component parts from which it emerges. That which differentiates an "integron" from the entities of a lower level that go to make it up, can only be the fact that the lower-level entities are combined according to a particular structure in the higher entity. It is the structure which makes the difference between higher and lower level. And it is the structure which explains the appearance, at the higher level, of properties which did not exist in the lower-level entities. This applies to social levels in which multilevel analysis is interested, just as much as it does to levels which have for a long time been identified in biology within living creatures. And we begin thus to form a more precise idea of what a hierarchy of social levels is.

Let's call the components of an emerging entity its *matter*. The structure to which the relations between these components conforms we can call the *form* of the emerging entity. We can then say that the relation between two social levels is one of matter to form, and of form to matter, depending on whether we are ascending or descending the hierarchy of levels.

That which is the *form* of a *matter* of a lower level is the *matter* of a *form* on a higher level. The same social entity is thus both *matter* and *form* depending on whether we place it in relation to the social entity on the higher level or the lower level. Aristotle was the first to show that things are both matter and form at once. This is what we call *hylemorphism* : "hyle" means matter and "morphe" means form. I attempt, for my part, to benefit from aristotelian hylemorphism insofar as it can clarify the nature of levels in social life, as can also be done for levels in biology.

8. FACTORS AND SYSTEMS

The nature of levels such as they may be conceived by the aid of the philosophical concept of hylemorphism can help us clear up the question of the relations which occur between factors and systems. This question was raised by Diez Roux, and the need for epidemiology to return to systems analysis has been endorsed by a number of writers in recent years. The need is not less great as regards other disciplines, I think. But how are we to understand the attraction of systems analysis? Often we expect from systems analysis a sort of extension of causal analysis. This would mean increasing the number of variables to which one can impute an influence over the phenomenon one wishes to explain, and then establishing between these variables a network of causal relations or relations of functional dependence which would allow us to understand how the various influences work together.

But a quite different benefit comes from conducting systems analysis in the light of hylemorphism. We can seek to know which determinations are worked by the system upon the factors which belong to this system, and which exercised by the factors upon the system. It is, then, the relation between factors and the system they belong to which must be clarified. How does the system influence the factors, and how do the factors influence the system? The following treatment applies to this second version of systems analysis.

Let's link the concept of system to that of emergent entity which we used up to now. A system emerges from the combination of its elements. These act upon each other, some in a unidirectional way, others in a reciprocal one, and we call them factors. These are the matter of the system. The system is nothing other than the factors which compose it, except that in a system the action of factors on each other conforms to a definite structure, a structure that we call the form of the system. It is because of this form that the system acquires properties the factors which compose the system don't have. Now that we have linked these concepts, system and emergent entity, we will be able to treat the relation between factors and their system as one of matter to form.

8.1. The factors influence the system

Our examination of the INUS condition of Mackie can help us now. We saw that the INUS condition's necessity was based on another kind of necessity. It was based on the combination of functions which is necessary for the production of the observed effects. For example, the necessity of the short-circuit with regard to the fire breaking out—in the absence of other causes—is based on the necessity of some flammable materials being ignited. The functions (that of igniting some flammable material and the function of catching fire) were performed by the short circuit and the curtains, let's say. These functions could have been performed by other factors. The short circuit and the curtains are the matter of the system. The form (the structure) of the system is the combination of the short-circuit and the curtains, and it is also the combination of their functions. We must take care not to confuse these two aspects of the form of a system : this form is at once a combination of factors (let us call this combination *empirical*) and a combination of functions (let us call this a *theoretical* combination).

If the short-circuit had not set the curtains on fire, the fire would not have occurred. We have here a case of conjunctive multiple causation : the fire is the effect of a conjunction of the short and the curtains. But this is also a case of another kind of determination : if the short-circuit had not caught the curtains on fire the system, that of the causal conjunction of short and curtains, would not have emerged. Within conjunctive multiple causation, there is a different kind of determination : the determination of the conjunction of factors (that is, of the system itself) by the factors themselves.

The distinction made here between production, by the factors, of the system which connects them, and the production of the properties of the system (here, the fire) may seem a bit fine in the example, but its importance appears when the production of the system covers a long time. For example, the railway system emerged and continues to emerge daily from its component parts (railway workers, a signalling system, the rails, freight trains, etc.) and it changes as a result of action by those parts, as when the introduction of new materials, new technologies, or new investment capital occurs. The railway system is determined by its parts, and this determination is not to be confused with the determination, by those same parts, of the properties of the railway system, for example its transport capacity. Another example: the school system is reproduced every day by its many parts, by the various job categories, budgets, learning techniques, administration, etc. One might study how these many parts or some of their characteristics (the number of students in class, the type of programs offered) contribute to the properties of the school system (for example the percentage of passing grades). But one could also study how these parts or characteristics, acting on each other, influence the evolution of the system itself. That is what the second version of systems analysis proposes. For example, has the introduction of computers in classes transformed the school system's structure (i.e. the *theoretical* combination of functions and/or the *empirical* combination of factors)?

Let us specify what this influence of the factors over the system consists. We return to Mackie's example. If the fire had been started, not by a short, but by a leak from a gas tank and the striking of a match, the emergent system would have been different. The theoretical form of the system (the combination of two functions, that of igniting some material and the function of catching fire) would be unchanged, but its empirical form (that is, the combination of factors) would no longer be the same, since the factors were different. It can also happen that the form of the functions of the system changes.

That would be the case if, for example, the introduction of computers into schoolrooms changed the combination of functions of the school, such as education, selection, socialisation, child care, professional training, etc.

8.2. The system influences the factors

Systems analysis, understood not as an extension of causal analysis but as the analysis of relations between the system and the factors from which it emerges, offers also the possibility of studying the influence of the form of the system upon its matter. This influence is of two kinds : one influence comes from the combination (which we have called *empirical*) of the factors making up the system, and another from the combination of the functions (*theoretical* combination) of the system. The first kind is illustrated by conjunctive multiple causation. Each of the causes which combine to produce an effect is incapable of producing it alone, yet if any of them is lacking in the causal combination, the effect will not occur. Thus it is the empirical combination of factors which determines the causal action of each one. In other words, the causal power of each factor is generated by the system of factors of which it is a part. No factor can exercise its causal power outside the system. For example, away from the curtains, the short-circuit is no longer the cause of a fire. This attests the quite large role systems analysis is destined to play (as analysis of relations between factors and their system) in causal analysis. Causal explanation can vary from one system (one environment of factors) to another. Systems analysis proposes to study the influence upon causal relations due to the system itself.

The influence exercised by the system's combination of functions upon the factors is even more important. The system defines those functions which must be carried out by the factors in order to produce the system properties. For example, the school system specifies a selection function for student tests. When a test fails to perform that function, it is dropped, or revised by its author, even if it still performs other functions properly, such as the function of evaluation. This happens when all the students get the same grade, for example. Inserting people (teachers, students, administrators) or any other thing (tests, school plays, science fairs) into their functions or suspending them from such functions—this is performed not by the system, but through other factors (for example by school rules, evaluation procedures, punishments from other acting persons etc.). But it is within the limits of their functions defined by the system that factors and persons, acting within the system, can exert causal force. In other words, the system's combination of functions limits the range of causal actions possible for actors and factors.

9. A SOCIAL PHILOSOPHY

Many aspire to better understand how the social and natural environment can influence behaviour, ideas, mores, and institutions, to say nothing of diseases, birth rates, immigration, etc. The burning question of the influence of the environment on our lives finds an answer—at least in conceptual terms—when we express the question in terms of a relation between a system and its elements in the manner of hylemorphism (form and matter). The environment (understood as system) does not act upon us or the world around us as a cause which produces an effect. The determination produced by the environment is of two kinds. First, the combination of factors (persons and things) composing a particular environment (the *empirical form* of the system), brings about for each of these factors some causal power. None of these factors could exercise the causal action proper to it outside of the environment to which it belongs. Second, that which is possible to do is limited by the combination of social functions of the system (its *theoretical form*). The combination of social functions of the system defines the range of possible actions which can be performed by its agents or by other factors.

By defining the range of possible actions, and in conferring upon human and non-human factors the causal power they are capable of exercising with regard to social life, the environment defines possible behaviours, ideas, mores and institutions, as well as possible diseases, birth rates, immigration rates, etc. Must these constraints imposed by the system be interpreted as predeterminations? No, because we have learned above that social systems and natural systems do not fall from the sky, and are not invented by gods or demons. They are emergent. They are the result of reciprocal actions performed by the elements which are the component parts of these systems. The social environment exists only because it is reproduced every day through the actions of humans and the things which surround them, and the social environment changes under these influences. A social system is nothing other than the emergent form of social life. This form is made up of an empirical form of relations between social elements, and a theoretical form of combinations of functions which the elements cooperate in carrying out. When social relations change, the environment changes.

As may be inferred, systems analysis comports a social philosophy, in the sense of a general conception of the place of humans in society. But we should not forget that this general conception was the result of an effort toward the elucidation of the concept of a system which has been continuing since the 18th century, beginning in the natural sciences. The concept of system does not result from this social philosophy; rather the reverse. This means that we can continue to improve the general philosophical conception of society if we continue to refine the concept of a system, basing ourselves on the natural and human systems studied by various sciences.

10. CONCLUSION. CAUSAL ANALYSIS, SYSTEMS ANALYSIS, AND MULTILEVEL ANALYSIS

The constraints exercised by the form, both empirical and theoretical, of the social environment upon everything which can occur in it are very strong. We have seen what they consist of: these are not causal determinations. The constraints consist in delimiting what is possible, furnishing humans and things with causal power for a moment, or preventing them from exercising it. Yet such constraints are little studied in social sciences. More often than not we are satisfied today to study individual characteristics in order to explain social life. Why? Many reasons could be adduced to explain this turn in research in social science. One particularly interests us here: we seem to lack a methodology capable of analysing the constraints imposed by the environment. Can multilevel analysis help us to achieve such analysis?

First, multilevel analysis allows us to discern the influence upon behaviour of group characteristics and of other characteristics of the environment. Multilevel analysis matches thus the ambition which originally characterised 19th and 20th century social science. One wished for example to understand why crime rates were higher in some urban areas, or why rural life was transformed by commercial exchange, or why Protestants committed suicide more frequently than Catholics. With multilevel analysis, we have an instrument which can combine individual characteristics and collective or natural characteristics, which might allow us to escape from the ecological fallacy, and from controversies about whether the individual or the collective is to be given priority in explanation (see Courgeau, Chapter 2 in this volume).

Multilevel analysis also allows us to measure the influence of the environment, taken as a whole, upon some characteristics of individuals or of groups or of things and upon the correlations observed between characteristics from different levels. This is accomplished through comparisons between observations from different geographical regions, or from different social environments, e.g., groups of students, schools, urban neighbourhoods, etc.

Yet it is important to distinguish the influence exercised by the structure of some environment (i.e. its empirical and its theoretical form) from the influence which a number of characteristics of the same environment may exercise. This distinction seems hitherto neglected. We generally interpret differences observed from one region to another, or from one social environment to another, in causal terms only, and we lose all benefit from the distinction proposed above between causal determinations and systemic determinations. Measuring the environment's influence is not yet explaining this influence. It is the structure of the environment which explains why the observed correlations may vary across regions or social environments. In order to explain the influence of the environment (especially of the environment's empirical form, as we saw in our discussion of Mackie's thesis) upon the correlations observed between social characteristics from different levels, multilevel analysis must open itself up to new procedures, those of the analysis of system functions. The study of the combination of functions which are carried out in different environments (group of students, school, company, sports team, labour union, urban neighbourhood, army, State, etc.) should permit, it seems to me, a considerable increase in the fruitfulness of multilevel analysis.[5]

NOTES

[1] John Stuart Mill (1891, Book III, ch. III, 2, 3), who had a decisive influence on empiricist philosophy, nonetheless affirmed that it is possible to establish a causal relation based on the observation of a single occurrence. One can do this, he writes, through the aid of the inductive method as established by Francis Bacon, not by settling for induction understood as enumeration.

[2] This argument was set forth in Franck (2002, Conclusion of Part II).

[3] Mario Bunge, in contrast, devotes an entire chapter to it (*op. cit.* ch. 7).

[4] "If the romantics had been better acquainted with Newtonian mechanics, they would not have felt justified in decrying it, but might have found in that science the germs of three categories of determination of which the *Naturphilosophen* had been very fond, namely, self-movement, reciprocal action, and inner 'strife' of opposites" (Bunge, 1979, p. 116).

[5] Is there a dependable way of knowing the combination of functions which governs the correlations we are able to establish? This question was the object of an in-depth examination in the first volume of the Methodos Series (Franck, 2002) and I refer the reader to that work. That book shows that we can construct the combination of functions of a system by studying its properties, and I drew attention to the fact that this procedure is common in natural science, and not different from the procedure which was called *induction* in the 17th century (Bacon, Galileo, Descartes, Newton, etc.) before the reinterpretation of induction by empiricist philosophy (Hume, Mill, Hempel, Popper, etc.).

REFERENCES

Boudon, R. (1967). *L'analyse mathématique des faits sociaux.* Paris: Plon.

Boudon, R. (1988). Individualisme ou holisme : un débat méthodologique fondamental. In H. Mendras, & M. Verret (Eds.), *Les champs de la sociologie française* (pp. 31-45). Paris: Armand Colin.

Bunge, M. (1979). *Causality and Modern Science.* New York: Dover Publications.

Durkheim, E. (1937). *Les règles de la méthode sociologique.* Paris: PUF, (original work published 1895).

Durkheim, E. (1930). *Le Suicide.* Paris: P.U.F., (original work published 1897).

Franck, R. (1994). Les explications causale, fonctionnelle, systémique ou structurale, et dialectique, sont-elles complémentaires?. In R. Franck (Ed.), *Faut-il chercher aux causes une raison? L'explication causale dans les sciences humaines* (pp. 275-302). Paris—Lyon: Librairie Philosophique Vrin.

Franck, R. (1995). Mosaïques, machines, organismes et sociétés. Examen métadisciplinaire du réductionnisme. *Revue Philosophique de Louvain, 93*, 67-81.

Franck, R. (Ed.). (2002). *The Explanatory Power of Models, Bridging the gap between empirical and theoretical research in the social sciences.* Boston/Dordrecht/London: Kluwer Academic Publisher (Methodos Series vol.1).

Frede, M. (1980). The Original Notion of Cause. in M. Schofield, M. Burnyeat, & J .Barnes (Eds.), *Doubt and Dogmatism—Studies in Hellenistic Epistemology.* Oxford: Clarendon Press.

Granger, G.-G. (1988). *Essai d'une philosophie du style.* Paris: Editions Odile Jacob.

Jacob, F. (1970). *La logique du vivant.* Paris: Gallimard.

Jones, K. (1993). *"Everywhere is Nowhere" : multilevel perspectives on the importance of place.* The University of Portsmouth Inaugural Lectures.

Kant, E. (1968). *Kritik der Urteilskraft.* Hamburg: Felix Meiner, (original work published 1790).

Koopman, J.S. (1996). Emerging objectives and methods in epidemiology. *American Journal of Public Health, 86,* 630-632

Loriaux, M. (1994). Des causes aux systèmes. In R. Franck (Ed.), *Faut-il chercher aux causes une raison? L'explication causale dans les sciences humaines* (pp. 41-86). Paris—Lyon: Librairie Philosophique Vrin

Mackie, J. L (1965). Causes and conditions. *American Philosophical Quarterly*, , 245-264.

Mackie, J. L. (1974). *The cement of the Universe. A Study of Causation.* Oxford: Clarendon Press.

Marc-Wogau K. (1962). On Historical Explanation. *Theoria. 28,* 213-233.

Mill, J.S. (1891). *A System of Logic ratiocinative and inductive.* London: Longmans, Green, and Co., (original work published.1843).

Nowak, S. (1975). Causal interpretations of statistical relationships in social research. In Blalock H. M. & al. (Eds.), *Quantitative Sociology.* New York: Academic Press.

Susser, M., & Susser, E. (1996). Choosing a future for epidemiology : II. From black box to Chinese boxes and eco-epidemiology. *American Journal of Public Health*, *86*, 674-7

Valade, B. (2001). De l'explication dans les sciences sociales: holisme et individualisme. In J.-M. Berthelot (Ed.), *Epistémologie des sciences sociales* (pp. 357-405). Paris: Presses Universitaires de France.

Wunsch, G. (1988). *Causal Theory and Causal Modeling, Beyond Description in the Social Sciences.* Leuven: Leuven University Press.

Daniel COURGEAU

GENERAL CONCLUSION

The preceding chapters have illustrated the validity, the contribution, and the fertility of the multilevel approach applied to different social sciences; but they have also described the main criticisms levelled at the approach as well as the limits encountered when it is applied with excessive rigour. The multilevel approach provides a solution to the problems that occur when working on a single level. It avoids the risks of the ecological and atomistic fallacies by accommodating the effects of characteristics operating at different aggregation levels. By contrast, when we want to examine the set of dynamic, reciprocal, and non-linear relationships that exist inside each level and between levels, the multilevel approach still seems too limited in its present form. We see the need to extend its scope to other analytical strategies introducing new hypotheses. We should investigate and verify whether more complex multilevel models might not offer a fuller approach for the social sciences examined here.

The authors have described—with great clarity and detail—the complex interplay between the contributions and limits of the multilevel approach in their respective social sciences. There is thus no need for us to rehearse these issues in our conclusion. Some authors have even explored ways of handling systems more complex than those which the multilevel approach usually makes it possible to treat; these investigations have shown that such a treatment still requires major advances in the social sciences. In particular, Robert Franck has focused on the concept of structure, which gives us an understanding of how the levels connect from the top down and from down up—a point to which we shall return in greater detail below.

Our aim here will be to take the authors' findings one step further by asking ourselves broader questions on the field opened up by multilevel analysis, on the nature of the concept of probability used, and on the difficulty of defining relevant levels and their interconnections in the widest sense. In other words, how should we implement a fuller theory of human behaviour?

1. EXPERIMENTAL OR NON-EXPERIMENTAL APPROACH

We begin by showing how the multilevel approach revitalises the very old debate between the experimental approach, used in the natural sciences and some social sciences, and the non-experimental approach, often imposed for ethical reasons in the social sciences. Let us first define the problem.

In social sciences, the experimental approach, when experiments are ethically permissible, consists in distributing the subjects at random between two groups: in epidemiology, for example, the first undergoes the treatment to be

D. Courgeau (ed.) Methodology and Epistemology of Multilevel Analysis, 199-213.

tested (target group), the second is totally excluded from the treatment (control group). We can easily see that such a procedure, applied to a sufficiently large sample, makes it possible to keep parasite risk factors—including unknown ones—under control, except for random variation. This property is crucial and seems to allow an effective neutralisation of the influence of parasite variables (Schwartz, 1989). But we will see that in some cases, most notably in a multilevel analysis, this method is not without dangers.

Of course, such an approach cannot be implemented unless the scientific protocol does not clash with the interest of interviewees. This sharply curtails the number of such tests in the social sciences, but some experiments along these lines have been conduced in epidemiology, demography, economics, and education: for example, in epidemiology, the test of the effectiveness of the Salk polio vaccine (Francis *et al.*, 1955) and, in demography, the tests of the effectiveness of new contraceptive methods (Wunsch, 1994).

When the experimental approach is unfeasible for ethical or cost reasons, the researcher must resort to a non-experimental approach, in which the subjects cannot be distributed at random. Broadly speaking, there are two major types of non-experimental studies in the social sciences.

The first is the prospective or retrospective cohort study, which allows a measurement of selected characteristics of subjects, but cannot yield information on the unknown factors. When a single event is studied, cohort analysis is the direct analogue of the experimental approach, where different groups are compared, but in this case the investigator cannot designate individuals at random for the experiment.

The second is the case-control study, in which the cases observed (the target individuals) are matched by controls exhibiting similar characteristics; we then compare the relative risks obtained for the target individuals and for the control ones. The case-control study differs from the longitudinal study in the initial choice of cases tracked, as it requires a selection of controls in addition to that of cases for observation.

This difference aside, both procedures operate identically and do not permit a neutralisation of the hidden parasite variables, as in the experimental approach. We can never be sure of knowing all the causes of the phenomenon studied, and there will always remain variables that cannot be included in the experimentation protocol. Hence the non-experimental approach is generally considered less satisfactory than the experimental approach.

Despite its superiority, we will now see that the experimental approach carries risks of incorrect assignment, in particular when we want to use a multilevel analysis.

First, we can show that the experimental approach is not fully effective unless the hidden variables act in a strictly unrelated manner (Wunsch, 1994). If an interaction exists between the experimental treatment and the hidden variables, randomisation will not enable us to clearly discern the treatment's specific effect; all we will see is the conjunction of the specific effect and of its interaction with the hidden variables. When the context changes, the effect identified in a randomised test may be altered by the interaction, even though the treatment's effect remains the same. Thus a multilevel analysis on experimental data, involving groups in which the context changes, could mistakenly indicate an effect of the treatment that may not exist in reality.

To give a more eloquent example, let us take the case of a contraceptive, whose specific effectiveness is independent of the country of use, but whose correct use depends heavily on the degree of user motivation, which varies from one country to another: the degree of motivation acts as a hidden variable here. If we perform a multilevel analysis of the effectiveness of this contraceptive method on an experimental sample where the first level is the individual and the second is the country of use, we may very well find a strong effect of the country owing to the hidden variable, whereas there is no reason for the specific effectiveness to vary between countries. The interaction between the treatment and user motivation is the only explanation for the incorrect observation of the effect. Here the use of a non-experimental approach, with a correct measurement of female users' motivation, would reveal the motivation effect and eliminate the country-of-use effect. An experimental approach with a random assignment scheme—naturally implemented without explicit recourse to that measurement—could not show the country-of-use effect.

Second, an experimental approach of this kind, used in a multilevel study, can also lead to erroneous conclusions, as the random protocol for sampling the individuals may give free rein to the effects of the composition of the group in which the individuals are included—effects that will be attributed to the phenomenon studied. To illustrate this, let us take a very clear example suggested by Harvey Goldstein (1998). Suppose we want to demonstrate an effect of class size on students' scholastic progress. We can construct a perfectly controlled sample by randomly distributing students into small and large classes, and observing their progress over a given period of time. Under these conditions, randomisation should enable us to conclude whether size does or does not influence student progress.

Now, let us suppose that there is also an effect due to the existence of a particular group—for example, low-attaining children, who represent an average 10% of the student population. Let us consider the extreme case where class progress is reduced when low-attaining children make up at least 33% of the total class, with no effect of class size on the result. It is easy to show that the probability of being in a disadvantaged class will be fairly high in the sample of small classes, whereas it will be negligible in the sample of large classes. The randomised sample is thus very likely to display a class-size effect that does not actually exist, simply because the small classes alone will contain a high percentage of low-attaining children.

Our example is thus "an instance where a key rationale for randomisation, namely the equalisation (on average) of initial characteristics within the "treatments" being studied, undermines the possibility of valid inferences" (Goldstein, 1998, p. 14). By contrast, a survey of a representative sample of classes would have made it possible to work with a sufficient number of small and large classes containing high proportions of low-attaining children; this approach would have led to the right conclusions by factoring in the percentages of low-attaining children.

Lastly, an experimental approach is virtually impossible to use when we want to perform a multilevel event-history analysis, which incorporates the many events in an individual's life—events that appear at different aggregation levels. Such an analysis does not concentrate on a single effect of interest, on which the random sample will be centred; rather, the analysis will seek to interlink the events in an individual's life by placing them in the settings where they have been experienced. Here, of course, the best observation will consist in a comprehensive documentation of all the events for the entire population, of their timing, and of all the relevant contexts in which each individual has lived. Unfortunately, such a gathering of data is impossible, and the researcher will have to make do with a sample supplying the best possible information for the purpose.

Examining the case of a simple event-history survey—where individuals are regarded as independent units—Jan Hoem (1985) has already shown that the sampling plan needs to be non-informative, to ensure that it can be disregarded in the life-history analysis. If the survey is prospective, this will not be a problem; if the survey is retrospective, a selection will occur because one can only question survivors. In most cases, survival-based selection is not too problematic, as the data from a Swedish survey confirms (Lyberg, 1983).

A multilevel event-history survey raises more complex problems, and a general solution is not available. For example, if we want to monitor a cohort using a division of national territory into regions, the sample will initially need to be non-informative for each region. By contrast, if we want to track a sample of students from the beginning to the end of their schooling, and if we want to include class attainment in the analysis, we need to survey all the students—or at least a sample of the students—of each class during their stay in a given class. Only a prospective survey is possible in this case, and, if the sample of students tracked is small, it requires a much larger sample of the classes they successively attended.

In conclusion, we should mention a survey carried out in France, "Biographies et entourage" (life histories and contact circle, see: Lelievre *et al.*, 1998), which managed to follow a sample of individuals and their contact circles by questioning only the sampled individuals (the contact circle is defined as the set of members of the different households to which the individuals have belonged in their lifetime and of key family members who are not necessarily coresidents). This method reduces the sample to be questioned, but does not yield a detailed life history of contact-circle members. By contrast, it will be far more detailed than a conventional event-history survey, as it documents the households in which the individuals have lived from birth to death. The only requirement is for the sampling plan to be non-informative.

We can therefore conclude from this outline of various types of multilevel surveys that the experimental approach is not necessarily the most effective, even when it is acceptable to the population surveyed. The choice will accordingly depend on the aggregation levels to be examined and on whether the sample is to be monitored over time or not.

2. PROBABILITY: OBJECTIVIST, SUBJECTIVIST, OR LOGICIST APPROACH

As well as redefining the comparison between the experimental and non-experimental methods, the multilevel approach requires us to reconsider the use of probability. In mathematics, foundation-related issues are usually solved once satisfactory axiomatics have been developed. But that is not the case in probability theory. Although the latter has now been completely axiomatised for more than half a century (Kolmogorov, 1933), the controversies rage on—without a break—concerning the nature of probability and how much inference it allows. We must therefore begin by identifying the nature of these issues before examining what the multilevel approach can contribute.

The objectivist or frequentist approach rests on the law of large numbers defined by Bernoulli (1713), which tells us that the ratio of (1) the number of events observed to (2) the number of individuals exposed to the risk tends towards the probability of the event when the population exposed to the risk tends towards infinity. We can therefore assign an objective status to the probability of event that may occur indefinitely in identical conditions. This condition seems very constraining, particularly in the social sciences, although some of them have adopted it for specific studies. The objectivists also refuse to extend probability theory to any notion of uncertainty other than that involved in the occurrence of such indefinitely repeatable events—an uncertainty that can be verified empirically. In particular, the notion of a probability that a given proposition is true has no meaning for an objectivist, as we cannot define the probability of an intrinsically unique event.

Under these conditions, and from the observation of a sample, we may use statistical inference to test the validity of a given hypothesis for the population from which the sample has been picked, but not the probability that the hypothesis will materialise. This is possible if we assume that the observed sample belongs to a much vaster set of samples picked at random in that population. The analysis will consequently focus on the probability of obtaining the observed sample if the hypothesis is true—not on the probability that the hypothesis is true, which, as we have seen, is meaningless for an objectivist.

As the frequentist approach precludes an examination of the probability of different hypotheses that could explain a given empirical result, we are led to adopt a more subjectivist point of view. We will thus seek to show that if an individual behaves consistently in the presence of uncertainty, then the degrees of plausibility that he or she assigns to the various possible hypotheses can be expressed by real numbers compatible with the axioms of probability theory. This starting point depends on the significance that each of us assigns to consistent behaviour and leads to different axiomatic definitions of the "rational", which we cannot elaborate here. Readers interested in this approach can read Matalon's chapter on the epistemology of probability (1967).

In the subjectivist approach, statistical inference can rely on Bayes's theorem (1763). The problem addressed by the theorem consists in determining how the prior probability of a hypothesis can be revised by the observation of a later experience. It is easy to see why the frequentists reject this method of statistical inference, as they refuse to envisage the probability of a hypothesis that is a unique event, which can only be true or false. By contrast, for the subjectivists, the notion of the probability of a hypothesis is central to probability theory, and Bayes's theorem allows them to interpret inference as a decision-making process.

A third, "logicist" approach agrees with the subjectivists that probability is an indicator of a degree of belief. However, this degree is not regarded as a personal feeling, but as a logical relationship valid for everyone. Advocates of the third point of view therefore propose assigning probabilities using a logical analysis of incomplete information typically encountered in problems of statistical analysis. The latter originated in the work of Laplace (1812), was developed by Jeffreys (1939), Cox (1946), and Polya (1954), and was elaborated more fully by Jaynes (1996). It is determined by a small number of properties, which provide a foundation for probability theory:

- Divisibility and comparability—The degrees of plausibility are represented by real numbers and depend on the information available on the subject.
- Common sense—A greater plausibility must correspond to a larger number, and vice versa.
- Consistency—If any conclusion can be reached in different ways, each must lead to the same result.

The "logicist" approach leads to a generalisation of the mathematical rules of probability theory, and makes it possible to perform not only all the "frequentist" calculations, when the problems are sufficiently simple and idealised, but also "Bayesian" calculations in more complex situations, such as special cases. Moreover, when frequentist and Bayesian methods cannot be employed, the logicist approach allows the use of the principle of maximum entropy, to create an optimal model using all the information available. Lastly, because it is broader in scope than the first two approaches, it erases the distinction between "probability theory" and "statistical inference"—paving the way for a more general theory of inductive reasoning (Jaynes, 1996).

Let us now see what becomes of the three approaches to probability in a multilevel analysis.

In objectivist terms, we can regard the different levels as a random sample of contexts whose effects are distributed, say, in an approximately normal manner. For example, in education, when we have grades for students distributed in different classes (Goldstein, 1995), we can regard the classes observed in the sample as a random selection from a much larger population of classes, while the students are drawn from an equally larger population of students. This sample—examined at the student level as well as the class level—will give us much more specific information on both levels than when we examine them separately. At the same time as the effect of individual characteristics on grades, we have statistical information on (1) the effect of the characteristics of a class on its students' progress (contextual model) and (2) the effect of the students' characteristics on their progress taking into account the class they are attending (multilevel model).

What inference does such an analysis allow concerning an individual not observed in the sample, whose characteristics are known but whose grade is unknown? A useful insight here is provided by Fisher (1956), who expresses the ideas of an objectivist on these issues:

> This fundamental requirement [of no recognisable subset] for the applicability to individual cases of the concepts of classical probability shows clearly the role of subjective ignorance, as well as that of objective knowledge in a typical probability statement. It has been often recognised that any probability statement, being a rigorous statement involving uncertainty, has less factual content than an assertion of a certain fact would have, and at the same time has more factual content than a statement of complete ignorance. The *knowledge* required for such a statement refers to a well-defined aggregate, or population of possibilities within which the limiting frequency ratio must be exactly known. The necessary *ignorance* is specified by our inability to discriminate any of the different subaggregates having different limiting frequency ratios, such as must always exist (p. 33).

We see here that the identification of a "subaggregate" would enable us to infer the grade that an individual not observed in the survey might obtain, although the inference would naturally be associated with an estimated confidence interval. When we are working on a classic regression model we can say that, knowing the characteristics of a new individual, we can estimate the theoretical grade that we might expect from the model: we must assume that the individual would behave in the same manner as an individual in the initial sample possessing the same characteristics, and we must introduce the model's randomness. In a multilevel regression model, we need to introduce not only the model's individual randomness, but also the randomness of the parameters included in the model. This enables us to generalise the notion of statistical individual, described in the introduction, by considering the individual in each of the aggregation levels used for the analysis. But if we examine a real individual, then we have grounds for assuming that many characteristics, not taken into account by the survey, prevent the individual from being situated (as before) in a specific sub-population, as Fisher notes.

As long as the aggregation levels introduced (classes, schools, localities, etc.), can be regarded as being drawn from an infinite population, or at least a sufficiently vast population, the objectivist approach can be applied to such multilevel models. By contrast, let us suppose we are working on a comprehensive division of national territory into regions—as in human geography—and that we have taken a sample of the population from each region to determine, for example, if an individual is a chronic smoker or not, on the basis of individual and regional characteristics (Jones, 1993). Here, it is hard to consider that the regions have been picked from a bigger sample of regions, since they cover the entire territory. We can, of course, add regions of other countries to enlarge the sample, but the normality condition may well be broken and there is a strong likelihood of obtaining a distribution that will display, for example, two or more local maxima, owing to substantial differences between countries. In such circumstances, it is useful to examine whether a subjectivist point of view might solve the problem.

We show in this case that an empirical Bayes estimator, for example, can be used without having to bring in an infinite number of regions. From a prior estimation covering the entire country, and applying Bayes's theorem to the regional observations, we obtain an empirical Bayes estimator of the fact that the individual is a chronic smoker. We show that this estimator is far more accurate than a conventional estimator is. However, the empirical Bayesian method is inappropriate here unless we can assume the exchangeability of the prior estimators. We must therefore examine the implications of such a hypothesis in greater detail, so that we can justify the approach.

The concept of exchangeability was introduced by de Finetti (1974); later on, we shall see that it plays a role comparable to that of membership of a sub-population in the objectivist approach. Exchangeability, construed here in its subjective sense, implies judgements of similarity in the behaviour of individuals, which allow forecasts based on observations. We can regard two unknown quantities as exchangeable if, for any judgement involving one of them or both simultaneously, the probability assignments do not change when the two quantities are exchanged. In the previous example, we will assume that before observing the regional data, we cannot tell whether there are differences between regional data sets or not simply by looking at the national data. We can thus legitimately regard the regional data sets as exchangeable. By contrast, the *a posteriori* estimators may, of course, be non-exchangeable if major differences are found between the regions. We can show that these estimators would in any event be far more precise than conventional estimators, even if the hypotheses of prior-estimator exchangeability are grossly incorrect (Greenland, 2000).

The notion of exchangeability can be generalised to that of conditional exchangeability, if the joint distribution of n random variables, X, conditioned by the value of another random variable, Y, which can be multidimensional, is invariant whatever the permutation of the units (Lindley and Novik, 1981; Draper *et al.*, 1993; Greenland, 1998a). In the example above, if we observe two individuals whom we cannot identify as chronic smokers or not, but who possess identical characteristics regarded as influencing the fact of being a chronic smoker or not, then we can regard their chronic-smoker statuses as exchangeable.

This approach also leaves room for statistical inference from the sample. When the random variable X depends on a set of characteristics Y, for n individuals, a new individual whose characteristics Y are all identical to those of the n individuals may also be regarded as exchangeable in X. Let us take an individual whose chronic-smoker status is undetermined, but all of whose characteristics known to influence chronic-smoker status (such as age, sex, occupation, marital status, etc.) are identical to those of n individuals, judged to be exchangeable in regard to their being smokers or not. The new individual's status as smoker will also be exchangeable with that of the n individuals.

The notion of conditional exchangeability of individuals thus resembles Fisher's notion of their membership in a "subaggregate", where the discrimination described by Fisher hinges on the condition that they should belong to the sub-population whose characteristics Y are identical. However, there are two key differences between these concepts (Lindley and Novik, 1981). First, the exchangeability of individuals refers explicitly to a random variable, whereas a sub-population cannot refer to it. Individuals can be exchangeable in Y given X, but not in X: if we select a new individual living in another country we can, for example, postulate that the propensity to smoke differs significantly from country to country, but that the characteristics examined have an identical influence on the propensity, i.e., that $P(Y|X)$ and $P(Y|\bar{X})$ are the same in the two countries studied. But we will not be able to estimate the propensity to be a smoker exhibiting characteristics Y. The reason is that Bayes's theorem gives us: $P(X|Y) \approx P(Y|X)P(X)$; thus, without a judgement of exchangeability in X, we can no longer obtain the probability that individuals with characteristics Y in the new country examined will be smokers. Second, we have pointed out that it is difficult, if not impossible, to assign a real individual to a sub-population well defined in objectivist terms. Exchangeability, on the other hand, is a judgement on an individual, so it allows that assignment. Statistical inference is now seen "as a passage from data to a unit and not, except as an intermediary, to a parameter" (Lindley and Novik, 1981, p. 48).

Naturally, there is not enough room here to convey the full potential of this Bayesian multilevel approach, which can use far more levels and introduce very diverse and complex analytical methods (Lindley and Smith, 1972; Gelman *et al.*, 1995; Lee, 1997). These technical advances, made possible by the subjective approach, lie outside the scope of this volume and will not be described here. Rather, we will try to show how the subjective approach can be transcended by the "logicist" approach—which, as indicated earlier, formalises the degree of personal belief involved in the subjective approach into a logical relationship valid for all.

The logicist approach, of course, incorporates all the contributions of the Bayesian approach, but enables us to go beyond, particularly in an exploratory phase that all social scientists encounter. Specifically, it offers a precise method for assigning a prior probability distribution in cases where the frequentist hypotheses are invalid and Bayesian methods are not yet available; it permits a precise assignment of the distribution when only fragmentary information is available. For this purpose, it relies on the principle of maximum entropy: this makes it possible to assign a single model using all the information available—without any hypothesis other than what is contained in the data; but it avoids our having to assume that the information we lack is nevertheless usable. The logicist model is optimal under a very large number of criteria. We can say, for example, that it is the simplest one for capturing all the information contained in the constraints; it is the only model for which those constraints would have been sufficient statistics; etc. (Jaynes, 1996). It permits a satisfactory prior distribution in a multilevel model.

More generally, the logicist approach enables us to work on incomplete information, by codifying it logically and numerically in the form of probabilities. These do not describe a state of reality, as in the frequentist approach, but a state of knowledge. They are not "measured", but assigned according to an evidence-based process that yields the same probability assignment regardless of who performs the assignment—contrary to the subjective approach.

Thus far, the logicist approach has been used mainly in the hard sciences, but it could bring a greater consistency to the social sciences. The first attempts by Jaynes (1991) to apply the maximum-entropy principle to economics, by distinguishing between macroeconomics and microeconomics, do not yet enable us to say what the approach can contribute in this area, as Jaynes was launching ideas to stimulate a discussion with economists rather than putting forward a well-developed theory. Only further studies will show if the logicist approach can achieve new advances in multilevel analysis.

3. A BETTER DEFINITION OF LEVELS AND A BETTER INTERCONNECTION BETWEEN THEM

We turn now to the definition of levels and to the possible interconnection between them—one of the trickiest and most hotly debated issues in the multilevel approach. Some chapters of this volume have partly addressed the question: Are the levels considered relevant for the subject studied? Might not other breakdowns give more satisfactory results? What linkages between levels should we regard as relevant? How should we explain the changes observed at levels more aggregated than the individual level?

First, if in some cases the definition of aggregation levels is obvious and straightforward, in other cases it is far more delicate, and the choice between possible segmentations becomes an acute dilemma. Let us take a more detailed look at how this happens.

For example, as shown by Harvey Goldstein, in education it is obvious that the class is a wholly relevant level, as is the school. The teacher's impact on the behaviour of his or her students must also be taken into account to understand their scholastic performance; the functioning of the school they attend should also influence their behaviour. Similarly, in demography, an individual's membership in a given family or contact circle will have a significant effect on his or her future demographic behaviour, and the changes he or she experiences in the contact circle may well influence his or her future behaviour. These levels describe powerful interactions between the individuals enmeshed in each level; the analysis that focuses on the levels at the same time as on the individuals studied is perfectly justified.

By contrast, can an individual's membership in an administrative unit, such as the British districts considered by Mark Tranmer David Steel and Ed Fieldhouse, have an effect on his or her behaviour and, if so, through what channel? In our western societies, such divisions play a largely administrative role, and we can be sceptical of their effective influence on, say, the demographic behaviour of their members. Of course, in some specific cases, the effect can be measured by local legislation favouring a given population group over another—for instance, the racist measures taken in some French towns where the far right holds the political majority. Also, in some social sciences such as human geography, it may be useful to adopt the town or the region as organisational geographical levels. By and large, however, the legislation concerning individuals is essentially national. Yet many multilevel analyses have shown the existence of sometimes major differences between administrative units, and the perceptible role of aggregate variables on the behaviour of individuals living in those areas. How should we go about investigating such an effect?

One possible angle is that, underneath the effect of these administrative levels, we are actually witnessing the effect of the underlying social organisation of the communities present in the areas. If so, we should form a clearer picture of this social organisation, which will be located not in a specific administrative division, but in a much more diffuse area. For example, the earlier-mentioned survey, "Biographies et entourage", should allow an identification of a contact circle that may be, in part, close to the location of the individual studied, but also more distant in physical space, while remaining a major influence on his or her behaviour. If the contact circle manages to cancel the effect of the town or district of residence of the surveyed individual, then we will have made progress in understanding human behaviour. Likewise, if we study individuals' working careers, the role of the "employment catchment area" where they live, or of their personal-contact networks, may provide a far more effective substitute for the role of the town or *département*, which appeared in a study on these administrative divisions.

Identifying social organisation in the manner described above thus seems necessary for defining the levels relevant to each phenomenon studied. This is a long-term undertaking that will require teamwork between specialists in a number of social sciences, as we will not be dealing with simple administrative, geographic, economic, and other divisions, but with complex, intertwined segmentations that vary over time.

The issue of identifying relevant segmentations is closely linked to that of the true connections between these levels. Whether the levels are ranked or nested in a more complicated pattern, they are regarded—in the multilevel models described here—as acting on individual behaviour. Should we not, therefore, take a more general view of the interactions and examine more complex effects?

Let us take the case of a student who is a member of a class, which, in turn, forms part of a school. On the face of it, a hierarchical model seems to be the obvious choice: the school principal will have effects on the class teachers and on their students; the teacher in a class will have effects on the behaviour of his or her students, each of whom possesses individual characteristics. But how, in this case, do we explain a possible effect of one or more students on a teacher's resignation, in the wake of a series of actions by the student(s) against that teacher? The hierarchical model cannot account for such effects of the students on the class or rather on the teacher; it can only describe an effect in the opposite direction, of the teacher on the student(s).

This particular example shows the great variety of cases we may encounter, in which the processes are much more complex than those studied with conventional multilevel models are, and in which the interactions may operate in all directions. This does not, of course, prevent us from obtaining very useful information on the process with the aid of simple multilevel models. But there is a visible need to attempt a formulation of models that come closer to the underlying reality. For this purpose, is it useful to introduce a fuller theory.

4. TOWARDS A FULLER THEORY

The multilevel approach followed by the social sciences discussed here consists in explaining human behaviours with reference to the different social contexts where they occur. For example, Harvey Goldstein shows that the improvement of a student's grades depends not only his or her own characteristics, but on the schools or classes the student attends and on their characteristics. Likewise, an individual's chances of migrating depend on his or her occupation, but also on the region in which the individual resides and on the aggregated variables linked to that region. As Robert Franck says—in the general conclusion of the preceding volume in the present series on *The Explanatory Power of Models* (2002)— we try to explain, in such cases, an empirical process by one or more hypothetical factors present in its environment. Such an explanation is limited as it refers to a given period and country, and does not supply an answer when we work on data from another country or another period in the same country, where the contexts can be very different.

We must therefore seek to transcend this approach by trying to discover the more general social mechanisms underlying the behaviour. Robert Franck (2002) proposes two kinds of approaches, complementary to each other: "First, properties of a social system are explained with reference to a formal (conceptual) structure which is necessary in order for the properties to be present. This explanation can be called *theoretical*. Second, the properties of a social system are explained with reference to the (empirically determined) social mechanism, which generates them. This second type of explanation can be called *empirical*" (p. 296). The roles of these two approaches are inseparable in that neither can be successfully undertaken without the other.

However, as he states in the chapter he has contributed to this volume, it is not possible to view such a system as standing on a single level as this would make all explanation impossible. This leads to the concept of emergence, which permits to say that the relation between two levels is one of matter to form, and the reverse, depending on whether we are ascending or descending the hierarchy of levels, and to the notions of reciprocal influence of factors and systems. These concepts may permit to generalise knowledge in the social field, even if it does not yet appear clearly how this can be put into practice.

Multilevel analysis is one of the means of revealing this functional structure, by observing how different contexts influence the emergence of a given phenomenon, in very varied circumstances, such as attendance in different schools or residence in different regions of a given country. Here, the goal is not to explain the behaviour of an individual in a given environment, but to look for the effect produced by the context, before trying to identify the causal mechanism that will come into play in each situation. We could thus identify a functional structure that—depending on the contexts prevailing in specific situations—leads to a particular causal structure.

We can ask ourselves, however, if this theoretical explanation of a phenomenon, examined in a single functional structure, is satisfactory. Should we not take the process one step further and introduce a fuller theory into the social sciences? A useful tool here is the distinction we made in our introduction between virtual lived experience and the theoretical virtual representation, which is the object of the social sciences. As we noted, virtual lived experience cannot be entirely eliminated from the social sciences, as it manifests itself in the form of the significances that characterise the "human fact" as such: "accordingly, a given gesture by a human being will be perceived as a possible « expression » of a « person », and a given institution will be seen as a possible « expression » of a « society »"(Granger, 1994, p.261). The earlier theoretical approach ignores the problem of these significances or solves it by equating them directly with functions, whose dynamics or statics are tacitly designed as rather crude imitations of those used by physicists, such as the method of "reverse engineering" applied to social sciences or the Durkheimian theory of suicide.

A fuller approach, which would make explicit allowance for the significances, could be developed in two stages.

First, the significances should be transcribed into specific abstract concepts, which would allow the virtual lived experience to be coded into one or more formal systems. The use of a single formal system would remove all the richness of lived experience, which can be grasped only through a greater variety of dimensions: indeed, as we pointed out in our introduction, if we want to reproduce the totality of lived experience, the number of those dimensions may not be exhausted. In a scientific approach, of course, we must restrict the dimensions to those that seem most relevant for the study of the phenomenon of interest, even if this means leaving the others in the shadows, given their negligible effect. This is yet another instance of the generalisation of the multilevel approach, which, from different perspectives on a virtual lived experience, would seek to construct a stereoscopic view resembling that experience as closely as possible.

In the second stage, we take the theoretical explanation of a phenomena examined in a fully multilevel structure and we superimpose a so-called information circuit, which enables us to alter some factors involved in the theoretical explanation by means of the specific functioning of the system studied. This is tantamount to introducing a loop in a multilevel model, with which we can redefine the characteristics and the resulting behaviours at each aggregation level. For example, isolated individual actions in a given community may create awareness of a problem that concerns the entire community. This may lead to political measures at a more aggregated level—measures that will affect the behaviour of individuals by giving them new opportunities. But these opportunities may generate new perverse effects, which will bring new actions to counteract these problems, and so on. Incorporating information circuits clearly leads to multilevel models that are far more complex than those we have examined until now, and that remain largely unexplored.

The issue on which the social sciences are having the greatest trouble moving forward today consists in finding the main levels from which we can best observe human facts, and in finding the relevant concepts that go with those levels. This is partly due to the lack of comparisons between the results obtained by each science. Most often, the social sciences ignore each other because of their different attitudes to human behaviour. But it is precisely by exploiting these different points of view that we will be able to build the foundations needed to bring the social sciences closer to the synthetic approach recommended here. It is important to realise that all human phenomena are overdetermined and can be regarded as the product of a diverse range of social strategies (family, economic, psychological, cultural, and so on). Moreover, these strategies are not frozen in time, and the multilevel approach will assign a proper role to the information circuit that allows a society to evolve.

The multilevel vision lies at the heart of all these advances (both past and future), which are shaping the social sciences. By overcoming the opposition between the macro and micro approaches, it has shown that the choice between holism and individualism no longer makes sense: the task now is to learn how to interconnect the different levels. By allowing the shift from an empirical approach to a theoretical approach, and reciprocally, it has enabled the social sciences to generalise their results and place them in a broader perspective. By making it possible to examine simultaneously the effects of a large number of significances of human facts, in a model incorporating an active temporality, it should facilitate progress towards the objectivation of lived human experience. The road is still long and fraught with obstacles, but the multilevel vision of people in society has brought that goal closer.

REFERENCES

Bayes, T. R. (1763). An essay towards solving a problem in the doctrine of chances. *Philosophical Transactions of the Royal Society of London*, *53*, 370-418.

Bernoulli, J.I. (1713). *Ars conjectandi.* Bâle: Impensis Thurnisiorum fratrum.

Cox, R. (1946). Probability, frequency, and reasonable expectation. *American Journal of Physics*, *14*, 1-13.

de Finetti, B. (1974). *Theory of probability, 2 vols.* London—New York: Wiley & Sons.

Draper, D., Hodges, J. S., Mallows, C. L. & Pregibon, D. (1993). Exchangeability and data analysis. *Journal of the Royal Statistical Society A*, *156*, 9-37.

Fisher, R. A. (1956). *Statistical methods and scientific inference.* Edimburgh: Oliver and Boyd.

Francis, T. F., Korns, R. F., & Voight, R. B. (1955). An evaluation of the 1954 poliomyelitis vaccine trial. *American Journal of Public Health*, *45, [suppl.]*, 1-63.

Franck, R. (Ed.). (2002). *The explanatory power of models. Bridging the gap between empirical and theoretical research in the social sciences.* Boston / Dordrecht / London: Kluwer Academic Publishers (Methodos Series, vol. 1).

Gelman, A., Karlin, J. B., Stern, H. S., & Rubin, D. B. (1995). *Bayesian data analysis.* New York: Chapman and Hall.

Goldstein, H. (1995). *Multilevel statistical models.* London: Edward Arnold.

Goldstein, H. (1998). *Model for reality: new approaches to the understanding of educational processes.* Professorial lecture, London: Institute of Education.

Granger, G.-G. (1994). *Formes, opérations, objets.* Paris: Librairie Philosophique J. Vrin.

Greenland, S. (1998a). Probability logic and probabilistic induction. *Epidemiology*, *9*, 322-332.

Greenland, S. (1998b). Induction versus Popper: substance versus semantics. *International Journal of Epidemiology*, *27*, 543-548.

Greenland, S. (2000). Principles of multilevel modelling. *International Journal of Epidemiology*, *29*, 158-167.

Hoem, J. (1985). Weighting, misclassification, and other issues in the analysis of survey samples of life histories. In Heckman J. and Singer B. (Eds.), *Longitudinal analysis of labour market data* (pp. 259-293). Cambridge: Cambridge University Press.

Holland, P. (1986). Statistics and Causal inference (with Comments). *Journal of the American Statistical Association, 81*, 945-970.

Jaynes, E.T. (1991). *How should we use entropy in economics?*. Unpublished paper. Retrieved October 13, 2001 from: http://www.leibniz.imag.fr/LAPLACE/Jaynes/prob.html.

Jaynes, E. T. (1996). *Probability theory: the logic of science.* Unpublished book. Retrieved October 13, 2001 from: http://www.leibniz.imag.fr/LAPLACE/Jaynes/prob.html.

Jeffreys, H. (1939). *Theory of probability.* New York: Clarendon Press.

Jones, K. (1993). *Everywhere is nowhere: Multilevel perspectives on the importance of place.* The University of Portsmouth Inaugural Lectures.

Kolmogorov, A. (1933). Grundbegriffe der wahrscheinlichkeitsrenung. In *Ergebisne der mathematik, vol.2*, Berlin.

Laplace, P.S. (1812). *Théorie analytique des Probabilités, 2 vols.* Paris: Coursier Imprimeur.

Lee, P. M. (1997). *Bayesian statistics, 2d ed.* London: Arnold.

Lelièvre, E., Bonvalet, C. & Bry, X. (1998). Event history analysis of groups. The findings of an ongoing research project. In Courgeau D. (Ed.), *Population, An English selection, 10*, 11-37.

Lindley, D. V., & Novick, M. R. (1981). The role of exchangeability in inference. *The Annals of Statistics, 9*, 45-58.

Lindley, D.V., & Smith, A. F. M. (1972). Bayes estimates for the linear model. *Journal of the Royal Statistical Society, Series B (Methodological), 34*, 1-41.

Lyberg, I. (1983). *The effects of sampling and nonresponse on estimates of transition intensities: Some empirical results from the 1981 Swedish fertility survey.* Stockholm Research Reports in Demography, n° 14. Stockholm: University of Stockholm.

Matalon, B. (1967). Epistémologie des probabilités. In Piaget J. (Ed.), *Logique et connaissance scientifique* (pp. 526-553), Paris: Gallimard.

Polya, G. (1954). *Mathematics and plausible reasoning, 2 Vols.* Princeton: University Press.

Rosenbaum, P. R. (1984a). The consequence of adjustment for a concomitant variable that has been affected by the treatment. *Journal of the Royal Statistical Society A, 147*, 656-666.

Rosenbaum, P .R. (1984b). From association to causation in observational studies: the role of tests of strongly ignorable treatment assignment. *Journal of the American Statistical Association, 79*, 41-48.

Rosenbaum, P. R., & Rubin, D. B. (1984). Reducing bias in observational studies using subclassification on the propensity score. *Journal of the American Statistical Association, 79*, 516-524.

Rubin, D. B. (1978). Bayesian inference for causal effects: the role of randomization. *The Annals of Statistics, 6*, 34-58.

Schwartz, D. (1989). L'explication en épidémiologie. In Duchêne J., Wunsch G., & Vilquin E. (Eds.), *L'explication en sciences sociales. La recherche des causes en démographie* (pp. 127-140). Louvain-la-Neuve: Editions Ciaco.

Wunsch, G. (1994). L'analyse causale en démographie, in Franck R. (Ed.), *Faut-il chercher aux causes une raison ? L'explication causale dans les sciences humaines* (pp. 24-40). Paris: Librairie Philosophique J. Vrin.

SUBJECT INDEX

D

E

F

O

P

AUTHOR INDEX

THE EXPLANATORY POWER OF MODELS

First volume in the *Methodos Series*, edited by Robert Franck

The outstanding points of this book are the following:

As empirical research often lacks theory, this book progressively works out a method of constructing models which can bridge the gap between empirical and theoretical research in social sciences. This might improve the explanatory power of models. The issue is quite novel, and it benefits from a thorough examination of statistical and mathematical models, conceptual models, diagrams and maps, machines, computer simulations and artificial neural networks. These modelling practices have been approached through different disciplines. The proposed method is partly inspired by reverse engineering. The standard covering law approach is abandoned, and classical induction restored to its rightful place. It helps to solve several difficulties which weigh upon the social sciences today, for example how to extend an explanatory model to new phenomena, how to establish laws, and how to guide the choice of a conceptual structure. This book can be used for advanced courses in research methods in the social sciences and in philosophy of science.

HIERARCHY IN NATURAL AND SOCIAL SCIENCES

Third volume in the *Methodos Series*, will be edited by Denise Pumain

The outstanding points of this book are the following:

There is a paradoxical situation about hierarchy in the modern world. One the one hand, the hierarchy is denied or fought in the political or social fields through ideas of democracy, equality or equity. As an organisational pattern for administrations or firms, hierarchy has been questioned in terms of efficiency by a newly marked preference for networks. But on the other hand there are many evidences of hierarchical differentiation in social as well as in natural systems. The concept of hierarchy may become relevant for interpreting a complex system when constructive or evolutionary processes are related to this type of organisation or structure. We suggest a careful survey of the explanations which have been given, for example in the case of the size distribution of firms, or the hierarchical differentiation of urban systems, or the size or number of living species. This can be done by comparing precisely the characteristic of hierarchical structures and of explanatory models existing both for natural and social phenomena. Discussions and comparisons of their models between social and natural scientists can help in identifying possible common processes and specific feature of each system offering hierarchical properties.

Printed in the United Kingdom
by Lightning Source UK Ltd.
120110UK00004B/184

9 781402 014758